Bloom's Classic Critical Views

THE BRONTËS

Bloom's Classic Critical Views

Bloom's Classic Critical Views

THE BRONTËS

Edited and with an Introduction by
Harold Bloom
Sterling Professor of the Humanities
Yale University

BLOOM'S
LITERARY CRITICISM
An imprint of Infobase Publishing

Bloom's Classic Critical Views: The Brontës

Copyright © 2008 Infobase Publishing

Introduction © 2008 by Harold Bloom

All rights reserved. No part of this publication may be reproduced or utilized in any form or by any means, electronic or mechanical, including photocopying, recording, or by any information storage or retrieval systems, without permission in writing from the publisher For more information contact:

Bloom's Literary Criticism
An imprint of Infobase Publishing
132 West 31st Street
New York NY 10001

Library of Congress Cataloging-in-Publication Data
The Brontës / edited and with an introduction by Harold Bloom.
      p. cm. — (Bloom's classic critical views)
   A selection of important older literary criticism on the Brontës.
   Includes bibliographical references and index.
   ISBN 978-1-60413-136-9
   1. Brontë family. 2. English fiction—19th century—History and criticism. I. Bloom,
Harold. II. Title. III. Series.

   PR4169.B77 2008
   823'.809—dc22
                                    2008014069

Bloom's Literary Criticism books are available at special discounts when purchased in bulk quantities for businesses, associations, institutions, or sales promotions. Please call our Special Sales Department in New York at (212) 967-8800 or (800) 322-8755.

You can find Bloom's Literary Criticism on the World Wide Web at
http://www.chelseahouse.com

Contributing editor: Tabitha Sparks
Series design by Erika K. Arroyo
Cover design by Takeshi Takahashi
Printed in the United States of America
Bang EJB 10 9 8 7 6 5 4 3 2 1

This book is printed on acid-free paper.

All links and Web addresses were checked and verified to be correct at the time of publication. Because of the dynamic nature of the Web, some addresses and links may have changed since publication and may no longer be valid.

Contents

Series Introduction

Bloom's Classic Critical Views is a new series presenting a selection of the most important older literary criticism on the greatest authors commonly read in high school and college classes today. Unlike the Bloom's Modern Critical Views series, which for more than 20 years has provided the best contemporary criticism on great authors, Bloom's Classic Critical Views attempts to present the authors in the context of their time and to provide criticism that has proved over the years to be the most valuable to readers and writers. Selections range from contemporary reviews in popular magazines, which demonstrate how a work was received in its own era, to profound essays by some of the strongest critics in the British and American tradition, including Henry James, G.K. Chesterton, Matthew Arnold, and many more.

Some of the critical essays and extracts presented here have appeared previously in other titles edited by Harold Bloom, such as the New Moulton's Library of Literary Criticism. Other selections appear here for the first time in any book by this publisher. All were selected under Harold Bloom's guidance.

In addition, each volume in this series contains a series of essays by a contemporary expert, who comments on the most important critical selections, putting them in context and suggesting how they might be used by a student writer to influence his or her own writing. This series is intended above all for students, to help them think more deeply and write more powerfully about great writers and their works.

Introduction by Harold Bloom

—◦◦◦— —◦◦◦— —◦◦◦—

1

The three Brontë sisters—Charlotte, Emily Jane, and Anne—in retrospect form a literary movement that created a genre all their own: let us call it "northern romance." George Gordon, Lord Byron, was its precursor, and its continuators, with a difference, include Thomas Hardy and D.H. Lawrence. Byron was more than a literary forerunner for the Brontës: he gave them their ideal of masculine passion. I do not know what the noble Byron would have made of his two grand parodies: Rochester in *Jane Eyre* and Heathcliff in *Wuthering Heights*. But Charlotte and even more Emily seem to have intuited some of the secrets of Byron's psychosexuality. The closest friend of Shelley, who himself always kept falling in love with one idealized charmer after another, the equally High Romantic Byron (in matter of love, revolution, and war, rather than literary outlook) was a veritable sexual anthology. The notoriously handsome poet (a dead-ringer for the film actor Tyrone Power) was a passive-aggressive narcissist. His varieties included sadomasochism, homoeroticism, incest with his half-sister, and heterosexual sodomy. He died a more or less heroic death in Greece on April 19, 1824, aged thirty-six years, three months, while leading his hireling band of brigands against the Turks.

When the noble Lord Byron died, Charlotte was eight, Emily Jane six, and Anne four. As Britain's reigning celebrity, the death of Byron was reported everywhere, probably even in the remote Haworth Parsonage, in Yorkshire. Rochester in *Jane Eyre* and Heathcliff in *Wuthering Heights* palpably are Byronic hero-villains.

Since *Jane Eyre* is narrated in the first person by Jane herself, the Byronic aura of Rochester is augmented. Going on seventy-eight, I am appalled at how many novels and prose romances I have read. Because of a preternatural reading speed (progressively slowing down as I age) and rather too retentive a memory, I can feel oppressed by overload in my darker moods. All this is preamble to remarking that no other fictive character is so given to cudgeling male readers as is Jane Eyre, surrogate for Charlotte Brontë, who out-Byrons Byron in exuberant aggressivity. I admire *Jane Eyre* and have reread it many times, but I fear that it gratifies my sadomasochism.

Jane is the aesthetic splendor of her novel, and her release of her will-to-power over Rochester is overwhelming: rhetorically, psychologically, all but cosmologically. This portrait of the artist as a young woman (Jane is a visionary painter whose subject matter is her own dreams) is so composed that the novel, with its allusions to John Bunyan's *The Pilgrim's Progress*, becomes a full-scale visionary painting, curiously in the mode of William Blake. I think that Blake would have loathed and feared *Jane Eyre*, because it depicts the triumph of the mythological entity he named the Female Will.

As an exhausted old male literary critic, I no longer like to provoke academic feminists, so I am wary in expressing my simultaneous aesthetic admiration for *Jane Eyre*, and my annoyance that Jane/Charlotte enjoys bashing me. Rochester calls Jane "indomitable," but that may not be the right word for her ferocity. Poor Rochester dwindles into a virtuous, highly dependent husband, in Charlotte's ultimate triumph over Lord Byron.

2

Wuthering Heights transcends *Jane Eyre* and takes a place near *Moby-Dick*, another nineteenth-century masterpiece that breaks free of genre. The best contemporary reaction to Emily Brontë's sublime originality was by Dante Gabriel Rossetti:

> It is a fiend of a book, an incredible monster, combining all the stronger female tendencies from Mrs. Browning to Mrs. Brownrigg. The action is laid in Hell,—only it seems places and people have English names there.

This nasty but accurate reflection upon female sadism in *Wuthering Heights* invokes a parallel between the heavy moralism of Elizabeth Barrett Browning and the eighteenth-century Mrs. Brownrigg, executed for her enthusiasm in whipping young women to death. Beyond his hyperbole, Rossetti caught the strange quality of the love between Heathcliff and Catherine Earnshaw, which is *contra naturam*. The romance's deepest affinities are with William Blake, though Emily Brontë may never have heard of him. Like Blake, she developed an original Gnosis, a religion entirely her own.

Catherine Earnshaw exemplifies this creedless knowing in her longing to escape the prison-houses of nature and of society:

> "Oh, you see, Nelly! he would not relent a moment, to keep me out of the grave! *That* is how I'm loved! Well, never mind! That is not *my* Heathcliff. I shall love mine yet; and take him with me—he's in my soul. And," added she, musingly, "the thing that irks me most is this shattered prison, after all. I'm tired, tired of being enclosed here. I'm wearying to escape into that glorious world, and to be always there; not seeing it dimly through tears, and yearning for it through the walls of an aching heart; but really with it, and in it. Nelly, you think you are better and more fortunate than I; in full health and strength. You are sorry for me—very soon that will be altered. I shall be sorry for *you*. I shall be incomparably beyond and above you all. I *wonder* he won't be near me!" She went on to herself. "I thought he wished it. Heathcliff, dear! you should not be sullen now. Do come to me, Heathcliff."

The mystery of *Wuthering Heights* is that Emily Brontë refuses to forge any connecting structure between the two worlds of her novel. Reason, nature, and society constitute one world; the preternatural, transcendental, and ghostly inform quite another. The reader is caught between the two, an impasse which is the aesthetic splendor that is permanent.

CHARLOTTE BRONTË

BIOGRAPHY

CHARLOTTE BRONTË
(1816–1855)

Charlotte Brontë was born at Thornton in Yorkshire on April 21, 1816. She was the third daughter born in her family, sisters Maria (1814–1825) and Elizabeth (1815–1825) dying as children. Charlotte's younger siblings were Branwell (1817–1848), Emily (1818–1848), and Anne (1820–1849). She spent most of her life with her family in Haworth, Yorkshire, where her father was perpetual curate. Charlotte's mother died in 1821, and in 1823 her mother's sister Elizabeth Branwell moved in with the family to take care of the children. In 1824, Maria, Elizabeth, Charlotte, and Emily entered the Clergy Daughters' School at Cowan Bridge, where soon after the elder two sisters contracted tuberculosis and died. Charlotte and Emily were taken home to be taught by their father and aunt. In 1831, Charlotte was enrolled at Miss Wooler's School in Roe Head. She returned home to tutor her sisters in 1832 and in 1835 returned to Roe Head as a teacher. Charlotte resigned her position in 1838, moved home, and in 1842 went with Emily to study at the Pensionnat Héger in Brussels; they returned later that year after the death of their aunt Elizabeth Branwell. Charlotte revisited Brussels in 1843 to teach English and to study, and on her return in 1844 she and her sisters attempted unsuccessfully to open a school.

Perhaps because they spent so much time alone together at Haworth, in a remote and isolated part of Yorkshire, as children Charlotte, Emily, Anne, and Branwell shared an active imaginative life. From an early age, they wrote verse and stories collaboratively, and Charlotte and Branwell created the world of Angria, which figured in many of Charlotte's early tales. In 1845 Charlotte began gathering some of this juvenilia, and the following year the three sisters published a slim volume of sixty-one poems titled *Poems by Currer, Ellis and Acton Bell* (the pseudonyms, respectively, of Charlotte, Emily, and Anne). This collection did not sell well, and Charlotte was unsuccessful in finding a publisher for her first novel, *The Professor*, which she had completed in 1846; it appeared after her death. Charlotte's second novel, *Jane*

Eyre, was published pseudonymously in 1847 and became an immediate success, arousing much speculation as to the identity and sex of its author.

Charlotte was not, however, able to enjoy this newfound success for very long. In 1848 both Branwell and Emily died, and in the following year Anne died also. Despite these tragedies, Charlotte completed another novel, *Shirley,* again published under the name Currer Bell in 1849. Her fourth novel, *Villette,* appeared in 1853, also under the name Currer Bell, even though her identity was by then widely known. In 1854 Charlotte married Arthur Bell Nicholls, her father's curate, and was said to be happy with the match. Less than a year later, on March 31, 1855, she died of complications resulting from the early stages of pregnancy.

After her death, Charlotte Brontë's fame increased with the publication of her friend Elizabeth Gaskell's *Life of Charlotte Brontë* (1857). Charlotte's first novel, *The Professor,* was published in 1857, and in the twentieth century several volumes of her juvenilia and miscellaneous writings have appeared, including *Five Novelettes* (1971; ed. Winifred Gerin), *Emma and Another Lady* (1980; J.M. Dent), *An Edition of the Early Writings of Charlotte Brontë* (1987; ed. Christine Alexander), and *Tales of Angria* (2006; ed. Heather Glen).

PERSONAL

From her lifetime until today, there has been a critical tendency to read Charlotte Brontë's (and Emily and Anne's) novels as thinly veiled autobiographies. This interpretation evolved from the early fascination with the Brontës' isolation and perceived loneliness in Haworth and the attendant assumption that their fiction would have to be drawn from their own limited scope of experience. There are, however, several problems with this reading. The first is that it largely ignores the inventive record of their juvenilia, which, in all of its fantastic, adventurous, and heroic style, was never presumed to be inspired by daily life in the Haworth parsonage. The second omission revealed by an autobiographical treatment of the Brontës' fiction is that it undervalues Charlotte's (and briefly, Emily's) experiences in Belgium, which broadened her scope in literal and figurative ways. It also eclipses the sisters' intellectual resources from childhood on: the extensive reading (in the form of newspapers, magazines, novels, biographies, and histories, among other genres) that their father made available to the household.

As the following excerpts reveal, Charlotte's shyness and countrified appearance certainly helped to inspire the views of her as unworldly and guileless, someone whose fictions must be the records of her own personal feelings rather than the inventions of a complex mind. The ingenuousness that so many perceived in her certainly leant her work an air of sincerity. But it also has the tendency to underrate her creative powers.

The most significant nineteenth-century treatment of Brontë's life is Elizabeth Gaskell's biography, *The Life of Charlotte Brontë* (1857). Gaskell compiled this biography from numerous letters and interviews with the Brontës' friends, as well as with their father, Patrick Brontë. Gaskell's work encouraged a long phase of criticism that was overshadowed by a fascination with the Brontës' personal lives.

Robert Southey (1837)

Robert Southey (1774–1843) was one of the Lake Poets, a literary set that included Wordsworth and Coleridge. In 1813, he became England's poet laureate. Southey was also an accomplished historian and biographer and the biographer of Horatio Nelson, one of the Brontë children's heroes.

Charlotte's early admiration of Southey inspired her, at age 21, to write a letter to him in which she expressed her literary ambitions and solicited his advice. In his reply, Southey was famously discouraging. Specifically, he cautioned Brontë against investing too much energy in her poetry, as he wrote that "Literature cannot be the business of a woman's life, and it ought not to be." While he acknowledges that her poetry (examples of which she included in her letter to him) showed evidence of talent, he believed that she should write for herself rather than try to appeal to a general public. While the end of his letter is gracious and even warm, his advice to check her ambitions remains the overwhelming message.

———— ———— ————

It is not my advice that you have asked as to the direction of your talents, but my opinion of them, and yet the opinion may be worth little, and the advice much. You evidently possess, and in no inconsiderable degree, what Wordsworth calls the "faculty of verse." . . . But it is not with a view to distinction that you should cultivate this talent, if you consult your own happiness. I, who have made literature my profession, and devoted my life to it, and have never for a moment repented of the deliberate choice, think myself, nevertheless, bound in duty to caution every young man who applies as an aspirant to me for encouragement and advice, against taking so perilous a course. You will say that a woman has no need of such a caution; there can be no peril in it for her. In a certain sense this is true; but there is a danger of which I would, with all kindness and all earnestness, warn you. The day dreams in which you habitually indulge are likely to induce a distempered state of mind; and in proportion as all the ordinary uses of the world seem to you flat and unprofitable, you will be unfitted for them without becoming fitted for anything else. Literature cannot be the business of a woman's life, and it ought not to be. The more she is engaged in her proper duties, the less leisure will she have for it, even as an accomplishment and a recreation. To those duties you have not yet been called, and when you are you will be less eager for celebrity. You will not seek in imagination for excitement, of which the vicissitudes of this life, and the anxieties from which you must not hope to be exempted, be your state what it may, will bring with them but too much.

But do not suppose that I disparage the gift which you possess; nor that I would discourage you from exercising it. I only exhort you so to think of it, and so to use it, as to render it conducive to your own permanent good. Write poetry for its own sake; not in a spirit of emulation, and not with a view to celebrity; the less you aim at that the more likely you will be to deserve and finally to obtain it. So written, it is wholesome both for the heart and soul; it may be made the surest means, next to religion, of soothing the mind and elevating it. You may embody in it your best thoughts and your wisest feelings, and in so doing discipline and strengthen them.

Farewell, madam. It is not because I have forgotten that I was once young myself, that I write to you in this strain; but because I remember it. You will neither doubt my sincerity nor my good will; and however ill what has here been said may accord with your present views and temper, the longer you live the more reasonable it will appear to you. Though I may be but an ungracious advisor, you will allow me, therefore, to subscribe myself, with the best wishes for your happiness here and hereafter, your true friend,

—Robert Southey, letter to Charlotte Brontë,
March 1837, from Elizabeth Gaskell,
The Life of Charlotte Brontë, p. 119

ROBERT SOUTHEY (1837)

In the letter to Caroline Bowles, Southey refers to the letter from Brontë and his reply (above). Caroline Bowles (1786–1854) was a poet who later became Southey's second wife.

I sent a dose of cooling admonition to the poor girl whose flighty letter reached me at Buckland. It was well taken, and she thanked me for it. It seems she is the eldest daughter of a clergyman, has been expensively educated, and is laudably employed as a governess in some private family. About the same time that she wrote to me, her brother wrote to Wordsworth, who was disgusted with the letter, for it contained gross flattery to him, and plenty of abuse of other poets, including me. I think well of the sister from her second letter, and probably she will think kindly of me as long as she lives.

—Robert Southey, letter to Caroline Bowles, 1837,
*The Correspondence of Robert Southey with
Caroline Bowles*, ed. Edward Dowden, 1881, p. 348

Charlotte Brontë (as "Currer Bell") (1850)

The biographical statement that Brontë included in the joint publication of *Wuthering Heights* and *Agnes Grey* recalls the sisters' early literary aspirations and their decision to publish their work under male (or
gender-neutral) pseudonyms. Their adolescent notion that "authoresses"
were "liable to be looked on with prejudice" was correct, as Southey's
previously cited letter testifies.

———

We had very early cherished the dream of one day becoming authors. This
dream, never relinquished even when distance divided and absorbing tasks
occupied us, now suddenly acquired strength and consistency: it took the
character of a resolve. We agreed to arrange a small selection of our poems,
and, if possible, to get them printed. Averse to personal publicity, we veiled
our own names under those of Currer, Ellis, and Acton Bell; the ambiguous
choice being dictated by a sort of conscientious scruple at assuming Christian
names positively masculine, while we did not like to declare ourselves women,
because—without at that time suspecting that our mode of writing and
thinking was not what is called "feminine"—we had a vague impression that
authoresses are liable to be looked on with prejudice; we had noticed how
critics sometimes use for their chastisement the weapon of personality, and
for their reward, a flattery, which is not true praise.

—Charlotte Brontë (as "Currer Bell"),
"Biographical Notice of Ellis and Acton Bell,"
Wuthering Heights and Agnes Grey, 1850

George Eliot (1853)

George Eliot was the pseudonym of Mary Ann (later Marian) Evans (1819–
1880), one of the nineteenth century's greatest novelists and intellectu-
als. After translating several works from German in the 1840s and 1850s
and contributing to *The Westminster Review*, her first literary publication
was *Scenes of Clerical Life* in *Blackwood's Magazine* (1857), followed by a
string of celebrated novels, starting with *Adam Bede* (1859) and including *The Mill on the Floss* (1860), *Silas Marner* (1861), *Middlemarch* (1871–72)
and *Daniel Deronda* (1874–76). She also wrote poetry, short stories, and
numerous letters, many of which have been published. Eliot lived with
the political historian and intellectual George Lewes in an unconventional relationship for many years (Lewes was already married and could

not obtain a divorce), and, at the end of her life, she married her much younger financial adviser, John Walter Cross.

Eliot's description of Brontë is notable for two things: It illustrates Brontë's conspicuous appearance, and it documents the meeting of perhaps the two most significant women writers of the Victorian age.

Lewes was describing Currer Bell to me yesterday as a little, plain, provincial, sickly-looking old maid. Yet what passion, what fire in her! Quite as much as in George Sand, only the clothing is less voluptuous.

—George Eliot, letter to Mr. and
Mrs. Charles Bray, March 5, 1853

Elizabeth Gaskell (1857)

Elizabeth Cleghorn Gaskell (1810–1865) was a celebrated novelist. Many of her works—such as *Mary Barton* (1848), *Ruth* (1853), and *North and South* (1855)—take a reformist and humanitarian attitude to the social discrepancies of industrial England. Her other major works—*Cranford* (1853), *Sylvia's Lovers* (1863), and *Wives and Daughters* (1866)—explore a wide range of domestic and social relationships. Gaskell met Brontë in 1850 at the Lake District home of Sir James Kay-Shuttleworth, and the two novelists formed an instant rapport, so that after Brontë's death Gaskell was selected by Patrick Brontë to write his late daughter's biography. Gaskell's biography makes use of a great number of Brontë family letters that constitute the bulk of what we know about their life at Haworth. But Gaskell also carefully edited those letters in order to show a specific side of her subject.

In particular, Gaskell's biography directed Brontë scholarship toward a bleak and tragic interpretation of the sisters' lives, and Gaskell reflected later that she may have exaggerated these elements of Charlotte Brontë's life. One of her primary motives in writing Brontë's autobiography was to counter the many critics who accused the novelist—and especially *Jane Eyre*—of being "coarse." By emphasizing the personal tragedy in Brontë's life, Gaskell offset this charge by instead trying to show how suffering, not immorality, shaped her subject's vision. Other aspects of Gaskell's *Life* that have been criticized are her portrait of Patrick Brontë as unrealistically harsh and her failure to discuss the relationship between Brontë and Constantin Héger in Belgium, the inspiration of Paul Emmanuel in *Villette*.

Gaskell's description of Charlotte Brontë that follows is characteristic in its emphasis on Brontë's meekness and seriousness, a description that would be moderated by T. Wemyss Reid in his 1877 biography, *Charlotte Brontë: A Monograph*, of which an excerpt is included later in the volume.

This is perhaps a fitting time to give some personal description of Miss Brontë. In 1831, she was a quiet, thoughtful girl, of nearly fifteen years of age, very small in figure—'stunted' was the word she applied to herself,—but as her limbs and head were in just proportion to the slight, fragile body, no word in ever so slight a degree suggestive of deformity could properly be applied to her; with soft, thick, brown hair, and peculiar eyes, of which I find it difficult to give a description, as they appeared to me in her later life. They were large, and well shaped; their colour a reddish brown; but if the iris was closely examined, it appeared to be composed of a great variety of tints. The usual expression was of quiet, listening intelligence; but now and then, on some just occasion for vivid interest or wholesome indignation, a light would shine out, as if some spiritual lamp had been kindled, which glowed behind those expressive orbs. I never saw the like in any other human creature. As for the rest of her features, they were plain, large, and ill set; but, unless you began to catalogue them, you were hardly aware of the fact, for the eyes and power of the countenance over-balanced every physical defect; the crooked mouth and the large nose were forgotten, and the whole face arrested the attention, and presently attracted all those whom she herself would have cared to attract. Her hands and feet were the smallest I ever saw; when one of the former was placed in mine, it was like the soft touch of a bird in the middle of my palm. The delicate long fingers had a peculiar fineness of sensation, which was one reason why all her handiwork, of whatever kind—writing, sewing, knitting— was so clear in its minuteness. She was remarkably neat in her whole personal attire; but she was dainty as to the fit of her shoes and gloves.

I can well imagine that the grave serious composure, which, when I knew her, gave her face the dignity of an old Venetian portrait, was no acquisition of later years, but dated from that early age when she found herself in the position of an elder sister to motherless children. But in a girl only just entered on her teens, such an expression would be called (to use a country phrase) 'old-fashioned'; and in 1831, the period of which I now write, we must think of her as a little, set, antiquated girl, very quiet in manner, and very quaint in dress . . . ."

—Elizabeth Gaskell, *The Life of Charlotte Brontë*, 1857, p. 74

Caroline Fox (1857)

Caroline Fox (1819–1871) was an English diarist whose collection *Memories of Old Friends* (1881) recounts her acquaintance with a host of important Victorians, including John Stuart Mill, Thomas Carlyle, William Wordsworth, Elizabeth Fry (Fox's cousin), and Alfred, Lord Tennyson.

———— ———— ————

We are reading the *Life of Charlotte Brontë*, a most striking book. Genius as she was, she is beautifully attentive to the smallest practical matters affecting the comforts of others. She is intensely true, and draws from actual life, cost what it may; and in that remote little world of hers—a village, as it seems, of a hundred years back—facts came to light of a frightful unmitigated force; events accompanied them, burning with a lurid glow and setting their very hearts on fire. She is like her books, and her life explains much in them which needs explanation.

—Caroline Fox, *Journal*, July 9, 1857,
Memories of Old Friends, ed.
Horace N. Pym, 1881, p. 336

T. Wemyss Reid (1877)

Sir Thomas Wemyss Reid (1842–1905) was a publisher, editor, and writer whose works included the biography *Charlotte Brontë* (1876), which among important nineteenth-century Brontë biographies is second only to Gaskell's 1857 *The Life of Charlotte Brontë*. For his version, Reid worked closely with Brontë's friend from Roe Head School, Ellen Nussey. Reid revised the biography in 1877, and, despite objections from Brontë's widower Arthur Nicholls, he included details and speculations about the novelist's personal life. The biography also portrays Patrick Brontë as a harsh and neglectful father, a view that has been somewhat reassessed.

Reid's biography of Brontë is also noteworthy for its various corrections to Gaskell's *The Life of Charlotte Brontë*. In particular he draws upon Ellen Nussey's memories to argue that Charlotte was a more spirited and cheerful person than the dour portrait that emerges from Gaskell's study. Reid also disagrees with Gaskell about the greatest influence on Brontë as a writer. While Gaskell claims it was the tragic and successive deaths of her siblings Branwell, Emily, and Anne, Reid argues that her experience in Belgium had more authority over her artistic vision.

———— ———— ————

[Mrs. Gaskell] seems to have set out with the determination that her work should be pitched in a particular key. She had formed her own conception of Charlotte Brontë's character, and with the passion of the true artist and ability of the practiced writer she made everything bend to that conception. The result was that whilst she produced a singularly striking and effective portrait of her heroine, it was not one which was absolutely satisfactory to those who were oldest and closest friends of Charlotte Brontë. If the truth must be told, the life of the author of *Jane Eyre* was by no means so joyless as the world now believes it to have been. That during the later years in which this wonderful woman produced the works by which she has made her name famous, her career was clouded by sorrow and oppressed by anguish both mental and physical, is perfectly true. That she was made what she was in the furnace of affliction cannot be doubted; but it is not true that she was throughout her life the victim of that extreme depression of spirits which afflicted her at rare intervals, and which Mrs. Gaskell has presented to us with so much vividness and emphasis. On the contrary, her letters show that any rate up to the time of her leaving for Brussels, she was a happy and high-spirited girl, and that even to the very last she had the faculty of overcoming her sorrows by means of that steadfast courage which was her most precious possession, and to which she was so much indebted for her successive victories over trials and disappointments of no ordinary character. Those who imagine that Charlotte Brontë's spirit was in any degree a morbid or melancholy one do her a singular injustice.

—T. Wemyss Reid, *Charlotte Brontë:
A Monograph*, 1877, pp. 2–3

Harriet Martineau (1877)

Harriet Martineau (1802–1876) was a social reformer whose writing career spanned several decades and many different genres: political economy, fiction, philosophy, children's literature, memoir and autobiography, and travel writing. Her most famous work is a multivolume series, *Illustrations of Political Economy* (1832–1834), which models concepts of economic reform in fictional scenarios. Her causes also include the abolition of slavery in the United States and the economic independence of women. Martineau suffered from a variety of health problems and conditions, including deafness, and she wrote about the experience of being an invalid. This description of her meeting with Brontë in 1850 reiterates her interest in the physical condition, and particularly in Martineau's belief that health is an extension of one's mental state.

Between the appearance of *Shirley* and that of *Villette*, she came to me;—in December, 1850. Our intercourse then confirmed my deep impression of her integrity, her noble conscientiousness about her vocation, and her consequent self-reliance in the moral conduct of her life. I saw at the same time tokens of a morbid condition of mind, in one or two directions;—much less than might have been expected, or than would have been seen in almost any one else under circumstances so unfavourable to health of body and mind as those in which she lived; and the one fault which I pointed out to her in *Villette* was so clearly traceable to these unwholesome influences that I would fain have been spared a task of criticism which could hardly be of much use while the circumstances remained unchanged. . . . She might be weak for once; but her permanent temper was one of humility, candour, integrity and conscientiousness. She was not only unspoiled by her sudden and prodigious fame, but obviously unspoilable. She was somewhat amused by her fame, but oftener annoyed;—at least, when obliged to come out into the world to meet it, instead of its reaching her in her secluded home, in the wilds of Yorkshire.

—Harriet Martineau, *Autobiography*, ed.
Maria Weston Chapman, 1877, vol. 2, p. 24

SIR LESLIE STEPHEN (1877)

Sir Leslie Stephen (1832–1904) was a Victorian man of letters whose contribution to literature ranged from his editorship of *The Cornhill* (1871–1882) to his massive undertaking in editing the *Dictionary of National Biography*, which he began in 1882 and is still compiled and revised today. Stephen is also famous for being the father of Virginia Woolf.

The personal orientation of Stephen's analysis of Brontë reflects his biographical approach. His discussion of the novelist is also one of the more negative assessments of her from this period. In particular Stephen construes a fragile psyche informing Brontë's literature, arguing that the "feverish disquiet" that marks her style extends from her emotional fragility. He goes even further in this speculation when he writes that her tragic view of life "speaks of a mind diseased." Stephen's reading of *Jane Eyre* is clearly dated in its remarks on the appeal of Mr. Rochester, who, Stephen claims, personifies "a true woman's longing . . . for a strong master."

Although the secret of Miss Brontë's power lies, to a great extent, in the singular force with which she can reproduce acute observations of character from without, her most esoteric teaching, the most accurate reflex from her familiar idiosyncrasy, is of course to be found in the characters painted from within. We may infer her personality more or less accurately from the mode in which she contemplates her neighbours, but it is directly manifested in various avatars of her own spirit. Among the characters who are more or less mouthpieces of her peculiar sentiment we may reckon not only Lucy Snowe and Jane Eyre, but, to some extent, Shirley, and, even more decidedly, Rochester. When they speak we are really listening to her own voice, though it is more or less disguised in conformity to dramatic necessity. There are great differences between them; but they are such differences as would exist between members of the same family, or might be explained by change of health or internal circumstances. Jane Eyre has not had such bitter experience as Lucy Snowe; Shirley is generally Jane Eyre in high spirits, and freed from harassing anxiety; and Rochester is really a spirited sister of Shirley's, though he does his very best to be a man, and even an unusually masculine specimen of his sex.

Mr. Rochester, indeed, has imposed upon a good many people; and he is probably responsible in part for some of the muscular heroes who have appeared since his time in the world of fiction. I must, however, admit that, in spite of some opposing authority, he does not appear to me to be a real character at all, except as a reflection of a certain side of his creator. He is in reality the personification of a true woman's longing (may one say it now?) for a strong master. But the knowledge is wanting. He is a very bold but necessarily unsuccessful attempt at an impossibility. The parson's daughter did not really know anything about the class of which he is supposed to be a type, and he remains vague and inconsistent in spite of all his vigour. He is intended to be a person who has surfeited from the fruit of the tree of knowledge, and addresses the inexperienced governess from the height—or depth—of his worldly wisdom. And he really knows just as little of the world as she does. He has to impose upon her by giving an account of his adventures taken from the first novel at hand of the early Bulwer school, or a diluted recollection of Byron. There is not a trace of real cynicism—of the strong nature turned sour by experience—in his whole conversation. He is supposed to be specially simple and masculine, and yet he is as self-conscious as a young lady on her first appearance in society, and can do nothing but discourse about his feelings, and his looks, and his phrenological symptoms, to his admiring hearer. Set him beside any man's character of a man and one feels at once that he has no real solidity or vitality in him. He has, of course, strong nerves and muscles, but those are articles which can be supplied in unlimited quantities with little expense to the imagination. Nor can one deny that his conduct to Miss Eyre is abominable. If he had proposed to her to ignore the existence of the mad Mrs. Rochester, he would have acted like a rake, but not like a sneak. But the attempt to entrap Jane into a bigamous connection by concealing the wife's existence is a piece of treachery for which it is hard to forgive him. When he challenges the lawyer and the clergyman to condemn him after putting themselves in his place, their answer is surely obvious. One may take a lenient view of a man who chooses by his own will to annul his marriage to a filthy lunatic; but he was a knave for trying to entrap a defenceless girl by a mock ceremony. He puts himself in a position in which the contemptible Mr. Mason has a moral advantage.

This is by far the worst blot in Miss Brontë's work, and may partly explain, though it cannot justify, the harsh criticisms made at the time. It is easy now to win a cheap reputation for generosity by trampling upon the dead bodies of the luckless critics who blundered so hopelessly. The time for anger is past; and mere oblivion is the fittest doom for such offenders. Inexperience, and consequently inadequate appreciation of the demands of the situation, was Miss Brontë's chief fault in this matter, and most certainly not any want of true purity and moral elevation. But the fact that she, in whom an instinctive nobility of spirit is, perhaps, the most marked characteristic, should have given scandal to the respectable, is suggestive of another inference. What, in fact, is the true significance of this singular strain of thought and feeling, which puts on various and yet closely-allied forms in the three remarkable novels we have been considering? It displays itself at one moment in some vivid description, or—for "description" seems too faint a word—some forcible presentation to our mind's eye of a fragment of moorland scenery; at another, it appears as an ardently sympathetic portrayal of some trait of character at once vigorous and tender; then it utters itself in a passionate soliloquy, which establishes the fact that its author possessed the proverbial claim to knowledge of the heavenly powers; or again, it produces one of those singular little prose-poems—such as Shirley's description of Eve—which, with all their force, have just enough flavour of the "devoirs" at M. Heger's establishment to suggest that they are the work of an inspired schoolgirl. To gather up into a single formula the meaning of such a character as Lucy Snowe, or, in other words, of Charlotte Brontë, is, of course, impossible. But at least such utterances always give us the impression of a fiery soul imprisoned in too narrow and too frail a tenement. The fire is pure and intense. It is kindled in a nature intensely emotional, and yet aided by an heroic sense of duty. The imprisonment is not merely that of a feeble body in uncongenial regions, but that of a narrow circle of thought, and consequently of a mind which has never worked itself clear by reflection, or developed an harmonious and consistent view of life. There is a certain feverish disquiet which is marked by the peculiar mannerism of the style. At its best, we have admirable flashes of vivid expression, where the material of language is the incarnation of keen intuitive thought. At its worst, it is strangely contorted, crowded by rather awkward personifications, and degenerates towards a rather unpleasant Ossianesque. More severity of taste would increase the power by restraining the abuse. We feel an aspiration after more than can be accomplished, an unsatisfied yearning for potent excitement, which is sometimes more fretful than forcible.

The symptoms are significant of the pervading flaw in otherwise most effective workmanship. They imply what, in a scientific sense, would be an inconsistent theory, and, in an aesthetic sense, an inharmonious representation of life. One great aim of the writing, explained in the preface to the second edition of *Jane Eyre,* is a protest against conventionality. But the protest is combined with a most unflinching adherence to the proper conventions of society; and we are left in great doubt as to where the line ought to be drawn. Where does the unlawful pressure of society upon the individual begin, and what are the demands which it may rightfully make upon our respect? At one moment in *Jane Eyre* we seem to be drifting towards the solution that strong passion is the one really good thing in the world, and that all human conventions which oppose it should be disregarded. This was the tendency which shocked the respectable reviewers of the time. Of course they should have seen that the strongest sympathy of the author goes with the heroic self-conquest of the heroine under temptation. She triumphs at the cost of a determined self-sacrifice, and undoubtedly we are meant to sympathise with the martyr. Yet it is also true that we are left with the sense of an unsolved discord. Sheer stoical regard for duty is represented as something repulsive, however imposing, in the figure of St. John Rivers, and virtue is rewarded by the arbitrary removal of the obstacles which made it unpleasant. What would Jane Eyre have done, and what would our sympathies have been, had she found that Mrs. Rochester had not been burnt in the fire at Thornfield? That is rather an awkward question. Duty is supreme, seems to be the moral of the story; but duty sometimes involves a strain almost too hard for mortal faculties.

If in the conflict between duty and passion the good so often borders upon the impracticable, the greatest blessing in the world should be a will powerful enough to be an inflexible law for itself under all pressure of circumstances. Even a will directed to evil purposes has a kind of royal prerogative, and we may rightly do it homage. That seems to be the seminal thought in *Wuthering Heights*, that strange book to which we can hardly find a parallel in our literature, unless in such works as the *Revengers Tragedy*, and some other crude but startling productions of the Elizabethan dramatists. But Emily Brontë's feeble grasp of external facts makes her book a kind of baseless nightmare, which we read with wonder and with distressing curiosity, but with even more pain than pleasure or profit. Charlotte's mode of conceiving the problem is given most fully in *Villette*, the book of which one can hardly say, with a recent critic, that it represents her "ripest wisdom," but which seems to give her best solution of the great problem of life. Wisdom, in fact, is not the word to apply to a state of mind which seems to be radically inconsistent and tentative. The spontaneous and intense affection of kindred and noble natures is the one really precious thing in life, it seems to say; and, so far, the thought is true, or a partial aspect of the truth; and the high feeling undeniable. But then, the author seems to add, such happiness is all but chimerical. It falls to the lot only of a few exceptional people, upon whom fortune or Providence has delighted to shower its gifts. To all others life is either a wretched grovelling business, an affair of making money and gratifying sensuality, or else it is a prolonged martyrdom. Yield to your feelings, and the chances are enormously great that you are trampled upon by the selfish, or that you come into collision with some of those conventions which must be venerated, for they are the only barriers against moral degradation, and which yet somehow seem to make in favour of the cruel and the self-seeking. The only safe plan is that of the lady in the ballad, to "lock your heart in a case of gold, and pin it with a silver pin." Mortify your affections, scourge yourself with rods, and sit in sackcloth and ashes; stamp vigorously upon the cruel thorns that strew your pathway, and learn not to shrink, when they lacerate the most tender flesh. Be an ascetic, in brief, and yet without the true aim of the ascetic. For, unlike him, you must admit that these affections are precisely the best part of you, and that the offers of the Church, which proposes to wean you from the world and reward you by a loftier prize, are a delusion and a snare. They are the lessons of a designing priesthood, and imply a blasphemy against the most divine instincts of human nature.

This is the unhappy discord which runs through Miss Brontë's conceptions of life, and, whilst it gives an indescribable pathos to many pages, leaves us with a sense of something morbid and unsatisfactory. She seems to be turning for relief alternately to different teachers, to the promptings of her own heart, to the precepts of those whom she has been taught to revere, and occasionally, though timidly and tentatively, to alien schools of thought. The attitude of mind is, indeed, best indicated by the story (a true story, like most of her incidents) of her visit to the confessional in Brussels. Had she been a Catholic, or a Positivist, or a rebel against all the creeds, she might have reached some consistency of doctrine, and therefore some harmony of design. As it is, she seems to be under a desire which makes her restless and unhappy, because her best impulses are continually warring against each other. She is between the opposite poles of duty and happiness, and cannot see how to reconcile their claims, or even—for perhaps no one can solve that or any other great problem exhaustively—how distinctly to state the question at issue. She pursues one path energetically, till she feels herself to be in danger, and then shrinks with a kind of instinctive dread, and resolves not only that life is a mystery, but that happiness must be sought by courting misery. Undoubtedly such a position speaks of a mind diseased, and a more powerful intellect would even under her conditions have worked out some more comprehensible and harmonious solution.

For us, however, it is allowable to interpret her complaints in our own fashion, whatever it may be. We may give our own answer to the dark problem, or at least indicate the path by which an answer must be reached. For a poor soul so grievously beset within and without by troubles in which we all have a share, we can but feel the strongest sympathy. We cannot sit at her feet as a great teacher, nor admit that her view of life is satisfactory, or even intelligible. But we feel for her as for a fellow-sufferer who has at least felt with extraordinary keenness the sorrows and disappointments which torture most cruelly the most noble virtues, and has clung throughout her troubles to beliefs which must in some form or other be the guiding lights of all worthy actions. She is not in the highest rank amongst those who have fought their way to a clearer atmosphere, and can help us to clearer conceptions; but she is among the first of those who have felt the necessity of consolation, and therefore been stimulated to more successful efforts.

—Sir Leslie Stephen, from "Charlotte Brontë,"
1877, *Hours in a Library*, 1874–79 1904,
vol. 3, pp. 301–311

MILLICENT GARRETT FAWCETT (1889)

Millicent Garrett Fawcett (1847–1929) was one of Great Britain's most influential advocates for women's rights in the late nineteenth and early twentieth centuries. In 1871 she cofounded Newnham College, Cambridge, one of the first colleges to admit female students. From

1897 to 1919, she served as president of the National Union of Women's Suffrage Societies (NUWSS). Fawcett was also a writer, whose works include *Women's Suffrage: A Short History of a Great Movement* (1912), a biography of Josephine Butler (1927), and earlier, *Some Eminent Women of Our Times* (1889), from which this discussion of Brontë's marriage is extracted. Fawcett's criticism of Brontë's husband, Arthur Bell Nicholls, expands on Elizabeth Gaskell's idea that Nicholls was indifferent to his wife's literary career. Fawcett is much harsher than Gaskell, accusing Nicholls of an "essential meanness of soul" in his apparent disinterest in Brontë's genius. Of course, the short span of the Nicholls' married life (only eleven months) makes it difficult to cast such judgments, and we cannot know the degree to which Brontë participated in the curtailment of her work during her brief married life.

The loving admirers of Charlotte Brontë can never feel much enthusiasm for Mr. Nicholls. Mrs. Gaskell states that he was not attracted by her literary fame, but was rather repelled by it; he appears to have used her up remorselessly, in their short married life, in the routine drudgery of parish work. She did not complain, on the contrary, she seemed more than contented to sacrifice everything for him and his work; but she remarks in one of her letters, "I have less time for thinking." Apparently she had none for writing. Surely the husband of a Charlotte Brontë, just as much as the wife of a Wordsworth or a Tennyson, ought to be attracted by literary fame. To be the life partner of one to whom the most precious of Nature's gifts is confided, and to be unappreciative of it and even repelled by it, shows a littleness of nature and essential meanness of soul. A true wife or husband of one of these gifted beings should rather regard herself or himself as responsible to the world for making the conditions of the daily life of their distinguished partners favourable to the development of their genius. But pearls have before now been cast before swine, and one cannot but regret that Charlotte Brontë was married to a man who did not value her place in literature as he ought.

—Millicent Garrett Fawcett, *Some Eminent Women of Our Times*, 1889, p. 109

ANNE RITCHIE (1891)

Anne Thackeray Ritchie (1837–1919) was the elder daughter of Brontë's favorite novelist, William Makepeace Thackeray. She was herself a novelist, but is better known for her various reminiscences about her childhood (such as this piece); her father's fame enabled her to meet many noteworthy Victorians.

One of the most notable persons who ever came into our old bow-windowed drawing-room in Young Street is a guest never to be forgotten by me, a tiny, delicate, little person, whose small hand nevertheless grasped a mighty lever which set all the literary world of that day vibrating. I can still see the scene quite plainly!—the hot summer evening, the open windows, the carriage driving to the door as we all sat silent and expectant; my father (W. M. Thackeray), who rarely waited, waiting with us; our governess and my sister and I all in a row, and prepared for the great event. We saw the carriage stop, and out of it sprang the active, well-knit figure of young Mr. George Smith, who was bringing Miss Brontë to see our father. My father, who had been walking up and down the room, goes out into the hall to meet his guests, and then after a moment's delay the door opens wide, and the two gentlemen come in, leading a tiny, delicate, serious, little lady, pale, with fair straight hair, and steady eyes. She may be a little over thirty; she is dressed in a little *barege* dress with a pattern of faint green moss. She enters in mittens, in silence, in seriousness; our hearts are beating with wild excitement. This then is the authoress, the unknown power whose books have set all London talking, reading, speculating; some people even say our father wrote the books—the wonderful books. To say that we little girls had been given *Jane Eyre* to read scarcely represents the facts of the case; to say that we had taken it without leave, read bits here and read bits there, been carried away by an undreamed-of and hitherto unimagined whirlwind into things, times, places, all utterly absorbing and at the same time absolutely unintelligible to us, would more accurately describe our states of mind on that summer's evening as we look at Jane Eyre—the great Jane Eyre—the tiny little lady. The moment is so breathless that dinner comes as a relief to the solemnity of the occasion, and we all smile as my father stoops to offer his arm, for, genius though she may be, Miss Brontë can barely reach his elbow.

—Anne Ritchie, "My Witches' Caldron,"
Macmillan's Magazine, February 1891,
pp. 251–252

WILLIAM WRIGHT (1893)

Dr. William Wright (1837–1899) was an Irish reverend and author whose volume *The Brontës in Ireland or Facts Stranger than Fiction* (1893, 1894) takes many creative liberties in its treatment of the family. He claims that the particular flavor of the Brontës' genius is derived from the family's Irish heritage. The following excerpt romanticizes the family's collective enthusiasm for storytelling with an intimacy that we have to question.

Story-telling, as we shall see, was a hereditary gift in the Brontë family, and Patrick (Charlotte's father) inherited it from his father. Charlotte's friend, Miss Ellen Nussey, has often told me of the marvelous fascination with which the girls would hang on their father's lips as he depicted scene after scene of some tragic story in glowing words and with harrowing details. The breakfast would remain untouched till the story had passed the crisis, and sometimes the narration became so real and vivid and intense that the listeners begged the vicar to proceed no farther. Sleepless nights succeeded story-telling evenings at the vicarage.

—William Wright, *The Brontës in Ireland*, 1893, pp. 15–16

CLEMENT K. SHORTER (1896)

Clement King Shorter (1857–1926) was a journalist and editor who wielded great influence over the literary tastes of late-nineteenth- and early-twentieth-century England. He was editor of both the *Illustrated London News* and the *English Illustrated Magazine* and founder of *The Tatler*, in 1901. The Brontës were a special project of Shorter's; his books include *Charlotte Brontë and Her Circle* in 1896 (later retitled *The Brontës and Their Circle*), *Charlotte Brontë and Her Sisters* (1905), and *The Brontës: Life and Letters* (1908).

As this excerpt demonstrates, Shorter's approach to Brontë (and her family) is popular and chatty rather than analytical. He was fascinated by the Brontës' austere upbringing, exaggerates the family's poverty, and describes Charlotte Brontë's life quite dramatically as a sequence of tragedy and disaster.

Taken as a whole, the life of Charlotte Brontë was among the saddest in literature. At a miserable school, where she herself was unhappy, she saw her two elder sisters stricken down and carried home to die. In her home was the narrowest poverty. She had, in the years when that was most essential, no mother's care; and perhaps there was a somewhat too rigid disciplinarian in the aunt who took the mother's place. Her second school brought her, indeed, two kind friends; but her shyness made that school-life in itself a prolonged tragedy. Of the two experiences as a private governess I shall have more to say. They were periods of torture to her sensitive nature. The ambition of the three girls to start a school on their own account failed ignominiously. The suppressed vitality of childhood and early womanhood made Charlotte unable to enter with sympathy and toleration into the life of a foreign city, and Brussels was for her a further disaster. Then within two years, just as literary fame was bringing its consolation for the trials of the past, she saw her two beloved sisters taken from her. And, finally, when at last a good man won her love, there were left to her only nine months of happy married life. "I am not going to die. We have been so happy." These words to her husband on her deathbed are not the least piteously sad in her tragic story.

—Clement K. Shorter, *The Brontës and Their Circle*, 1896, p. 21

GENERAL

The excerpts in this section refer to Charlotte Brontë's works and style broadly, or they place her in the literary context of the nineteenth century. The public fascination with Brontë's secluded life in Haworth and the tragic deaths of her siblings, as many of the excerpts in the preceding section reveal, seems to have made the passion and vigor attributed to her writing all the more noteworthy. Critic after critic, as this section shows, remarks on the forcefulness of Brontë's emotions. Sometimes this is a compliment, and sometimes it is not, but her critics largely praise the honesty of the emotions that they attribute to her, even when finding them overwrought.

Moreover, the emphasis on the seclusion of the Brontës' life on the moors of Haworth recycles a mainstay of the Romantic ideology: the notion of the isolated genius, reflecting the beliefs and impressions of his or her own mind rather than the currents of society and history. This reading of Charlotte Brontë (and her sisters) has largely been revised, or at least challenged, more recently. Modern critics have pointed out, for instance, that Haworth was not a lonely outpost but a growing industrial town and that the Brontë siblings were not raised in bookish seclusion but in a richly companionable and intellectually stimulating household, where they wrote their stories and later novels in dialogue. But in the nineteenth century, as many of these excerpts attest, most critics saw Brontë's genius as self-conceived and remote from historical causality.

SYDNEY DOBELL (1850)

Sydney Thompson Dobell (1824–1874) was an English poet and critic. He was a member of the spasmodic school of poetry, which was characterized by a discontented and skeptical sensibility and ornate style. He published *The Roman* in 1850 under the palindromic pseudonym of Sydney Yendys and a second long poem, *Balder*, in 1854. He also cowrote a set of sonnets about the Crimean War in 1855 that were followed by *England in Time 4 War*. Dobell was friends with such literary figures as Browning, Ruskin, Hunt, Mazzini, Tennyson, and Carlyle. He was a generous supporter of other writers and an advocate of reformist politics both at home and abroad.

In the following review Dobell offers an analysis of Charlotte Brontë as an author. As many critics did, Dobell assumed that *Jane Eyre* and *Wuthering Heights* were written by the same person, and he consequently treats the novels as the successive productions of one writer. Charlotte Brontë attempted to correct this misconception in her subsequent correspondence with him.

Dobell is hard on *Shirley*. He takes issue with its title, citing Caroline's innate moral superiority and Shirley's relatively unheroic character, and claims that Caroline Helstone is the one true heroine of the novel. His concerns with the book are not centered only on Brontë's characterizations, though. In general, he feels that she has not rested adequately between the writing of *Jane Eyre* and *Shirley* and that her creative exhaustion is apparent in every aspect of the latter novel. Where *Jane Eyre* has a rich and effortless originality, he sees *Shirley* as flimsy, self-conscious, and heavy handed. Despite these drawbacks, he nonetheless applauds the important moral and political agenda promoted in *Shirley*: a society organized around merit instead of material wealth.

While he finds much to criticize in *Shirley*, his overall assessment of Charlotte Brontë is very positive: He maintains that *Jane Eyre* deserves to be "universally read" and that Charlotte Brontë, if she allows her genius time to ripen, has the ability to achieve real greatness. Characteristically, Dobell offers the author both effusive praise and detailed instructions for improvement.

———

Any attempt to give, in a review, a notion of *Jane Eyre* would be injustice both to author and reviewer; and, fortunately for both, is now unnecessary. Few books have been, and have deserved to be, so universally read, and so well remembered. We shall not now essay even an analysis of the work itself, because we have in this article fixed our eyes rather upon the author than the reader; and whatever absolute superiority we may discover in *Jane Eyre,* we find in it only further evidence of the same producing qualities to which *Wuthering Heights* bears testimony. Those qualities, indurated by time, armed by experience, and harmonised by the natural growth of a maturing brain, have here exhibited, in a more favourable field, and under stronger guidance, the same virtues and the same faults. In *Shirley,* on the other hand, we see the same qualities—with feebler health, and under auspices for the time infelicitous—labouring on an exhausted soil. Israel is at work, indeed; but there is a grievous want of straw, and the groan of the people is perceptible. The book is misnamed *Shirley.* Caroline Helstone, the child of nature, should yield no pre-eminence to Shirley Keeldar, the daughter of circumstance.

The character of the one is born of womanhood; that of the other of 'Fieldhead, and a thousand a year.' Kant's formula, inefficient in morals, is sometimes useful in criticism. 'Canst thou will thy maxim to be law universal?' Place Caroline Helstone where you will, she is still exquisitely sweet, and, in element, universally true. To make Shirley Keeldar repulsive, you have only to fancy her poor. This absence of intrinsic heroism in the heroine, and some shortcomings on the part of the authoress—a consciousness of the reader, an evident effort, and an apparent disposition to rest contented with present powers, opinions, and mental status—would do much to damp the hopes of a critic, were they not the mere indications of overwork, and of a brain not yet subsided from success. One eloquent and noble characteristic remains to her unimpaired. Her mission [of social reform] is perpetually remembered ... There is much work here which the poets cannot do, and which the ungifted *may* not do. The poets, when they are prophets, should speak only to the highest minds. The giftless should not speak to any. They have a better duty and privilege—to work out the thoughts of the highest. But here is a doctrine and practice affecting every man—wise and foolish, rich and poor, young and old, the highest genius and the lowest drudge. And the evangelist, like the evangel, must be cosmopolitan. We believe that, among other high callings, this evangelism has fallen to Currer Bell; and we bid her God speed in her grand work, because we believe that in attempting to return to social reality—to harmonise the outward and the inward—to stamp the invisible character on the visible face of the age—we shall solve unconsciously many troublesome problems, and shall be preparing the way for Him, who, alone knowing the secrets of men, can alone construct and exhibit for us in its full perfection the ideal of society. But we cannot help thinking, with all admiration for Currer Bell, and all respect for her artistic competence, that on those ram's horns she has blown so vigorously before walls that must surely come down (those grim old feudal bastions of prejudice, and those arabesque barriers of fashion, which will fall in the wind of them), there are other tunes possible than that one of which she has already given us the air and variations—that to repeal the test and corporation acts of extinct castes, and to reconstruct society on the theory of an order of merit, something more is needed than a perpetual *pas de deux* between master and governess, mistress and tutor. True, the temptation was strong, and perhaps she has hitherto done well to yield to it. It is difficult to find in other positions than those she has drawn the precise ideal of the two classes she would invert in situations where the machinery of inversion would be so natural and easy, and where she could exhibit, at so little cost of skill, the conventional rank of outward circumstance bowing before the absolute rank of intrinsic superiority. Nevertheless, other cases exist, and it must be Currer Bell's to find them.

We have said that in *Shirley* we see the qualities of the author of *Jane Eyre* labouring on an exhausted soil. The fat kine and the lean are a fair emblem of the two books. Jane is in high condition; her 'soul runneth over with marrow and fatness;' in her sorriest plight she is instinct with superfluous life; all her 'little limbs' are warm, all her veins pulsate; she is full of unction; the *oleum vitœ* lubricates her brain day and night. The other book gives one the idea of a great sketch poorly filled in, or a Frankenstein skeleton finished in haste, at a proportionate economy in fat and flesh. *Jane Eyre* is the real spar—the slow deposit which the heart of genius filters from the daily stream of time and circumstance. *Shirley* is its companion, made to order, fair to look upon, but lacking the internal crystal. Open the earlier work where you will, this crystal sparkles in your eyes; break it up piecemeal, and every fragment glitters. Turn over the first chapter, and pause at hazard. There is no apparent consciousness of wisdom—no parading of truths or setting forth of paradoxes—no dealing in aphorisms, axioms, or generals of any kind. Yet one could preach a sermon from every sentence. Who that remembers early childhood can read without emotion the little Jane Eyre's night journey to Lowood? How finely, yet how unconsciously, are those peculiar aspects of things which cease with childhood developed in this simple history!—that feeling of unlimited vastness in the world around—that absence of all permanent idea of the extra-visible, which leaves everything not actually seen in outer fog, wherein all things are possible—that strange absence of all habitual expectations, which makes even a new room a field of discovery, wherein the infant perceptions go, slowly struggling and enlightening, like a faint candle in a dark night. There is something intensely, almost fearfully, interesting in the diary of a child's feelings. This 'I,' that seems to have no inheritance in the earth, is an eternity with a heritage in all heavens. This 'me,' which is thrown here and there as a thing of nought—the frail, palpitating subject of a schoolboy's tyranny, almost too fragile even to make sport for him—fear not for it. It can endure. This, that trembles at the opening of a parlour-door, quails at the crushing of a china plate, droops amid the daily cuffs and bruises of a household, and faints with fear in a haunted room, will pass alive through portals which the sun dare not enter, survive all kinds of temporal and spiritual wreck, move uninjured among falling worlds, meet undismayed the ghosts of the whole earth, pass undestroyed through the joys of angels—perhaps, also, through anguish which would dissolve the stars. Is there not something awful in these 'I's' and 'me's'? They go about the page in a kind of veiled divinity; and when the unjust hand strikes 'me,' or 'I' am reviled by the graceless lip of vulgar arrogance, we shrink involuntarily as from sacrilege.

But pass over the striking passages in these chapters; take some sentence which the circulating library will skip. It is full of the moralities of nature. Little, ill-used Jane Eyre does not hush her doll, but we are the better for it. 'I was happy,' says she, *believing it to be happy likewise.* Uncurl your lip, reader, and take this little sentence reverently, for it contains a great psychologic truth. We read, week by week, 'it is more blessed to give than to receive;' but how few of us recognise the reason, that the best abiding happiness must arise from the happiness of others. . . . Those few words are a masterstroke of genius. Only let Jane Eyre give you her nursery confessions, and they shall help you to read the heart of three-score and ten. . . . But we might multiply extracts as easily as turn the page. We have quoted these not for the reader, but the author; and—though it be a labour of love—must quote no more.

We sat down to this paper with no intention of what is ordinarily expected in a review. We look upon it as a morning talk with that accomplished young writer, with whose name we have graced it. Literally a half-hour *with* a best author. We rise to take leave, strengthened in the conviction with which we entered—that the authoress of *Jane Eyre* is the novelist of the coming time. . . .

It seems to us that the authoress *of Jane Eyre* combines all the natural and accidental attributes of the novelist of her day. In the ecclesiastical tendencies of her education and habits—in the youthful ambiguity of her politics—in a certain old-world air, which hangs about her pictures, we see her passports into circles which otherwise she would never reach. Into them she is carrying, unperceived, the elements of infallible disruption and revolution. In the specialties of her religious belief, her own self-grown and glorious heterodoxies—in the keen satiric faculty she has shown—in the exuberant and multiform vigour of her idiosyncrasy—in her unmistakeable hatred of oppression, and determination to be free—in the onward tendencies of a genius so indisputably original, and in the reaction of a time on which, if she lives, she cannot fail to act strongly, we acknowledge the best pledge that that passport, already torn, will be one day scattered to the winds. The peculiarities of her local position—evidently Lancashire or Yorkshire—give her opportunity for investigating a class of character utterly out of the latitude of the London *litterateur*—the manufacturing classes, high and low—the Pancrates of the future, into whose hands the ball of empire has now passed; and in the strange combination of factory and moorland, the complexities of civilisation and the simple majesty of nature, she has before her, at one glance, the highest materials for the philosopher and the poet—the most magnificent emblem of the inner heart of the time. One day, with freer hands, more practised eye, an ampler horizon, an enlarged experience, she must give us such revelations of that heart—of its joys, woes, hopes, beliefs, duties and destinies—as shall make it leap like a dumb man healed. But, above all other circumstantial advantages, there is one element in her diagnosis which, alas! in these times, is full of an ominous and solemn interest—her faith in the Christian Record is unshaken. If this were merely a passive faith, the ordinary accident of her youth and sex, we should look upon it, at best, with mournful prescience, as one might see the white plumes and unspotted braveries of a host in full march for a field of blood. But in Currer Bell this faith is evidently positive and energic. Self-supporting, also; for it is united with a vigour of private judgment, without which there is nothing for it but famine in these days. . . .

In bidding, for a while, farewell to an author towards whom we cannot feel too warmly, and of whom it is difficult, in the space of a review, to say enough, we would give one parting word of an advice which, for her, comprehends all others—*Wait*. Having learned that you have the power to labour, let that tremendous knowledge beget in you an unconquerable patience; stand and grow under the weight of your responsibilities; get accustomed to the knowledge of your powers. . . . What I say unto you, I say unto all—*Watch*. Do not try to give largesse out of an exhausted treasury, lest you exert your prerogative to depreciate the currency, and, being conscious of the will to do wonders, take, or gain, credit for the deed. Enrich your own soul, that the alms you give us shall not be of your penury but of your abundance. Be so long bare-headed under the dews of heaven that you shall need but to nod to scatter them on the earth. Send your heart long enough into the school of life, and its daily sayings shall be wisdom for us. Every tree has in its time dropped honey-dew: it is the happiness of genius that culture can make this a perpetual exhalation. There are few fruits which, more or less perfectly, cannot sustain the life of man; it is the prerogative of genius that its very leaves may be for the healing of the nations. There is a time in the excellence of genius, when, like the spheres, to move is music. It will be well for the possessor of genius if he can keep silence till that time. These things we commend in love to the authoress of *Shirley*.

The strength of Currer Bell lies in her power of developing the history, more or less amplified and varied by imagination, of her own individual mind. In saying this, we are not depreciating, for we are giving her the characteristic attribute of a poet—which, nevertheless, in some senses, she is not, and will not be. Before she writes another volume of that great history, in the shape of a new novel, she should live another era of that strong, original, well-endowed mind. She must go through the hopes and fears, passions and sympathies, of her age; and by virtue of her high privilege of genius, she must take not only the colour of her time, but that complementary colour of the future which attends it; she must not only hear the voice of her day, but catch and repeat its echoes on the forward rock of ages; she must not only strike the chord which shall rouse us to the battle of the hour, but seize and embody that sympathetic note on the unseen strings of the 'To come,' which it is the attribute of genius to recognise and to renew.

—Sydney Dobell, from "Currer Bell," 1850,
The Life and Letters of Sydney Dobell, ed.
Emily Jolly, 1878, vol. 1, pp. 176–186

PETER BAYNE (1857)

Peter Bayne was born in Aberdeenshire, Scotland, and studied theology at Edinburgh before turning to writing and journalism. His works include *The Christian Life* and two volumes of *Essays in Biography and Criticism* (1857 and 1859). He credited his style to Thomas Carlyle while claiming a total dissent from Carlyle's judgments. Bayne was briefly editor in chief of a Glasgow newspaper, the *Commonwealth*, but retired due to poor health. After living in Berlin, Bayne returned to Scotland to take up editorship of *The Witness*, a political-religious journal, in 1857. His *Essays in Biography and Criticism* (vol. 1) includes, in addition to discussion of Currer Bell, essays on Thomas de Quincey; Alfred, Lord Tennyson; as well as individual works such as *Paradise Lost* and *Aurora Leigh*, among others.

Like other Victorian critics included in this volume, Bayne draws
attention to Charlotte Brontë's "nobly English" style, which he uses to
exemplify directness and honesty.

The style of Currer Bell is one which will reward study for its own sake. Its
character is directness, clearness, force. We could point to no style which
appears to us more genuinely and nobly English. Prompt and businesslike,
perfectly free of obscurity, refining, or involution, it seems the native garment
of honest passion and clear thought, the natural dialect of men that can work
and will. It reminds one of a good highway among English hills: leading
straight to its destination, and turning aside for no rare glimpse of landscape,
yet bordered by dewy fields, and woods, and crags, with a mountain stream
here rolling beneath it, and a thin cascade here whitening the face of the
rock by its side: utility embosomed in beauty. Perhaps its tone is somewhat
too uniform, its balance and cadence too unvaried. Perhaps, also, there is
too much of the abruptness of passion. We should certainly set it far below
many styles in richness, delicacy, calmness, and grace. But there is no writer
whose style can be pronounced a universal model; and for simple narrative,
for the relation of what one would hear with all speed, yet with a spice of
accompanying pleasure, this style is a model as nearly perfect as we can
conceive. And its beauty is so genuine and honest! You are at first at a loss
to account for the charm which breathes around, filling the air as with the
fragrance of roses after showers; but the secret cannot long remain hidden
from the poor critic, doomed to know how he is pleased. It lies in the perfect
honesty, combined with the perfect accuracy, of the sympathy with nature's
beauty which dwelt in the breast of the author; in the fact that she ever loved
the dew-drop, the daisy, the mountain bird, the vernal branch. Uncalled for
and to her unconsciously, at the smile of sympathy, the flowers and the dew-
drops come to soften and adorn her page. . . .

The peculiar strength of Currer Bell as a novelist can be pointed out in a
single word. It is that to which allusion was made in speaking of *Wuthering
Heights;* the delineation of one relentless and tyrannizing passion. In hope, in
ardor, in joy, with proud, entrancing emotion, such as might have filled the
breast of him who bore away the fire of Jove, love is wooed to the breast. But
a storm as of fate awakens: the blue sky is broken into lightnings, and hope
smitten dead; and now the love which formerly was a dove of Eden is changed
into a vulture, to gnaw the heart, retained in its power by bands of adamant.
As the victim lies on his rock, the whole aspect of the world changes to his eye.

Ordinary pleasures and ordinary pains are impotent to engage the attention, to assuage the torment. No dance of the nymphs of ocean attracts the wan eye, or for a moment turns the vulture aside. Such a passion is the love of Rochester for Jane, perhaps in a somewhat less degree, that of Jane for Rochester; such, slightly changed in aspect, is the passion beneath which Caroline pines away, and that which convulses the brave bosom of Shirley. With steady and daring hand, Currer Bell depicts this agony in all its stages; we may weep and tremble, but we feel that her nerves do not quiver, that her eye is unfilmed. So perfect is the verisimilitude, nay the truth, of the delineation, that you cannot for a moment doubt that living hearts have actually throbbed with like passion. It is matter, we believe, of universal assent, that Currer Bell here stands almost alone among the female novelists of Britain, and we doubt whether, however they surpass her in the variety of their delineations, there is any novelist of the other sex who, in this department, has exhibited greater power.

—Peter Bayne, "Currer Bell," *Essays
in Biography,* 1857, pp. 409–415

ELIZABETH GASKELL (1857)

Gaskell depicts Brontë's approach to writing as exceptional in its patience, diligence, and precision. She also suggests a portrait of Brontë as fully consumed by her writing. This latter emphasis contributes to the Romantic notion of the driven, even obsessive, genius.

Any one who has studied her writings,—whether in print or in her letters; any one who has enjoyed the rare privilege of listening to her talk, must have noticed her singular felicity in the choice of words. She herself, in writing her books, was solicitous on this point. One set of words was the truthful mirror of her thoughts; no others, however apparently identical in meaning, would do. She had that strong practical regard for the simple holy truth of expression, which Mr. Trench [Richard Chenevix Trench, *Study of Words* (1851)] has enforced, as a duty too often neglected. She would sit patiently searching for the right term, until it presented itself to her. It might be provincial, it might be derived from the Latin; so that it accurately represented her idea, she did not mind whence it came; but this care makes her style present the finish of a piece of mosaic. Each component part, however small, has been dropped into the right place. She never wrote down a sentence until she clearly understood what she wanted to say, had deliberately chosen the words, and arranged them in their right order. Hence it comes that, in the scraps of paper covered with her pencil writing which I have seen, there will occasionally be a sentence scored out, but seldom, if ever, a word or an expression. She wrote on these bits of paper in a minute hand, holding each against a piece of board, such as is used in binding books, for a desk. This plan was necessary for one so short-sighted as she was; and, besides, it enabled her to use pencil and paper, as she sat near the fire in the twilight hours, or if (as was too often the case) she was wakeful for hours in the night. Her finished manuscripts were copied from these pencil scraps, in clear, legible, delicate traced writing, almost as easy to read as print.

—Elizabeth Gaskell, *The Life of Charlotte Brontë*, 1857, p. 234

John Skelton (1857)

Sir John Skelton (1831–1897) was an author, essayist, and frequent contributor to *Blackwood's Edinburgh Magazine,* a periodical known for its social orthodoxy, as well as other publications including *Fraser's.* Skelton published works under the pseudonym "Shirley" in a gesture to his appreciation for Brontë's heroine. Skelton's review of Brontë, excerpted here, focuses on *Shirley* and *Villette* and is idiosyncratic in its praise of the former; *Shirley* is often considered the weakest of Brontë's three major novels. Skelton praises the unflinching honesty of Brontë's writing, calling it earnest in its directness, which marks a critical tendency that assigns clarity and force to English writing in contrast to the more flowery and metaphorical styles attributed to Continental prose.

Shirley presents a notable contrast to Miss Brontë's other novels. In them there is a profound and frequently overmastering sense of the intense dreariness of existence to certain classes. The creative spirit of poetry and romance breaks at times through the dull and stagnant life; but as a rule it is different; and *Villette,* especially, becomes monotonous from the curb maintained upon the imagination. But *Shirley* is a Holiday of the Heart. It is glad, buoyant, sunshiny. The imagination is liberated, and revels in its liberty. It is the pleasant summer-time, and the worker is idling among the hills. The world of toil and suffering lies behind, but ever so far away. True, it must be again encountered, its problems resolved, its sores probed; the hard and obstinate war again waged manfully; but in the mean time the burn foams and sparkles through the glen; there is sunshine among the purple harebells; and the leaves in the birken glade dance merrily in the summer wind.

> Surely, surely, slumber is more sweet than toil, the
>   shore
> Than labour in the deep mid ocean, wind, and wave,
>   and oar;
> O, rest ye, brother mariners, we will not wander
>   more.

In *Villette* Miss Brontë returns to the realities of life; but with power more conscious and sustained. She is less absorbed, and more comprehensive. There is the same passionate force; but the horizon is wider.

Villette is by no means a cheerful book; on the contrary, it is often very painful, especially where the central figure—the heroine—is involved. *Her* pain—her tearless pain—is intense and protracted. And in this connexion *Villette* may be regarded as an elaborate psychological examination— the anatomy of a powerful but pained intellect—of exuberant emotions watchfully and vigilantly curbed. The character of this woman is peculiar, but drawn with a masterly hand. She *endures* much in a certain Pagan strength, not defiantly, but coldly and without submission. Over her heart and her intellect she exercises an incessant restraint—a restraint whose vigilant activity curbs every feeling, controls every speculation, becomes as it were engrained into her very nature. *She,* at least, will by all means look at the world as it is—a hard, dry, practical world, not wholly devoid of certain compensating elements—and she will not be cajoled into seeing it, or making others see it, under any other light. For herself, she will live honestly upon the earth, and invite or suffer no delusions; strong, composed, self-reliant, sedate in the sustaining sense of independence. But cold and reserved as she may appear, she is not without imagination—rich, even, and affluent as a poet's. This is in a measure, however, the root of her peculiar misery. The dull and cheerless routine of homely life is not in her case relieved and penetrated by the creative intellect, but on the contrary, acquires through its aid a subtle and sensitive energy to hurt, to afflict, and to annoy. Thus she is not always strong; her imagination sometimes becomes loaded and surcharged; but she is always passionately ashamed of weakness. And through all this torture she is very solitary: her heart is very empty; she bears her own burden. There are cheerful hearths, and the pleasant firelight plays on the purple drapery that shuts out the inhospitable night; but none are here who can convey to her the profound sympathy her heart needs pitifully; and so she passes on, pale and unrelenting, into the night. Undoubtedly there is a very subtle, some may say obnoxious, charm in this pale, watchful, lynx-like woman—a charm, certainly, but for our own part we have an ancient prejudice in behalf of *Shirley's* piquant and charming ferocity.

Miss Brontë always wrote earnestly, and in *Villette* she is peremptorily honest. In it she shows no mercy for any of the engaging *ruses* and artifices of life: with her it is something too real, earnest, and even tragic, to be wantonly trifled with or foolishly disguised. She will therefore tolerate no hypocrisy, however decent or fastidious; and her subdued and direct insight goes at once to the root of the matter. She carries this perhaps too far—it may be she lacks a measure of charity and toleration, not for what is bad—for *that* there must be no toleration—but for what is humanly weak and insufficient. Graham Bretton, for instance, with his light hair and kind heart and pleasant sensitiveness, is ultimately treated with a certain implied contempt; and this solely because he happens to be what God made him, and not something deeper and more devout, the incarnation of another and more vivid kind of goodness, which it is not in his nature to be, and to which he makes no claim. It is the patience, the fortitude, the endurance, the strong love that has been consecrated by Death and the Grave, the spirit that has been tried in fire and mortal pain and temptation,—it is these alone she can utterly admire. We believe she is wrong. But as we recall the lone woman sitting by the desolate hearthstone, and remember all that she lost and suffered, we cannot blame very gravely the occasional harshness and impatience of her language when dealing with men who have been cast in a different mould.

Villette excels Miss Brontë's other fictions in the artistic skill with which the characters are—I use the word advisedly—*developed.* She brings us into contact with certain men and women with whom she wishes to make us acquainted. She writes no formal biography; there is no elaborate introduction; the characters appear incidentally during the course of the narrative, and by degrees are worked into the heart of the every-day life with which the story is concerned. But the dissection goes on patiently all the time—so leisurely and yet so ruthlessly—one homely trait accumulated upon another with such steady, untiring pertinacity, that the man grows upon us line by line, feature by feature, until his idiosyncrasy is stamped and branded upon the brain. Probably the most genuine power is manifested in the mode in which the interest is shifted from Graham Bretton to the ill-favoured little despot—Paul Emmanuel. No essential change takes place in *their* characters, *they* remain the same, the colours in which they were originally painted were quite faithful, perfectly accurate—not by any means exaggerated for subsequent effect and contrast. It is only that a deeper insight has been gained by *us,* and if our original judgment undergoes modification, it is not because any new or inconsistent element has been introduced, but because, the conditions remaining the same, *we* see further. Leaf after leaf has been unfolded with a cold and impartial hand, until we have been let down into the innermost hearts of the men, and taught by the scrutiny a new sense of their relative value and worthiness. And Paul Emmanuel is surely a very rich and genuine conception. 'The Professor' will ever be associated in our memory with a certain soft and breezy laughter; for though the love he inspires in the heroine is very deep and even pathetic after its kind, yet the whole idea of the man is wrought and worked out in a spirit of joyous and mellow ridicule, that is full of affection, however, and perhaps at times closely akin to tears.(. . .)

To ourselves, one of the most surprising gifts of the authoress of these volumes is the racy and inimitable English she writes. No other Englishwoman ever commanded such language—terse and compact, and yet fiercely eloquent. We have already had occasion to notice the absence of comparison or metaphor in her poetry; the same is true of her prose. The lava is at white heat; it pours down clear, silent, pitiless; there are no bright bubbles nor gleaming foam. A mind of this order—tempered, and which cuts like steel—uses none of the pretty dexterities of the imagination; for to use these infers a pause of satisfied reflection and conscious enjoyment which it seldom or never experiences. Its rigorous intellect seeks no trappings of pearl or gold. It is content to abide in its white veil of marble—naked and chaste, like 'Death' in the Vatican. Yet, the still severity is more effective than any paint could make it. The chisel has been held by a Greek, the marble hewed from Pentelicus.

—John Skelton, from "Charlotte Brontë,"
Fraser's Magazine, May 1857, pp. 579–582

ANTHONY TROLLOPE (1883)

Anthony Trollope (1815–1882) is one of the most beloved British novelists of the nineteenth century. He wrote 47 novels and many collections of short stories, travel books, and miscellanies, as well as his celebrated *An Autobiography* (1883). During this remarkable career as a novelist and writer, Trollope was also employed by the General Post Office for most of his adult life, working his way into increasingly important positions.

To Trollope, Brontë's great gift is her acuity in creating realistic characters. Many critics say the same thing about Trollope: His fiction inspires more enthusiasm for its characterization than its plotting.

Trollope's forecasts about *Jane Eyre*'s lasting impact were prescient. His other predictions, however, are uneven: Along with *Jane Eyre* and George Eliot's *Adam Bede* (1859), Trollope imagines the future popularity of W.M. Thackeray's *The History of Henry Esmond*, 1852, which is seldom read today. Of the novels he thinks will be forgotten, he is correct about Edward Bulwer-Lytton's *Pelham: or the Adventures of a Gentleman* (1828) and Charles James Lever's *The Confessions of Harry Lorrequer* (1839), but he underestimates the recognition accorded to Dickens's first novel, *The Pickwick Papers* (1837).

―――――――――――――――――

Charlotte Brontë was surely a marvellous woman. If it could be right to judge the work of a novelist from one small portion of one novel, and to say of an author that he is to be accounted as strong as he shows himself to be in his strongest morsel of work, I should be inclined to put Miss Brontë very high indeed. I know no interest more thrilling than that which she has been able to throw into the characters of Rochester and the governess, in the second volume of *Jane Eyre*. She lived with those characters, and felt with every fibre of her heart, the longings of the one and the sufferings of the other. And therefore, though the end of the book is weak, and the beginning not very good, I venture to predict that *Jane Eyre* will be read among English novels when many whose names are now better known shall have been forgotten. *Jane Eyre*, and *Esmond*, and *Adam Bede* will be in the hands of our grandchildren, when *Pickwick*, and *Pelham*, and *Harry Lorrequer* are forgotten; because the men and women depicted are human in their aspirations, human in their sympathies, and human in their actions.

In *Villette*, too, and in *Shirley*, there is to be found human life as natural and as real, though in circumstances not so full of interest as those told in *Jane Eyre*. The character of Paul in the former of the two is a wonderful study. She must herself have been in love with some Paul when she wrote the book, and have been determined to prove to herself that she was capable of loving one whose exterior circumstances were mean and in every way unprepossessing

—Anthony Trollope, *An Autobiography*,
1883, ch. 13

A. Mary F. Robinson (1883)

Agnes Mary Frances Robinson (1857–1945) was an English-born poet and writer, known after her first marriage to James Darmesteter as Agnes-Marie-François Darmesteter and after her second, to Emile Duclaux, as Agnes Mary Frances Duclaux, but she usually published under the name Robinson. In addition to several volumes of poetry, Robinson wrote novels, biographies, and criticism. She achieved some fame, but her poetry was considered derivative and often preachy. The author of the first biography of Emily Brontë, from which this excerpt is taken, Robinson extols Brontë's literary power and analyzes her character and family relationships, especially that with her brother, Branwell, in great detail. Robinson surmises that Branwell's death in September 1848 precipitated Emily's death in December of the same year.

Robinson's comparison of Charlotte and Emily draws a rigid line between the sisters' artistic styles. Robinson credits Charlotte with measured social observance and realism and infers that Emily apprehends the world in a way that resembles, disturbingly, a mythologized hell.

Say that two foreigners have passed through Staffordshire, leaving us their reports of what they have seen. The first, going by day, will tell us of the hideous blackness of the country, but yet more, no doubt, of that awful, patient struggle of man with fire and darkness, of the grim courage of those unknown lives; and he would see what they toil for, women with little children in their arms; and he would notice the blue sky beyond the smoke, doubly precious for such horrible environment. But the second traveller has journeyed through the night; neither squalor nor ugliness, neither sky nor children, has he seen, only a vast stretch of blackness shot through with flaming fires, or here and there burned to a dull red by heated furnaces; and before these, strange toilers, half naked, scarcely human, and red in the leaping flicker and gleam of the fire. The meaning of their work he could not see, but a fearful and impressive phantasmagoria of flame and blackness and fiery energies at work in the encompassing night.

So differently did the black country of this world appear to Charlotte, clear-seeing and compassionate, and to Emily Brontë, a traveller through the shadows. Each faithfully recorded what she saw, and the place was the same, but how unlike the vision!

—A. Mary F. Robinson,
Emily Brontë, 1883, pp. 5–6

ANDREW LANG (1889)

Andrew Lang (1844–1912) was a versatile writer whose fields of interest included poetry, anthropology, Greek scholarship, and fiction. His best-known works were a series of fairy tales, each named for a different color. The first was the *Blue Fairy Book*, published in 1889. Lang's predilection for fantasy is evident in his discussion of Brontë, as he emphasizes the dreamy, otherworldly quality of her work. Lang considers *Jane Eyre* to be Brontë's best work and characterizes her style as fantastical and even mythopoetic, comparing her to Poe. He takes a familiar route in reading Brontë's works as distillations of her own feelings and in his speculation about how her married life might have changed or ended her career.

Miss Brontë's novels are day-dreams and memories rather than stories. In *Jane Eyre* she is dealing with the eternal day-dream of the disinherited; the unfortunate guest at life's banquet. It is a vision that has many shapes: some see it in the form of a buried treasure to make them suddenly wealthy—this was the day-dream of Poe; or of a mine to be discovered, a company to be formed—thus it haunted Balzac. The lodging-house servant straight of foundlings dreams, and behold she is a young countess, changed at nurse, and kept out of her own. The poor author dreams of a "hit," and (in this novel) Miss Brontë dwelt in fantasy on the love and the adventures that might come to a clever governess, who was not beautiful. The love and the adventures—these led her on in that path of story-telling where, perhaps, she might have done more and more fortunate work. *Jane Eyre* is her best story, and far the most secure of life, because it has plenty of good, old-fashioned, foolish, immortal romance. The shrieks, and cries, and nocturnal laughters, the wandering vampire of a mad woman, the shadow of a voice heard clamouring in lonely places, the forlorn child, the demon lover (for Mr. Rochester is a modern Euhemerised version of the demon lover)—these are all parts and parcels of the old romantic treasure, and they never weary us in the proper hands. Mr. Rochester is a mere child of dreams, of visions that sprang out of forty French novels, devoured at Haworth's in one winter! But *Shirley* is a day-dream far less successful. The heroine is Emily Brontë, as she might have been if the great god, Wünsch, who inspires day-dreamers, had given her wealth and health. One might as readily fancy the fortunes of a stormy sea-petrel in a parrot's gilded cage. *Shirley* cannot live with *Jane Eyre*, and *Villette* appears to be a thing of memories rather than of dreams; of bitter memories, too, and of despairing resignations. If people do not read it, one can only say, like the cook in "Ravenshoe," that one "does not wonder at it."

Miss Brontë had few strings to her bow as a novelist. She had not, apparently, the delight in invention, in character, in life, which inspires a writer like Scott, and she never would have been a manufacturer of fiction. She only said what she had to say, and her vitality was so depressed by sorrow and thwarting circumstances, that she could not wander into fresh and happier fields of thought and experience. Perhaps if she had lived longer as a clergyman's wife, she might have become the prose Crabbe of English literature. It is only a guess; almost as probably, like other ladies happy mothers made, she might have ceased to write altogether.

About her poetry, it is not easy to speak, so much has her poetry been overshadowed by her prose. Mr. Birrell calls it "the poetry of commerce," but then this critic detects the commercial element, unless he be venturing some kind of joke, in the author of *Atalanta*. To myself it appears that Miss Brontë often made verses as they ought to be made, that she had an accent of her own. These lines . . . have, unless one's ear is quite mistaken, the firm foot of Mr. Matthew Arnold's reflective poetry.

—Andrew Lang, "Charlotte Brontë,"
Good Words, 1889, p. 239

FREDERIC HARRISON (1895)

Frederic Harrison (1831–1923) was a law professor who wrote widely on political, literary, and historical topics and was one of the foremost proponents of Auguste Comte's positivism in England. His major contribution to British literature is *Early Victorian Literature* (1896). In this essay, Harrison quite conventionally reads Brontë's works as "artistic and imaginative autobiographies" that exude a rare frankness in their portrayal of suffering and passion.

It is quite natural and right that Thackeray, Mrs. Gaskell, indeed all who have spoken of the author of *Jane Eyre*, should insist primarily on the personality of Charlotte Brontë. It is this intense personality which is the distinctive note of her books. They are not so much tales as imaginary autobiographies. They are not objective presentations of men and women in the world. They are subjective sketches of a Brontë under various conditions, and of the few men and women who occasionally cross the narrow circle of the Brontë world. Of the three stories she published, two are autobiographies, and the third is a fancy portrait of her sister Emily. Charlotte Brontë is herself Jane Eyre and Lucy Snowe, and Emily Brontë is Shirley Keeldar. So in *The Professor,* her earliest but posthumous tale, Frances Henri again is simply a little Swiss Brontë. That story also is told as an autobiography, but, though the narrator is supposed to be one William Crimsworth, it is a woman who speaks, sees, and dreams all through the book. The four tales, which together were the work of eight years, are all variations upon a Brontë and the two Brontë worlds in Yorkshire and Belgium. It is most significant (but quite natural) that Mrs. Gaskell in her *Life of Charlotte Brontë* devotes more than half her book to the story of the family before the publication of *Jane Eyre.* The four tales are not so much romances as artistic and imaginative autobiographies.

To say this is by no means to detract from their rare value. The romances of adventure, of incident, of intrigue, of character, of society, or of humor, depend on a great variety of observation and a multiplicity of contrasts. There is not much of Walter Scott in *Ivanhoe* or of Alexandre Dumas in the *Trois Mousquetaires;* and Dickens, Thackeray, Trollope, Bulwer, Miss Edgeworth, Stevenson, and Meredith—even Miss Austen and George Eliot—seek to paint men and women whom they conceive and whom we may see and know, and not themselves and their own home circle. But Charlotte Brontë told us her own life, her own feelings, sufferings, pride, joy, and ambition. She bared for us her own inner soul, and all that it had known and desired, and this she did with a noble, pure, simple, but intense truth. There was neither egoism, nor monotony, nor commonplace in it. It was all coloured with native imagination and a sense of true art. There is ample room in Art for these subjective idealisations of even the narrowest world. Shelley's lyrics are intensely self-centered, but no one can find in them either realism or egoism. The field in prose is far more limited, and the risk of becoming tedious and morbid is greater. But a true artist can now and then in prose produce most precious portraits of self and glowing autobiographic fantasies of a noble kind.

And Charlotte Brontë was a true artist. She was also more than this: a brave, sincere, high-minded woman, with a soul, as the great moralist saw, "of impetuous honesty." She was not seduced, or even moved, by her sudden fame. She put aside the prospect of success, money, and social distinction as things which revolted her. She was quite right. With all her genius it was strictly and narrowly limited; she was ignorant of the world to a degree immeasurably below that of any other known writer of fiction; her world was incredibly scanty and barren. She had to spin everything out of her own brain in that cold, still, gruesome Haworth parsonage. It was impossible for any genius to paint a world of which it was as ignorant as a child. Hence, in eight years she only completed four tales for publication. And she did right. With her strict limits both of brain and of experience she could not go further. Perhaps, as it was, she did more than was needed. *Shirley* and *Villette*, with all their fine scenes, are interesting now mainly because Charlotte Brontë wrote them, and because they throw light upon her brain and nature. *The Professor* is entirely so, and has hardly any other quality. We need not groan that we have no more than we have from her pen. *Jane Eyre* would suffice for many reputations and alone will live. . . .

It is true that a purely subjective work in prose romance, an autobiographic revelation of a sensitive heart, is not the highest and certainly not the widest art. Scott and Thackeray—even Jane Austen and Maria Edgeworth—paint the world, or part of the world, as it is, crowded with men and women of various characters. Charlotte Brontë painted not the world, hardly a corner of the world, but the very soul of one proud and loving girl. That is enough: we need ask no more. It was done with consummate power. We feel that we know her life, from ill-used childhood to her proud matronhood; we know her home, her school, her professional duties, her loves and hates, her agonies and her joys, with that intense familiarity and certainty of vision with which our own personal memories are graven on our brain. With all its faults, its narrowness of range, its occasional extravagances, *Jane Eyre* will long be remembered as one of the most creative influences of the Victorian literature, one of the most poetic pieces of English romance, and among the most vivid masterpieces in the rare order of literary "Confessions."

—Frederic Harrison, "Charlotte Brontë's
Place in Literature," *Forum*, March 1895,
pp. 30-40

George Saintsbury (1895)

George Saintsbury (1845–1933) was one of the first critics of the nineteenth century responsible for the period's canon formation, the identification of "great" writers and works that define the age. His major works, *A History of Nineteenth-Century Literature, 1780–1895* (1896) and *The English Novel* (1913), appear dated today in their emphasis on appreciation rather than critique. "Three Mid-Century Novelists," which discusses George Eliot and Anthony Trollope in addition to Charlotte Brontë, makes several arguments about Brontë that, as befits his status as an originator of the Victorian canon, would become standard. Saintsbury infers that the subject of Brontë's novels is really Brontë herself and uses this argument

to denigrate her work from what may on first glance appear as "genius"
to what, in his opinion, is merely the gloss of personal investment. The
claim that Brontë's fictional portraits were self-portraits became a conventional way for critics to explain the perceived gap between her relatively narrow life and scope and the force of her novels, but it is one that
has been substantially challenged and revised in recent criticism.

—————

The author of *Jane Eyre* has had one indisputable reward for the shortness of
her brilliant career. She has become a classic; she has been recently reprinted
as such with authors the youngest of whom was her senior by nearly half a
century; and though it cannot be said that she had ever quite fallen out of
even popular knowledge, any one with a tolerably sharp eye for criticism must
have perceived that not a few readers come to her, as they come to a classic,
with a more or less respectful ignorance. She was protected from that most
ungracious stage of depreciation which attacks many of her kind immediately
after, if not even before, their death, first by the earliness of that event in
her case, and secondly by the fact that it happened at a peculiar period. In
1855 the English world had not yet become literary; and though I do not
know that the quality of the best literary criticism was much better or much
worse than it is now, the volume of it was infinitely smaller. There were far
fewer newspapers; and the young person who, on the strength of a modern
education, a comfortable confidence in his own judgment, and a hand-book
or two of authorities quotable and pillageable, commences critic, existed in
smaller numbers, and had very much fewer openings. Moreover, Currer
Bell had held one of those literary positions which expose the holder to more
hardships at first than afterwards. She belonged to no school; she was not
involved in any literary parties; she rose with few rivals, and she died before
she had time to create any. So that, though she had great difficulties in making
her way, and was subjected to some unfair and ungenerous comments at first,
when she had begun to make that way she had little direct detraction to fear.

I do not think that she was exactly what can be called a great genius,
or that she would ever have given us anything much better than she did
give; and I do not think that with critical reading *Jane Eyre* improves, or
even holds its ground very well. It has strength, or at any rate force; it
has sufficient originality of manner; it has some direct observation of life
within the due limits of art; and it has the piquancy of an unfashionable
unconventionality at a very conventional time. These are good things, but
they are not necessarily great; and it is to me a very suspicious point that

quite the best parts of Charlotte Brontë's work are admittedly something like transcripts of her personal experience. It is very good to be able to record personal experience in this pointed and vivid way; and perhaps few great creators, if any, have been independent of personal experience. But they have for the most part transcribed it very far off; and they have intermixed the transcription with a far larger amount of direct observation of others, and of direct imagination or creation. Those who have not done so fall into the second or lower place, and do not often rise out of it. This is an experience for confirmation of which I can, I think, confidently appeal to all competent reviewers and most competent editors. A book appears, or an article is sent in, wherein this or that incident, mood, character, what not, is treated with distinct vigour and freshness. The reviewer praises, and looks with languid interest tempered by sad experience for the second book; the editor accepts, and looks with eagerness tempered by experience still more fatal for the second article. Both come, and lo! there is either a distinct falling off from, or a total absence of, the first fine rapture. I think Charlotte Brontë is the capital example of this familiar fact, in a person who has actually attained to literature.

Not that she never did anything good after *Jane Eyre*. I think better than most people seem to have done of *Shirley*, somewhat less well perhaps of *Villette* and *The Professor*. But in all, from *Jane Eyre* itself downward, there is that rather fatal note of the presence and apparent necessity of the personal experience. It is portrait painting or *genre*, not creative art of the unmistakable kind, and in the one case where there seems to be a certain projection of the ideal, the egregious Mr. Rochester, even contemporary opinion—thankful as it was for a variation of type from the usual hero with the chiselled nose, the impeccable, or, if peccable, amiable character, and the general nullity—recognised at once that the ideal was rather a poor one. It was as much of a schoolgirl's or a governess's hero as any one of Scott's or Byron's. It is quite true that Rochester is not merely ugly and rude, but his ugliness and his rudeness are so much of him! And though Jane herself is much more than an underbred little hussy, I fear there is underbreeding and hussyness in her, where she is not a mere photograph. I used to think, years ago, that the finest touch in all Miss Brontë's work is where the boy in *Shirley* makes up his mind to ask Caroline for a kiss as the price of his services, and does not. I am not much otherwise minded now.

—George Saintsbury, "Three Mid-Century Novelists,"
Corrected Impressions, 1895, pp. 157–162

ANGUS M. MACKAY (1897)

Angus Mason MacKay was a Scottish writer who wrote on the Brontës in magazines including the *Westminster Review* and in books such as *The Brontës: Fact and Fiction*. MacKay here attends to the emotional suffering for which Brontë was so famous. While many critics find this topic overblown in her novels, MacKay praises its power and execution.

———— ———— ————

Charlotte Brontë's own art was the antithesis of that of Jane Austen. It was hers to depict love in its deeper, more tragic, more serious moods and aspects. She could give us the ordinary "love scene," and charm us with a spell such as few others can command—witness the passage in *The Professor*, in which Crimsworth claims Frances Henri—but it is the love agony which is her element. The pain of unrequited affection is the feeling she never tires of depicting, and in describing this she has no equal. Her novels may end happily, but not till they have been made the medium of exhibiting the suffering which the master passion brings with it when unaccompanied by hope. Nowhere else are to be found such piercing cries of lonely anguish as may be heard in *Shirley* and *Villette*. They are the very *de profundis* of love sunk in the abyss of despair. And their author insists throughout how much greater this suffering must be for women than for men, both because they are doomed to bear in silence, and because they have not the distraction of an active career.

—Angus M. MacKay, *The Brontës:*
Fact and Fiction, 1897, pp. 40–42

HUGH WALKER (1897)

Hugh Walker (1855–1939) was a prominent Scottish literary critic and scholar (at the University of Wales, Lampeter) whose works include *Three Centuries of Scottish Literature* (1893), *The Age of Tennyson* (1897), and *The Literature of the Victorian Era* (1910).

Walker takes a familiar approach in arguing that Brontë's literature was directly copied from life, but instead of channeling her own emotions, he sees many of her characters as uncomfortably faithful portraits of her friends, acquaintances, and family members. He considers this realistic approach to be limited and speculates that "if she had lived she would soon have exhausted her material." This interpretation recycles the familiar view of Brontë (and her sisters as well) as a sheltered original, unworldly to the extreme. On a more positive note, Walker notes that

Brontë's literary reputation has grown since her death, but we can presume that such honor is enhanced by views, like Walker's own, of her remoteness from the currents and influences of modern life.

———ᴠᴠᴠ— —ᴠᴠᴠ— —ᴠᴠᴠ—

For several reasons Charlotte Brontë holds a higher place in literature than her sister. She has not to be judged by one work only. *Jane Eyre* was followed by *Shirley* (1849), by *Villette* (1853), by *The Professor* (1857), published posthumously, and by the fragment *Emma* (1860). In none of these did she equal her first novel, but she exhibited different sides and aspects of her genius, she multiplied her creations, and she proved, as long as life was given her, that she had what in the language of sport is called 'staying power.' Moreover, Charlotte was decidedly more of the artist than Emily. She understood better the importance of relief. Her imagination too was prevailingly sombre; yet though *Jane Eyre* is sufficiently gloomy, it is less uniformly so than *Wuthering Heights*. The shadow is flecked here and there with light. Again, Charlotte is more versatile in her imagination and much more pictorial than Emily. All the members of the Brontë family had a love and apparently some talent for art; but it is in the works of Charlotte that this talent leaves the clearest traces. There are few things in *Jane Eyre* more impressive than her description in words of the picture her imagination, if not her brush, drew. More ample scope, greater variety, a more humane tone,—these then are the points in which Charlotte surpasses Emily. . . .

Probably no English writer of equal rank has transcribed so much from experience as Charlotte Brontë. Many of her characters were so like the originals as to be immediately recognised by themselves or by their neighbours. Shirley Keeldar was her sister Emily, Mr. Helstone was her father, the three curates were real men, and some of Charlotte's school friends were depicted, it is said, with the accuracy of daguerreotypes. This minute fidelity to fact occasionally brought Miss Brontë into trouble; for she was not particularly sagacious in estimating the effect of what she wrote. We may argue from it, moreover, that if she had lived she would soon have exhausted her material.

Charlotte Brontë was likewise deficient in humour. This might be safely inferred from her works, where there are hardly any humorous characters or situations; and the inference would be confirmed by her life. Her letters, often excellent for their common sense and their high standard of duty, and sometimes for their dignity, are almost destitute of playfulness. Neither does she seem to have readily recognised humour in others. She admired Thackeray above almost all men of her time, but she was completely puzzled by him when they met. She lectured him on his faults, and quaintly adds that his excuses made them worse. The humourist was playing with the too serious mind. Had Miss Brontë been as Irish in nature as she was by blood she would not have made this mistake.

In the case of the Brontës it would be peculiarly ungenerous to insist on defects. All life long they fought against odds. With inadequate means and imperfect training, without friends and without advice, they won by their own force and genius alone a position in literature which is higher now than it was forty years ago. Charlotte is one of the half-dozen or so of great English novelists of the present century.

—Hugh Walker, *The Age of Tennyson*, 1897, pp. 103–106

JAMES OLIPHANT (1899)

James Oliphant was one of the first critics to assess the Victorian novel as an art form with its own particular style and significance. The following description of Charlotte Brontë's fiction is excerpted from his study *Victorian Novelists* (1899). Oliphant emphasizes the dramatic tension that Brontë explored in relationships. His primary example is in the relationship between Jane Eyre and Rochester, which he considers her highest contribution to literary art. Oliphant refers to a common critique of the love affairs in Brontë's novels: that they are unrealistically dramatic. He does, however, defend and admire her original admittance of flawed, physically imperfect characters into her novels.

She shares with Hawthorne the merit of discovering the possibilities of what has been called the *motif*. She saw that in the relation between two people there lay a capacity for dramatic development which could scarcely be exceeded by the greatest wealth of incident or complexity of plot. It is true that, as we have seen, she had not the courage to throw aside entirely the more conventional properties of the novelist, but we have also seen that her stories lose more than they gain from these theatrical expedients. It is not the mysterious lunatic in *Jane Eyre* that enthralls our attention; it is simply the relation between Rochester and Jane. We are deeply interested in each of these characters by itself, and in close relation they move us many times more strongly. It seems so natural now for a novelist to depend on a situation of this kind, that we find it difficult to remember how entirely new the idea was when *Jane Eyre* was given to the world. Hawthorne's *motifs* were equally fresh and stimulating, but they were different from Charlotte Brontë's. He dealt mainly with the individual experiences of a human soul struggling with fate, while his English contemporary found her material in the action and reaction of two strongly-marked characters whose interchange of thought and emotion stirs our sympathy to its depths. It is this that constitutes the absorbing interest of her stories, and the discovery that such a firm foundation could be built with such simple materials was of the highest consequence in the development of the art of fiction.

It has been objected, and will no doubt be objected again, that Charlotte Brontë secured this unusually strong interest by attaching an importance to the passion of love which it does not possess, and ought not to possess, in real life, and which it is therefore wrong in a novelist to represent. But in the first place it may be fairly maintained that love, even in this restricted sense, is the most potent factor in human nature, and that if its significance is not realised in actual life as it is in fiction it is because reflection has been so largely and so unfortunately diverted from it. If this all-important element in the evolution of the race were in any adequate sense understood we should not have people marrying and giving in marriage in the haphazard and irresponsible and sordid fashion of our undeveloped civilisation. It is Charlotte Brontë's chief claim to greatness that she has ennobled the passion of love by triumphantly proving that it may be independent of physical attraction, and revealing its true basis in the subtle affinities of character. She has idealised love in the truest sense, by interweaving with its self-regarding instincts the golden threads of a spiritual and imaginative sympathy. We have all in some degree experienced, in friendship or in love, the unique delight of meeting a kindred soul whose whole being seems to vibrate in unison with our own. It is then that, in the words of Matthew Arnold:

A bolt is shot back somewhere in our heart,

And a lost pulse of feeling stirs again;

The eye sinks inward, and the heart lies plain,

And what we mean we say, and what we would we know.

If this mysterious feeling which reveals us to ourselves in the responsive sympathy of our spiritual counterpart has in any degree been strengthened by communion with the ideal types held together in such a bond in the realms of poetic fiction, we owe a debt of gratitude for the precious gift to the creator of Rochester and Jane Eyre, of Lucy Snowe and Paul Emanuel, of Louis Moore and Shirley Keeldar.

The discovery of the possibilities of such a *motif* would have been of little avail, however, if there had not been in Charlotte Brontë an unusual power of conceiving and representing characters that are at once entirely lifelike and thoroughly interesting. Her portraiture was not always perfect. We have seen that it sometimes became caricature (as it certainly does in the description of the curates in *Shirley)*, that in the case of children it was unreal and unsympathetic, that it was apt to err in a too literal transcript of insignificant peculiarities. Even her successes are not always beyond reproach. Fairfax Rochester has been called a woman's man, and it is perhaps true that there are some traits about him that are not entirely drawn as if from within. But as a whole he forms one of the most striking individualities in fiction. We follow all he says and does with the closest interest, knowing that he will constantly surprise us, but also knowing that every fresh revelation will be consistent with what we have already heard. We can have no deeper impression of reality and strength combined than to find our confidence uniformly justified in such a case. There is scarcely the same absolute success in her other heroes. Paul Emanuel certainly comes very near it, and Robert Moore is also thoroughly good, but his brother Lewis is a little shadowy, and his relation to Shirley Keeldar is not perfectly intelligible. There is indeed one mistake that runs through the relations of all the lovers. The assumption of authority on the part of the man, which the authoress supposed to be a proper attribute of the masculine character, and which she represents all her heroines as expecting and approving, is exaggerated till it approaches brutality. In Rochester it takes a specially ferocious form; in M. Paul it is an ungovernable temper; in Robert Moore it is a condescending superiority; in Lewis it is the privilege of a dominie. These are faults not so much in drawing as in the novelist's theory of the relations between men and women. They are to be regretted, but they can be allowed for without seriously interfering with the reader's enjoyment and appreciation. In her heroines Charlotte Brontë naturally achieves an even greater success. Here she had the knowledge of her own thoughts and feelings to guide her, and in two of her heroines, Jane Eyre and Lucy Snowe, she is understood to have largely reproduced not only her own mental experience but many of the scenes and events of her life. In Pauline and Caroline Helstone she drew partly from herself and partly from her sisters, while Shirley Keeldar is believed to be an idealised portrait of her sister Emily, as she might have been had fortune smiled on her. The two figures that most nearly represent the authoress herself are on the whole the most lifelike that she has drawn, and the interest which the novelist naturally takes in them is communicated to the reader. The two resemble each other rather too closely to attain separate and distinct individualities, but the model from which they are both evidently drawn is a perfectly definite as well as an entirely interesting character. She judged rightly when she put herself, literally as well as figuratively, into her novels. The portrait in each case is that of a girl of acute sensibility, made to be very happy or very miserable, but strong enough to bear either lot with firmness and self-control, in whom the discipline of early neglect or unkindness has caused a repression of feeling that might well have engendered bitterness, but has only intensified a noble pride and a stern sense of duty. It is a sad picture to be drawn from the life, this, for which the rule of conduct was the motto, "If you ever really wish to do anything, you may be sure it is wrong", but as material for imaginative treatment it could not easily have been surpassed. We follow the modest fortunes of this plain-looking girl with an absorbing interest, far greater than is called forth by the thrilling adventures of many a beautiful and romantic heroine. The secret of our sympathy lies in our consciousness of the intense capacity of emotion that underlies the calm face and self-contained manner, but it is a notable achievement of art to impress this consciousness upon us without departing from legitimate means of suggestion. Though in both cases the girl tells her own story, the reader is never bored by the confidences of the narrator, and no impression is left of egotism or undue expansiveness. But the most charming feminine characters are to be found, not in these autobiographical books, but in *Shirley*, in the person of the two friends, Caroline Helstone and Shirley Keeldar. Indeed the love episodes in the book are less interesting than the history of the friendship of the two girls. Caroline is perhaps the most charming of Charlotte Brontë's heroines, and this in spite of the fact that here the novelist has been decidedly less successful in endowing her characters with vivid natural speech. Some of the conversations between Shirley and Caroline are expressed in phraseology that is wholly out of keeping with the age and culture of the speakers. This must of course be distinguished from the much more serious error in a dramatic artist of making the characters *act* or *feel* in a way that is inconsistent with their general nature. Charlotte Brontë rarely makes that mistake, but in *Shirley* especially she allows them sometimes to talk more as the mouthpieces of the author than in their own proper persons. In spite of this, however, the relation between the two friends is very finely portrayed, and enlists our sympathies in a high degree. But notwithstanding the excellence of the chief characters, the book as a whole is scarcely equal to *Jane Eyre* or *Villette.* It attempts more. The canvas is larger, and the *motif is* wider, embracing not only the personal relations of the main figures, but the conflict of capital and labour in one of its striking phases. But the success is scarcely in proportion to the greater ambition, and there are more faults of detail than in the other novels. Some of the minor characters, such as Mrs. Prior and Mr. Yorke, cannot be believed in. A slight but irritating blemish which runs through all Charlotte Brontë's books may further be mentioned as illustrating curiously the want of taste for which her narrow circumstances were responsible—namely, her constant introduction of French words and phrases where English would have done as well. She had learned French thoroughly during her stay in Brussels, which must have been in many ways the most exciting period of her life, and as her mind was full of it she could not help putting it into her books. It is a mistake to call this affectation; it only proves the absence of a perfectly sure taste.

A study of Charlotte Brontë's novels suggests the judgment that while in all of them there is much that is of high value and interest, there is only one part of one of them that leaves the distinct impression of unmistakable greatness, namely, the relation between Rochester and Jane Eyre. This may seem a small achievement on which to base security of fame, but it is not to be measured by the number of pages in which it is contained. It struck a new note in the history of fiction—a note which has added many grand and subtle harmonies to itself in the works of succeeding writers, and the sweetness and power of which will never die away.

—James Oliphant, *Victorian Novelists,*
1899, pp. 72–77

Lewis E. Gates (1900)

Lewis Edwards Gates (1860-1924) was an American scholar who wrote on a variety of European and American nineteenth-century authors. He was an assistant professor at Harvard, first in English and later in comparative literature. Gates's essay on Brontë was published in *Studies and Appreciations* (New York, 1900), a text that spans the nineteenth century from romanticism to impressionism.

Gates's comprehensive knowledge of nineteenth-century literature informs his reading of Brontë. He compares her to several other nineteenth-century novelists and poets, placing her in the Romantic tradition and noting the "visionary" quality of her work, which does not naturally follow from her humble Yorkshire background or the unpretentious characters she creates. In contrast to the more "mild" Jane Austen, Gates emphasizes Brontë's passionate and poetic qualities, which position her in company of Romantics including Blake, Shelley, and Coleridge. Her "sensitiveness to natural beauty" underscores this connection for Gates. But he also situates Brontë in a later poetic school when he ties her to the Pre-Raphaelite Dante Gabriel Rossetti, whose work similarly reflects a "feverish" quality.

Finally, Gates interprets a "womanliness" in Brontë's art, claiming that the organizing principle of love in her novels testifies to a woman's constricted, emotional domain. When he wonders what Brontë "would have made of Marie Bashkirtzeff" he refers to the Russian émigrée, a poet, artist, and author best known for her detailed journals about the challenges faced by a woman artist in nineteenth-century society. Gates uses Bashkirtzeff (also spelled Bashkirtseff) to represent a more worldly perspective that contrasts to his reading of Brontë as narrowly, even obsessively, focused on love.

Unlike many of his contemporary critics, however, Gates's sense of Brontë's passion does not detract from her artistry. He writes that "the life that she puts before us is *actual* life, not a whimsical or fantastic or falsifying counterfeit of life." Her combination of emotionality and realism comprises, for Gates, Brontë's unique genius.

———— ———— ————

Charlotte Brontë was once reproached by the vivacious and ever-confident George Henry Lewes for not more nearly resembling, in her artistic methods, that favourite novelist of the gently cynical and worldly wise,— Jane Austen. Her answering letter, while in tone very prettily submissive, nevertheless justifies vigorously her own methods of writing and her treatment of life. "If I ever *do* write another book," she says, "I think I will have nothing of what you call 'melodrama'; I *think* so, but I am not sure. I *think*, too, I will endeavour to follow the counsel which shines out of Miss Austen's 'mild eyes,' 'to finish more and be more subdued'; but neither am I sure of that. When authors write best, or, at least, when they write most fluently, an influence seems to waken in them, which becomes their master,—which will have its own way,—putting out of view all behests but its own, dictating certain words, and insisting on their being used, whether vehement or measured in their nature; new-moulding characters, giving unthought-of turns to incidents, rejecting carefully elaborated old ideas, and suddenly creating and adopting new ones."

These words of Miss Brontë's carry with them a flash from eyes very different in quality from "Miss Austen's mild eyes," and they express more than a passing mood of protest. Charlotte Brontë really believed in her daemon. She had the faith which so many romantic poets from Blake to Shelley have confessed to, that her words and images were, not cleverly devised, but inevitably suggested. Novelists do not often take themselves so seriously, at least in public, particularly novelists who keep so sanely near the world of fact as Charlotte Brontë keeps. Your Poe and your Hoffmann may professedly dream out and set down their wildly fantastic tales with the same visionary glibness with which Coleridge wrote *Kubla Khan*. But the noteworthy fact is that Charlotte Brontë lays claim to much this same sort of inspiration for her narratives of actual Yorkshire life. Her visions of characters and incidents must have mastered her like veritable hallucinations to lead to such a claim; and this visionary eye of hers may well account, at least in part, for the astonishing vividness of her narratives and for their success in again and again imposing themselves for moments on our faith with a thoroughness that the more sophisticated art of to-day rarely attains. Charlotte Brontë has something of the seer's persuasiveness; she captures our faith at unawares.

In the letter already quoted Charlotte Brontë, while commenting on Jane Austen's work, puts to Lewes a very pertinent question. "Can there be a great artist," she asks, "without poetry?" She herself believed not, and her novels are from first to last faithful illustrations of her creed. It was not for nothing that she lived for so many years a lonely, introspective life between an overcrowded graveyard and the desolate expanses of the Yorkshire moors. The world, as she conceived of it, was not the world of conventional intrigue in drawing-rooms or pump-rooms or gossiping country-side towns; and the news of the world that she sent out through her novels was news that had come to her not by hearsay or tittle-tattle, or authenticated by painstaking watchfulness in the midst of tea-drinkers and scandal-mongers, but news that could bear the comment of the sweep of the moors by day and of the host of stars by night. She was a lyrical poet, and in each of her novels she set herself the task, or rather, her whole energy went into the task, of re-creating the world in such guise that it should have something of the intrinsic beauty of poetry conferred upon it.

Her interpretation of life was, first of all, a woman's interpretation. This is, of course, the conventional thing to say of Charlotte Brontë; but here, as so often, the conventional thing is the true thing, merely in need of a little exposition. Her novels are not feminine readings of life simply in the sense of portraying the passion of love from a woman's point of view. This she does, to be sure, with a power and a beauty that George Eliot, for example, with her impersonal point of view and her withering sense of the rights of intellect, never attains to. But vibrant Jane Eyrism is far from being the sole staple out of which Charlotte Brontë's novels are wrought. Intense sympathy with human love in all its myriad forms, together with an audacious belief in its power to bring happiness, or something better than happiness, is, one is tempted to assert, that sole staple. She has an obsession of reckless faith in the worth of love, and from first to last her novels are full of the pathos of craving hearts, and of the worth that life gains when their craving is contented. It is in the tenderness and strength of her loyalty to love in all its guises, and in her delicate perception and brave portrayal of all the fine ministrations of love to life, that the peculiar feminine quality of her novels resides.

For Charlotte Brontë, the struggle for life is the struggle for affection. There is a pathetic uniformity in the development of her stories when one stops to analyze them. In each, some creature striving for happiness is the central controlling character, and the plot of the story is the process by which this needy pensioner of the author is ultimately made heir to unexpected stores of appreciation and sympathy and love. Jane Eyre, at the opening of her history, is a tragically isolated little figure, without a sincere friend in the world, and symbolically busy over a woodcut of the lonely and frigid arctic regions. At the close, she has three excellent cousins—the two girls are as good as sisters; she casually gets, at the same time with her relatives, a very decent fortune; and above all, she falls heir to the vast hoard of passion long secreted in the caverns of Rochester's heart. Lucy Snowe in *Villette* has much the same fate; after long months or years of loneliness, she gets back old friends who are thrice as friendly as before; and the story of *Villette* is simply the history of Lucy's search for sympathy and of her acquisition of Monsieur Paul. The same is true of *Shirley*; the reader's vital interest in the story depends on his wish to see Caroline Helstone, Shirley, and Louis Moore duly fitted out with their fair share of love: Caroline wins a mother and a lover in a month; and Shirley also, as the reader doubtless remembers, fares sumptuously at the last. It is droll to note how little any of Charlotte Brontë's heroines care for literature or art. She herself was apparently hungry for fame as a writer, but all her heroines are lovers of life, and of life only; not one of them so much as coquets with art or literature except as she may write "exercises" for some favourite master. Very un-modern are all these young women, and the young men, too, for that matter, with no subtle dilettante theories, no morbid contempt for life, no erratic veins of enthusiasm or strange kinds of faculty or of genius. They are all simply bent on getting happiness through love of one sort or another.

Dorothea Brooke and her abstract ideal enthusiasm, Charlotte Brontë could not have conceived or created, any more than she could have traced out with relentless sociological and psychological detail the revenge that the "world" took on Dorothea for her fine passion of unconventionality. Not that Charlotte Brontë was less brave in her contempt of cheap worldly standards than George Eliot; but Dorothea's spiritual restlessness and ambition sprang from a complexity of moral and mental life that Charlotte Brontë's culture was too narrow to have suggested to her, and involves a passion for subtler kinds of goodness than Charlotte Brontë's simple, intense nature brought within her ken. Jane Eyre, when waxing discontented with the tameness of her early life at Thornfield Hall, describes her longing to get away in search of "other and more vivid kinds of goodness." *More vivid kinds of goodness* than those that the common run of mortals reach—these Charlotte Brontë ardently believed in and portrayed. Much of the permanent power of her stories comes from the "impetuous honesty" (to quote from Thackeray's characterization of her), and the fiery intensity of imagination with which she puts before even readers of the present day her sense and vision of what life may be made to mean for those who will live sincerely and resolutely. There is something elemental in her. She gives a new zest to life like the encounter with a bit of wild nature,—with a sea-breeze or the tense germinating silence in the depths of a wood. But she is elemental at the cost of being primitive,—primitive in her devotion to a few great interests, and in her lack of refining complexity of thought. Hence one's sense in reading her that one is moving in a world remote from the present. Her heroines indulge in no self-analysis, have no quarrels with their consciences, no torturing doubts about duty, no moral or spiritual struggles. They are curiously definite and resolute little persons, who at every crisis know in a trice just where duty lies and just what they want to do. Their minds are clear, their ideas about what makes life worth while are certain, their wills are intact; their only quarrel is with circumstance. They have no wish to play with life imaginatively, no sense of the cost of committing themselves to a single ideal, no critical fear of the narrowing effects of action. What would Charlotte Brontë have made, one wonders, of Marie Bashkirtzeff?

Life itself, then, not fancies or speculations about life,—life of an almost primitive intensity,—is what Charlotte Brontë's novels still offer to readers of to-day who may be surfeited with intellectual refinements of thought and feeling. Doubtless there is in her work something of the romantic false preference for savagery and barbarism over civilization, and of the romantic inclination to confuse crudeness with strength. She loathes conventional life and commonplace characters, and her art has to pay the penalty through growing now and then melodramatic and absurd. Her heroes, notably Rochester and Monsieur Paul, cannot always get themselves taken seriously.

Their grotesqueness is overaccentuated. They seem to study oddity. They drape themselves in extravagance as in a mantle. But although Miss Brontë's romantic bias—her fondness for the strange—may now and then distort the action and the characters of her stories, she never, unless rarely in her last novel, *Villette*, offends in her own style. She never rants; her taste is sure. Even in describing the most exciting scenes, her style has no strut and no stridency. And so it is easy to forgive the occasional grotesqueness of her incident and to yield to the sincerity of her art. Her romances deal with confessedly exceptional states of passion,—with almost such passions as a lyrical poet might deal with. And the imaginative truth and the beauty of phrase with which she realizes the moods of her heroines—moods which have the beat of the heart behind them, and are not mere fancies of brain-sick dilettantes—give to many passages in her stories almost the splendour and power of lyrical poetry.

It used to be said of Dante Gabriel Rossetti that life was, with him, always at a crisis. Much the same thing is true of Charlotte Brontë and of her heroines. Her novels—and this, when one stops to consider, helps largely to give them their peculiar tone—are perpetually busy with emotional crises; they are bent on portraying just the feverish expectation, the poignant grief, the joy, the glow of passion, which some special moment or incident stirs in the heart of the heroine. Very often the moods that colour her fiction are moods of anxiety, of breathless waiting, of nervous suspense. Jane Eyre's moods are continually of this sort. "I shall be called discontented," she says in one place. "I could not help it; the restlessness was in my nature; it agitated me to pain sometimes. Then my sole relief was to walk along the corridor of the third story, backward and forward, safe in the silence and solitude of the spot."

Early and late in *Jane Eyre,* these moments of eager waiting, sometimes for a definite sorrow or joy or excitement, sometimes merely with poignant longing for change, are described fully and vividly. When Jane, still a wee girl, has to make a start by coach before break of day for a distant school, the childish, half-haggard worry of the early morning is not taken for granted, but is put before the reader with almost oppressive truth. Jane's drive, many years later, across the country to Thornfield Hall, and her tremulous sensitiveness meantime to every new impression,—these also are keenly realized and faithfully reproduced. Throughout the story, wherever she is, Jane is continually aware of the sky-line and half-consciously quarrelling with the horizon. At Thornfield she often climbed to the leads of the Hall and "looked out afar over sequestered field and hill, and along dim sky-line," and "longed for a power of vision which might overpass that limit." And earlier, at Lowood, she speaks of "the hilly horizon," and adds: "My eye passed all other objects to rest on those most remote, the blue peaks; it was those I longed to surmount."

Lucy Snowe, whose fortunes make up the story of *Villette,* is not quite so fiery a young particle as Jane Eyre; but she has almost as many moods of thrilling restlessness to tell about. Her nerves vibrate to the "subtle, searching cry of the wind"; she answers half-superstitiously to all the skyey influences; she watches with a breathless exhilaration the Aurora Borealis,—its "quivering of serried lances," "its swift ascent of messengers from below the north star." And so throughout *Jane Eyre* and *Villette,—Shirley,* as will presently be noted, is somewhat differently conceived,—moods of acute and febrile intensity are imaginatively put before us. We are kept perpetually within sound of the heroine's breathing, and are forced to watch from hour to hour the anguished or joyful play of her pulse. The moods are not difficult moods, or subtly reflective moods; they are not the ingenious imitations of feelings which the pseudo-artistic temperament of to-day vamps up to while away the time and in emulation of the woes of special souls. They are the veritable joys and sorrows of eager and keenly sensitive natures that are bent above all upon living, and that never think of posing, or of mitigating the severity of life by artistic watchfulness over their own experiences. They are primitive, elemental, tyrannical emotions, and not to be disbelieved.

Another source of the almost lyrical intensity which runs through Charlotte Brontë's fiction is her sensitiveness to natural beauty. She had all a romantic poet's tremulous awareness of the bright and shadowed world of moor and field and sky. Her nerves knew nature through and through and answered to all its changing moods, and rarely do her stories, even when the scene is laid in a city, leave long out of notice the coursing of the clouds, the sound of the winds, the gay or ominous play of light and shade through the hours of the day, the look of the moon at night. The creativeness of her imagination, its searching inclusiveness, are not to be missed. It is a whole new world she gives us; she is not content with working out for us the acts or thoughts or looks of imaginary folk who may move satisfactorily across any sort of conventional stage. Her imagination is too elemental for this, too vital, includes too much of the universe within its sensitive grasp. Her people are knit by "organic filaments" to the nature they inhabit, and they can be thoroughly and persuasively realized only as their sensitive union with this nature-world which is their home is continually suggested. With the romantic poet, the individual is far more closely dependent on the vast instinctive world of nature for comfort and help and even for the life of the spirit, than on the conventional world of society, to which his relations seem to such a poet more nearly accidental. In her sympathy with this conception of man as intimately communing with the mysterious life of the physical universe, Charlotte Brontë shows once more her romantic bias.

Accordingly, the pages of her novels are full of delicate transcripts of the changing aspects of night and day, as these aspects record themselves on sensitive temperaments—more particularly on the temperaments of her heroines. *Jane Eyre* is perhaps most richly wrought with these half-lyrical impressions of what the earth and the sky have to say to the initiated. Yet, even through the more objective *Shirley*, Charlotte Brontë's love of nature follows her unmistakably,—the hero, Moore, owing his very name to her passion for the wild Yorkshire downs. In *Villette*, the scene is in Brussels; yet Charlotte Brontë's imagination, even when thus circumscribed, will not wholly give up the world of nature, and Lucy Snowe finds in the wind, in the sky, in the moon, companionable presences whose varying aspects and utterances symbolize again and again her joys or griefs or wringing anxieties. "It was a day of winter east winds," she says in one place, "and I had now for some time entered into that dreary fellowship with the winds and their changes, so little known, so incomprehensible, to the healthy. The north and the east owned a terrific influence, making all pain more poignant, all sorrow sadder. The south could calm, the west sometimes cheer; unless indeed, they brought on their wings the burden of thunder-clouds, under the weight and warmth of which all energy died." Of the moon as well as the winds, Lucy is strangely watchful; and often at some crisis in her externally placid but internally stormy life she describes its splendour or its sadness. So in Chapter xii: "A moon was in the sky, not a full moon, but a young crescent. I saw her through a space in the boughs overhead. She and the stars, visible beside her, were no strangers where all else was strange; my childhood knew them. I had seen that golden sign with the dark globe in its curve leaning back on azure, beside an old thorn at the top of an old field, in Old England, in long past days, just as it now leaned back beside a stately spire in this continental capital." Again: "Leaving the radiant park and well-lit Haute-Ville, I sought the dim lower quarter. Dim I should not say, for the beauty of the moonlight— forgotten in the park—here once more flowed in upon perception. High she rode, and calm and stainlessly she shone. The rival lamps were dying; she held her course like a white fate." Finally, a single passage may be quoted from *Shirley* because of the way it testifies, through the moon's subjugation of the surly and stormy temperament of old Yorke, to both the dramatic and the romantic power of Charlotte Brontë's imagination. Yorke, the brusque and violent Yorkshire squire, riding in the late evening over the downs with

Moore, the hero, has been betrayed into talk about a woman he had long ago loved; suddenly he breaks off. "'The moon is up,' was his first not quite relevant remark, pointing with his whip across the moor. 'There she is, rising into the haze, staring at us in a strange red glower. She is no more silver than old Helstone's brow is ivory. What does she mean by leaning her cheek on Rushedge i' that way, and looking at us wi' a scowl and a menace?' "

Charlotte Brontë's sensitiveness to the sinister or seductive beauty of the moon, illustrated by all these passages, may be taken as typical of her relation to all nature, and of her use of it throughout her stories. She has an almost transcendental faith in the meaning of natural sights and sounds; she reproduces them with a glamour that only a romantic imagination can catch and suggest; and the unmistakable sincerity of her moods and the lyrical intensity of her interpretations help to give to her novels a peculiarly vivid beauty that the modern instructed, scientific, and faithless novelist can rarely attain to. . . .

The new world, then, into which Charlotte Brontë's imagination inducts the modern reader and of which she makes him free, is a world where casuistry and philosophy are unknown, where they put no mist of abstractions between the reader and the poignant fact. It is a world where love and hate and the few great primary savage passions, of which recent literary folk of the first order fight so shy, are portrayed vigorously and convincingly. It is a world in which the elements, air and earth and water, flash and blossom and ripple, where the clouds and the winds, the sun and the moon, are never quite out of mind, and set the nerves a-tingle and put the imagination in play, even of the folk who are shut indoors.

And yet, though life, as Charlotte Brontë portrays it, is so passionate, and though the world is so primitive and elemental, the life that she puts before us is *actual* life, not a whimsical or fantastic or falsifying counterfeit of life, and the world in which her characters live and move and have their being, is the *actual* world, not a mystical dream-region, beautifully false in its colours and chiaroscuro and artificially filled like Hawthorne's world, for example, with omens and portents and moral symbolism. Her characters, too, are real men and women, not types, not figures in melodrama, not creatures of one idea, or one humour, or one passion. Doubtless they are not studied with the minuteness that modern realists use. Yet they have complex personalities and lead thoroughly individual lives. And they are flashed on the reader's retina with a vividness of colour and a dramatic truthfulness and suggestiveness in act and gesture that modern scientific novels rarely reach. Herein, perhaps, lies Charlotte Brontë's unique power,—in her ability to make her stories seem close to fact and yet strange and almost mystically imaginative. Her hallucinations are sane, and her victims of passion keep, after all, within the bounds of reason.

And indeed this is an aspect of Charlotte Brontë's genius that has not in general been insisted upon sufficiently—her self-control and her loyalty to reason, in all that is essential, whether in art or in morals, a loyalty that is none the less consistent and controlling because it is half-grudging. As a result of this loyalty she escapes in her stories much of the extravagance and absurdity that her sisters were led into. In some respects, Emily Brontë was a greater artist than Charlotte; she had an intenseness of vision, and an occasional beauty of image and phrase, that Charlotte Brontë never quite reaches. The vividness of some of her scenes and the acrid intensity of the counterfeit life in *Wuthering Heights* are beyond anything in *Jane Eyre* or *Shirley*. But the work of Emily Brontë is lacking in the moral and artistic sanity which is characteristic of Charlotte Brontë. *Wuthering Heights* has here and there greater lyrical beauty and power than anything that Charlotte Brontë has written. But Emily Brontë takes us wholly out of ordinary daylight into a region of nightmare horrors. Dante Rossetti used to say of *Wuthering Heights* that its scenes were laid in hell, though oddly enough the places and the people had English names. The story, too, is illogical and structureless, and hence fails to make a lastingly great impression; it spends itself in paroxysms and lacks sustained power and cumulative effect. . . .

Charlotte Brontë was liberally informed by the critics, and in her later stories she guards against them. Both *Shirley* and *Villette* are freer from absurdities than *Jane Eyre;* neither is quite so frankly devout toward the *outre*, and in both a certain insidious humour is cultivated. *Shirley* is a roundabout tribute to Thackeray. The point of view, the method, the tone, are the result of a hero-worshipping study of the novelist to whom *Jane Eyre* was finally dedicated. The story aims to be more a criticism of life than *Jane Eyre*, and less a personal confession; the point of view is that of "the author," and the tone is often whimsical or ironical. From the very first page the style betokens a changed attitude toward life. The novel is not to be a semi-lyrical record of moods of hope and grief and revolt and passion and joy; it is to portray with a certain delicate and at times ironical detachment the fortunes of a small group of characters whom the author lovingly but shrewdly watches. The brisk satire at the expense of the curates is something that lies quite out of the scope of *Jane Eyre*. The gain that *Shirley* shows in conscious breadth of outlook and in confidence of bearing,—in authority,—is noteworthy. *Jane Eyre* is the work of an audacious solitary dreamer; *Shirley* is the work of an author who has "arrived," who has made the world listen, and who feels sure that she has a right to speak. The monotonous poignancy *of Jane Eyre* gives place in *Shirley* to a wide range of moods; the story moves forward with a buoyant sense of the charm of life as well as with a half-indignant sense of its daunting and harrowing difficulty. The author escapes from the tyranny of a single, somewhat morbid, though courageous, temperament, and gives us incidents and characters with more of the checkered light upon them than ordinary mortals are from day to day aware of. . . .

It must, then, be admitted with all frankness that life is not for most people the sort of thing that Charlotte Brontë represents. The moods that fill the pages of *Jane Eyre* are no more the common moods with which the ordinary man or woman looks at life than are the lyrics of *In Memoriam* like the daily records of a clubman's thoughts. For most people, life is not perpetually at a crisis; nor are they all the time yearning intensely for love and sympathy. Petty personal rivalries and the pleasure that comes from success in them, silly little vanities that fancy themselves flattered, cheap bodily delights, a pleased ironical sense of the absurdities of other people,— these are the satisfactions that for half the world redeem the monotony of existence and make it no hardship to go on living; and these are precisely the phases of life that such novelists as Jane Austen delight to depict. Of all these frivolous feelings Charlotte Brontë's account of life contains scarcely a hint. *Shirley* now and then has glimpses of the absurd trivialities that the cynic likes to find and sneer at. But for the most part Charlotte Brontë is as oblivious as Shelley or Wordsworth of the possible delights of irony. Perhaps it is still an open question whether the ironical or the passionately sincere relation to life is the worthier in morals and in art. The imaginations that can reconcile the two are doubtless the most penetrating and potent. Miss Brontë showed that she could appreciate the ironical manner through her warm admiration of Thackeray,—an admiration, however, be it noted that expressly insists on the "sentiment, which, jealously hidden, but genuine, extracts the venom from that formidable Thackeray, and converts what might be corrosive poison into purifying elixir." As for her own work, however, she was too contemptuous of conventionality in all its forms to be a fit interpreter of the Spirit of Comedy.

Indeed, she now and then herself becomes in her art fair game for the Spirit of Comedy, because of the dulness of her conventional conscience. She does not always know when the laugh is bound to be against her. Her heroes often wax silly or grotesque. Rochester's smile which "he used but on rare occasions," his "ebon eyebrows," his "precious grimness," his "bursts of maniacal rage," all his extravagances of look and demeanour, are insisted upon absurdly. Paul Emmanuel's tricks of manner, his wilfulness, his self-conceit, his fidgetiness,—these are played upon out of all measure, and described with a fondness that must now and then seem ludicrous. And so, too, with the peculiarities of Louis Moore; his sardonic self-satisfaction, his somewhat pretentious iciness of demeanour, his satanic pride and so on, are made abundantly grotesque through overemphasis. Melodramatic incident, too, Miss Brontë shows a perilous fondness for. Not easy is it to take seriously the crazy wife of Rochester, who goes on all fours in an upper chamber, and now and then sallies forth to set fire to something or other. Excesses of this sort both in characterization and in incident are the penalty that Miss Brontë has to pay for her contempt for conventional standards and modes of judgment.

Gradually she doubtless came to recognize the danger involved in her fondness for the abnormal, and in her distrust of everyday virtues and modes of life. In her last novel, *Villette,* she tried to be fair to conventional types of men and women, and to portray worldly success sympathetically. In Dr. John Bretton she aims to draw the character of a well-bred, good-tempered, prosperous gentleman,—a man in no disgrace with fortune and men's eyes. And in Paulina she makes a brave effort to depict sympathetically a pretty and charming young society girl. Both Bretton and Paulina, however, are mere copperplate nonentities. Miss Brontë herself laments in one of her letters her failure with Paulina; and John Graham Bretton, the handsome young doctor at whom Lucy Snowe confesses she dare not look for fear of being dazzled for a half-hour afterward, is also a mere figment. Paul Emmanuel is the real hero of *Villette,*—a hero in his own way as *outre* as Rochester himself. In *Shirley,* the insufferable Sym0sons—Shirley's buckram uncle and his faultless daughters—together with Sir Philip Nunnely, the lily-fingered baronet, who writes sentimental verses, are the only really conventional folk portrayed. The daughters "knew by heart a certain young-ladies'-schoolroom code of laws on language, demeanour, etc.; themselves never deviated from its curious little pragmatical provisions; and they regarded with secret, whispered horror all deviations in others." Mr. Sympson's god was "the World," as Shirley tells him in a virago-like speech toward the close of the story. All these devotees of "correctness" Miss Brontë detests; "these things we artists hate," as Blake said of the *Mechanics' Magazine.* And her hatred of them gives a kind of dissenting bitterness to parts of her treatment of life,—a false note of acerbity like that of the professional heretic. This is another of the penalties she pays for that fervid unconventionality which was alike her strength and her weakness.

In morals, her unconventionality will hardly seem nowadays very startling, although in her own day there was much head-wagging among prim persons, male and female, over the vagaries and frank passionateness of Jane Eyre. Miss Brontë never pleaded for a moral revolution. She had no prophetic glimpses of "the modern woman," and she neither preached nor implied a gospel of woman's rights. She makes brisk war on Mrs. Grundy and on her notions of womanly propriety, but beyond this she never ventures. She limits herself expressly in the preface to the second edition of *Jane Eyre*. "Conventionality is not morality. Self-righteousness is not religion. To attack the first is not to assail the last. These things and deeds are diametrically opposed; they are as distinct as is vice from virtue. Men too often confound them; they should not be confounded; appearance should not be mistaken for truth." Never does one of Miss Brontë's heroines actually violate a moral law. Jane Eyre is a signal martyr to the sacredness of received ideas concerning marriage and divorce; and Rochester has to pay dearly for his lax notions about the rights of crazy wives. His Hall is burned and he just misses burning with it; he finally gets off with the loss of an arm and an eye and with several months of parboiled suffering. No; Charlotte Brontë is a relentless little conservative as regards all the essentials of the moral code. Her ideal for woman is the traditional domestic ideal freed from worldliness and hypocrisy,—the domestic ideal purged of non-essentials and carried to the nth degree of potency. All her women are merely fragments till they meet a man they can adore.

Perhaps, however, Shirley may be brought up as premonitory of the modern woman. In the "mutinous" Shirley, "made out of fire and air," frank and wilful and just a bit mannish, who parted her hair over one temple, who was not afraid of a musket, and who managed her own estate with a pretty air of self-sufficiency—surely, in *her,* so one is at first tempted to think, there is a suggestion of the new woman. Yet, after all, the suggestion is very slight. Shirley wears her mannishness merely as a challenging bit of colour. She is not intellectual; she has no theories; in her heart of hearts she longs to be bitted and ruled; in the core of her nature she is very woman of very woman, delighting in bravado, in playing at shrewishness, and then in suddenly obeying orders. She is merely a modern Rosalind masquerading for a summer's day in doublet and hose.

It nevertheless remains true that in one sense Charlotte Brontë prepared the way for the crusade of the modern woman. Her prodigiously vivid portrayal of the endless possibilities of woman's nature in power and passion and devotion inevitably suggests the rights of women to richer fields for the play of their faculties. "Women are supposed to be very calm generally," Jane Eyre exclaims; "but women feel just as men feel; they need exercise for their faculties and a field for their efforts as much as their brothers do; they suffer from too rigid a restraint, too absolute a stagnation, precisely as men would suffer. It is thoughtless to condemn them, or laugh at them, if they seek to do more or to learn more than custom has pronounced necessary for their sex." This passage in *Jane Eyre* is indeed almost revolutionary. And although it cannot readily be paralleled elsewhere in Miss Brontë's writings, the spirit that pervades it, the indignation of its protest against tyrannical and contemptuous limitations of woman's freedom, doubtless runs through all her novels. In this sense she may truly be described as preparing the way for the saner and more generous conceptions of woman and of her relations to man, that are characteristic of our own day.

What is true of Charlotte Brontë's ideas about women is true of her ethics in general. She has no radically new, no really revolutionary, doctrine. The great good in life—she is never weary of praising it and of illustrating its pricelessness—is pure human affection. Jane Eyre's cry, in a childish outbreak of feeling, is typical of all Miss Brontë's heroines: "If others don't love me, I would rather die than live." Each of her novels, as has already been noted, reduces in the last analysis to a pathetic quest after affection.

Callousness of heart, lack of "true generous feeling,"—this is for Miss Brontë the one fatal defect of character. Not even unflinching devotion to an abstract moral code or to a systematic round of religious observances can excuse in her eyes rigidity of nature and dearth of genuine human affection. Jane Eyre's cousin Eliza has her time parcelled out into ten minute intervals, which she spends day after day with splendid regularity on the same round of duties; yet she is to Jane Eyre, and to Charlotte Brontë as well, *anathema maranatha*, because she is "heartless." St. John Rivers, with whose fate the very last sentences in *Jane Eyre* concern themselves, is a still more striking case in point. He is consumed with religious zeal; he is absolutely sincere in his devotion to the cause of religion. Yet because he sacrifices love to the successful pursuit of his mission, and because he acts from severely conceived principle instead of from warm human feeling, the fiery little author can hardly keep her hand from angry tremulousness while she portrays him. She loathes him because he forgets "the feelings and claims of little people, in pursuing his own large views." Intense imaginative sympathy with life in all its forms,—even with animals and with nature,—this is what Miss Brontë demands of the characters she will approve. There must be no cheap sentiment; her heroes are apt to be stern or even ferocious in manner; but under a wilful exterior there must be a glowing spirit of human affection ready to flash out loyally, though capriciously, whenever there is real need.

And it is because she believes so unswervingly in the worth of life as ministered to by love, and because she sets forth with such manifold truth of detail and such visionary intensity the realities of life and love, that her novels, in spite of their obvious defects, keep their power, and are even in some ways doubly grateful in these latter days of cynical moralizing. She quickens faith in human nature and in human destiny. She gives the reader who will readily lend himself to her spell a new sense of the heights and depths of passion and of the unlimited possibilities of life. The finical reader will find in her much to shock him and bring his hand to his mouth, and the nicely intellectual reader will be sure that her *naivete* is by no means the finally satisfactory relation to life. The admirers of George Eliot and of Mrs. Ward will carp at her ethics or at her lack of them. Doubtless, her characters love love almost selfishly, and seem to struggle for it with something of the gambler's greed. George Eliot's analyses of the dangers of the self-centred and wilful pursuit even of love may lead to a much more scientifically accurate sense of the unimportance of the individual man or woman, and of the absurdity of hoping that the world will order itself to suit the needs of a single heart. George Eliot asserted the rights of the social order; Charlotte Brontë asserted the individual. And for that very reason her novels are tonic in these days when gently cynical resignation has become so largely a fashionable habit of mind in literature and art. George Eliot never tells of love at first hand, and always puts a mist of philosophizing and a blur of moral suasion between her readers and any passionate experience she recites. Charlotte Brontë tells of the joy and the terror and the tragedy of love and life with the intense directness of the lyric poet, and hence even the direst sufferings her characters undergo do not daunt or depress the reader, but rather quicken his sense of kinship with all forms of human experience and his realization of the dignity and scope of man's nature. The human will is never at a disadvantage with Charlotte Brontë. The struggle with circumstance and with fate is bitter, often exhausting; yet there is a curious constitutional buoyant courage in her work that more than counteracts any sympathetic sadness the story may for the moment carry with it.

—Lewis E. Gates, from "Charlotte Brontë,"
Studies and Appreciations, 1900, pp. 129–162

FRANCIS HOVEY STODDARD (1900)

Francis Hovey Stoddard (1847–1936) was a professor of English language and literature and also a dean at New York University. He published extensively on a variety of literary topics. His most famous work, from which this excerpt is taken, is *The Evolution of the English Novel* (1900). His other books include *The Modern Novel* (1883) and *The Study of the English Language* (1899). In a somewhat fervent style, Stoddard examines Brontë's emotionality and claims that it came to constitute a particular epoch in English fiction in which inner longings eclipse external appearance and experience as a novel's focal point.

Life was worth living to Charlotte Brontë only when it offered opportunity for such intense attachment as would make her willing to die for the object of her emotion. This intense, personal life went into the novels, and has made *Villette* and *Jane Eyre* as distinct and definite personalities as Charlotte Brontë herself. Indeed, perhaps they are more so, for I suspect it would be easier for most of us to draw a picture of the soul-life of the struggling teacher-governess of Haworth from the story of Jane Eyre, or from the story of Villette, than from the records of authentic history. The characters are creations, and their appearance marks an epoch in literature, marks a distinct and definite era in the history of the novel. Before their appearance we had had personages in fiction. In *Jane Eyre*, for the first time in English fiction, the intensity of life-craving which dominates a woman who loves is presented in the pages of the novel; and the voice of the outcry of her longing comes to the world. The story of Jane Eyre is familiar enough to all of us. She is a heroine of the inner life. In the depiction of her every advantage of the external is deliberately, almost defiantly, sacrificed. In our oldest English epic, the hero, Beowulf, fights a dragon, and when going to fight with a foe who cannot wear armor and cannot carry a sword, even though that foe is a fire-breathing dragon, Beowulf chooses to sacrifice every external advantage and fights without his armor and without his sword. In the *Orlando Furioso* of Ariosto, though the hero carries an enchanted ring and wields a magic sword at tournaments, yet when the conflict is for life, he throws away these adventitious and external aids and fights with simpler weapons. So, when Charlotte Brontë sets out to depict a stern struggle of the soul of a woman, she throws aside the external excellences by time-honored custom given to heroines. The heroine of her novel is small, dark, plain, almost insignificant, in person; she is poor; she is a governess serving under orders. How shall one make a heroine out of such as this? And the hero, what shall he be in a novel? Shall he not be beautiful, graceful, courteous, virtuous, and eligible? What say you to a hero who is ugly, who is awkward and brutal, who has been dissipated, and who has a wife? It is as if in the interest of the intenser life that Charlotte Brontë counted all external things but as dross, and would have us also count them as things not worth our care. The influences upon the heroine in *Jane Eyre* are not from the outside. She is moved, stirred, aroused, by the strength of her own emotion solely. The dominance of the external in the novel of personal life was ended when *Jane Eyre* was written. The one thing lacking in *Pride and Prejudice* is intensity of interest. The one thing thrilling through *Jane Eyre* and *Villette* is intensity of interest—interest in a system of life, interest in nature, interest in one's own soul-life, interest in emotion as emotion. When *Jane Eyre* is finished, passion has entered into the novel.

—Francis Hovey Stoddard, *The Evolution
of the English Novel,* 1900, pp. 62–65

WORKS

JANE EYRE: AN AUTOBIOGRAPHY

Brontë wrote *Jane Eyre* at home in Haworth between August 1846 and March 1847, in the wake of numerous publishers' rejections of her first novel, *The Professor*. *Jane Eyre*'s imaginative and exciting style was influenced by a critique repeatedly applied to *The Professor*: that the earlier novel was unappealingly somber. Her revised style was rewarded, as *Jane Eyre* was accepted by the first publishers she sent it to, Smith, Elder & Company, the firm that went on to publish her subsequent novels. The directors paid Brontë £100 for the novel's copyright and later paid her £500 for the three-volume editions.

Jane Eyre's popularity was immediate. Its first publication in October 1847 sold so well that a second edition came out in January 1848, this one dedicated to W.M. Thackeray, Brontë's favorite novelist, and a third edition followed in April 1848.

As the following criticism attests, *Jane Eyre*—despite its great popularity and almost universally acclaimed power—was routinely criticized for its moral license. Specifically, critics were surprised and often offended by Jane's willfulness, her perceived disrespect for figures of authority, and by her attraction to such an ethically suspect hero as Rochester. In terms of the book's composition, Brontë was praised for the excitement, suspense, and forcefulness of the novel but chided for her reliance on coincidence.

Another major strain of *Jane Eyre*'s early criticism was speculation as to "Currer Bell's" real identity and sex. Some critics (Lewes, for instance) claimed to know instantly that the novel reflected a woman's instinct and perspective, while others (such as Rigby) asserted that no woman would be responsible for such a bold and distasteful heroine. Further speculation surrounded the novel's possible ties to the other Bell brothers, Acton and Ellis, whose novels *Agnes Grey*, *The Tenant of Wildfell Hall*, and *Wuthering Heights* had already been published.

CHARLOTTE BRONTË (AS "CURRER BELL") (1847)

The following is a copy of the terse note that accompanied *Jane Eyre*, when Brontë first sent it to Smith, Elder & Company, the publishers that were to catapult the novel (and its somewhat reluctant author) to fame.

— ⁘ — ⁘ — ⁘ —

I now send you per rail a MS. entitled *Jane Eyre*, a novel in three volumes, by Currer Bell. I find I cannot prepay the carriage of the parcel, as money for that purpose is not received at the small station-house where it is left. If, when you acknowledge the receipt of the MS., you would have the goodness to mention the amount charged on delivery, I will immediately transmit it in postage-stamps. It is better in future to address Mr. Currer Bell, under cover to Miss Brontë, Haworth, Bradford, Yorkshire, as there is a risk of letters otherwise directed not reaching me at present. To save trouble, I enclose an envelope.

—Charlotte Brontë (as "Currer Bell"),
letter to Messrs. Smith, Elder & Co.,
August 24, 1847

HENRY F. CHORLEY (1847)

Henry Fothergill Chorley (1808–1872) was a journalist who worked primarily for *The Athenaeum* as a book reviewer. He was also a music reviewer and an unsuccessful fiction writer. His greatest commercial success came with three books: *Music and Manners in France and Germany* (1841), *Thirty Years' Musical Recollections* (1862), and *Memorials of Mrs. Hemens* (2 vols., 1836).

Chorley's highly descriptive reading of *Jane Eyre* somewhat mocks the novel's melodramatic resolution but is overall admiring of its diverting story.

There is so much power in this novel as to make us overlook certain eccentricities in the invention, which trench in one or two places on what is improbable, if not unpleasant. Jane Eyre is an orphan thrown upon the protection—or, to speak correctly, the cruelty—of relations living in an out-of-the-way corner of England; who neglect, maltreat, chastize, and personally abuse her. She becomes dogged, revengeful, superstitious: and at length, after a scene,—which we hope is out of nature now that "the Iron Rule" is over-ruled and the reign of the tribe Squeers ended,—the child turns upon her persecutors with such precocious power to threaten and alarm, that they condemn her to an *oubliette*—sending her out of the house to a so-called charitable institution. There she has again to prove wretchedness, hard fare, and misconstruction. The trial, however, is this time not unaccompanied by more gracious influences. Jane Eyre is taught, by example, that patience is nobler than passion; and so far as we can gather from her own confessions, grows up into a plain, self-sustained young woman, with a capital of principle sufficient to regulate those more dangerous gifts which the influences of her childhood had so exasperated. Weary of the monotonous life of a teacher, she advertises for the situation of a governess; and is engaged into an establishment—singular, but not without prototype—to take care of the education of the French ward of a country gentleman; which said girl proves, when called by her right name, to be the child of an opera *danseuse*. The pretty, frivolous, little faery Adele, with her hereditary taste for dress, coquetry, and pantomimic grace, is true to life. Perhaps, too—we dare not speak more positively—there is truth in the abrupt, strange, clever Mr. Rochester; and in the fearless, original way in which the strong man and the young governess travel over each other's minds till, in a puzzled and uncomfortable manner enough, they come to a mutual understanding. Neither is the mystery of Thornfield an exaggeration of reality. We, ourselves, know of a large mansion-house in a distant county where, for many years, a miscreant was kept in close confinement,—and his existence, at best, only darkly hinted in the neighbourhood. Some such tale as this was told in a now-forgotten novel—*Sketches of a Seaport Town*. We do not quarrel with the author of *Jane Eyre* for the manner in which he has made the secret explode at a critical juncture of the story. From that point forward, however, we think the heroine is too outrageously tried, and too romantically assisted in her difficulties:—until arrives the last moment, at which obstacles fall down like the battlements of *Castle Melodrame*, in the closing scene, when "avenging thunder strikes the towers of Crime, and far above in Heaven's etherial light young Hymen's flower-decked temple shines revealed." No matter, however:—as exciting strong interest of its old-fashioned kind *Jane Eyre* deserves high praise, and commendation to the novel-reader who prefers story to philosophy, pedantry, or Puseyite controversy.

—Henry F. Chorley, *Athenaeum,*
October 23, 1847, pp. 1,100–1,101

John Gibson Lockhart (1847)

John Gibson Lockhart (1794–1854) was a Scottish writer and editor known for his acid attacks on writers including Keats. Despite the harshness he was prone to, Lockhart was considered a perceptive reader whose interests focused on the novels of the day, Romantic poetry, and classics. His works include translations of German and Spanish works, a biography of Robert Burns, poetry, and some now obscure novels. His best-known work is a seven-volume biography of his father-in-law, Sir Walter Scott, published in 1837–1838 and revised in 1839 and 1848.

Lockhart was the editor of the *Quarterly Review* from 1825 until 1853 and, in that role, oversaw the publication of Rigby's scathing review of *Jane Eyre*. As this comment shows, however, he found the novel praiseworthy, if "brazen."

I have finished the adventures of Miss Jane Eyre, and think her far the cleverest that has written since Austen and Edgeworth were in their prime. Worth fifty Trollopes and Martineaus rolled into one counterpane, with fifty Dickenses and Bulwers to keep them company; but rather a brazen Miss.

> —John Gibson Lockhart, letter to
> Mrs. Hope, December 29, 1847, cited in
> Andrew Lang, *The Life and Letters of*
> *John Gibson Lockhart*, 1897, vol. 2, p. 310

ELIZABETH RIGBY (1848)

Elizabeth, Lady Eastlake, born Elizabeth Rigby (1809–1893), was a journalist, travel writer, and art critic and the first woman to write for the *Quarterly Review*. She also contributed to *The Edinburgh Review*, most notably with the Five Great Painters series (1883).

Rigby's review of *Jane Eyre* and *Vanity Fair*, excerpted here, is probably the most famous review of a Brontë novel. Rigby notoriously condemns *Jane Eyre* as "an anti-Christian composition" written in "horrid taste" and considers its heroine "unregenerate" and "ungrateful." For Rigby, the potential consequences of such a literary work are not only offensive but socially dangerous. The independence and willfulness that Jane Eyre embodies, she explains, is the same spirit that "fostered Chartism and rebellion at home." (Chartism was a British working-class political movement in the 1830s and 1840s that sought universal suffrage and a democratic representation of government; some factions of the movement embraced violent protest as a way to impress their demands.)

Reviews like Rigby's (and Whipple's, which follows) that identified *Jane Eyre* and, by extension, Currer Bell as immoral compelled Elizabeth Gaskell to use her biography, *The Life of Charlotte Brontë*, as a means of defending Brontë's integrity and correcting the charges of moral laxness lodged against her and her work.

As is in evidence here, much of Rigby's dissatisfaction with *Jane Eyre* comes from her grudging acknowledgement of the novel's power. The idea that a young woman (Jane herself) could be so independent and spirited obviously startled Rigby, who consequently uses the review to chastise such behavior as both asocial and irreligious.

Rigby's assertions of the male identity of "Currer Bell" reveal not only Rigby's essentialized view of femininity (based on the idea that no woman could be so bold or coarse as to write *Jane Eyre*) but are ironic in light of the male persona that she herself writes under here and which compels her to cite an imaginary "lady friend" as the authority on Brontë's fashion and cuisine inaccuracies.

Jane Eyre, as a work, and one of equal popularity, is, in almost every respect, a total contrast to *Vanity Fair*. The characters and events, though some of them masterly in conception, are coined expressly for the purpose of bringing out great effects. The hero and heroine are beings both so singularly unattractive that the reader feels they can have no vocation in the novel but to be brought together; and they do things which, though not impossible, lie utterly beyond the bounds of probability. On this account a short sketch of the plan seems requisite; not but what it is a plan familiar enough to all readers of novels—especially those of the old school and those of the lowest school of our own day. For Jane Eyre is merely another Pamela, who, by the force of her character and the strength of her principles, is carried victoriously through great trials and temptations from the man she loves. Nor is she even a Pamela adapted and refined to modern notions; for though the story is conducted without those derelictions of decorum which we are to believe had their excuse in the manners of Richardson's time, yet it is stamped with a coarseness of language and laxity of tone which have certainly no excuse in ours. It is a very remarkable book: we have no remembrance of another combining such genuine power with such horrid taste. Both together have equally assisted to gain the great popularity it has enjoyed; for in these days of extravagant adoration of all that bears the stamp of novelty and originality, sheer rudeness and vulgarity have come in for a most mistaken worship. . . .

This, to our view, is the great and crying mischief of the book. Jane Eyre is throughout the personification of an unregenerate and undisciplined spirit, the more dangerous to exhibit from that prestige of principle and self-control which is liable to dazzle the eye too much for it to observe the inefficient and unsound foundation on which it rests. It is true Jane does right, and exerts great moral strength, but it is the strength of a mere heathen mind which is a law unto itself. No Christian grace is perceptible upon her. She has inherited in fullest measure the worst sin of our fallen nature—the sin of pride. Jane Eyre is proud, and therefore she is ungrateful too. It pleased God to make her an orphan, friendless, and penniless—yet she thanks nobody, and least of all Him, for the food and raiment, the friends, companions, and instructors of her helpless youth—for the care and education vouchsafed to her till she was capable in mind as fitted in years to provide for herself. On the contrary, she looks upon all that has been done for her not only as her undoubted right, but as falling far short of it. The doctrine of humility is not more foreign to her mind than it is repudiated by her heart. It is by her own talents, virtues, and courage, that she is made to attain the summit of human happiness, and, as far as Jane Eyre's own statement is concerned, no one would think that she owed anything either to God above or to man below. She flees from Mr. Rochester, and has not a being to turn to. Why was this? The excellence of the present institution at Casterton, which succeeded that of Cowan Bridge near Kirkby Lonsdale—these being distinctly, as we hear, the original and the reformed Lowoods of the book—is pretty generally known. Jane had lived there for eight years with 110 girls and 15 teachers. Why had she formed no friendship among them? Other orphans have left the same and similar institutions, furnished with friends for life, and puzzled with homes to choose from. How comes it that Jane had acquired neither? Among that number of associates there were surely some exceptions to what she so presumptuously stigmatises as 'the society of inferior minds.' Of course it suited the author's end to represent the heroine as utterly destitute of the common means of assistance, in order to exhibit both her trials and her powers of self-support—the whole book rests on this assumption—but it is one which, under the circumstances, is very unnatural and very unjust.

Altogether the autobiography of Jane Eyre is preeminently an anti-Christian composition. There is throughout it a murmuring against the comforts of the rich and against the privations of the poor, which, as far as each individual is concerned, is a murmuring against God's appointment—there is a proud and perpetual assertion of the rights of man, for which we find no authority either in God's word or in God's providence—there is that pervading tone of ungodly discontent which is at once the most prominent and the most subtle evil which the law and the pulpit, which all civilized society in fact, has at the present day to contend with. We do not hesitate to say that the tone of mind and thought which has overthrown authority and violated every code human and divine abroad, and fostered Chartism and rebellion at home, is the same which has also written Jane Eyre.

Still we say again this is a very remarkable book. We are painfully alive to the moral, religious, and literary deficiencies of the picture, and such passages of beauty and power as we have quoted cannot redeem it, but it is impossible not to be spellbound with the freedom of the touch. It would be mere hackneyed courtesy to call it 'fine writing.' It bears no impress of being written at all, but is poured out rather in the heat and hurry of an instinct, which flows ungovernably on to its object, indifferent by what means it reaches it, and unconscious too. As regards the author's chief object, however, it is a failure—that, namely, of making a plain, odd woman, destitute of all the conventional features of feminine attraction, interesting in our sight. We deny that he has succeeded in this. Jane Eyre, in spite of some grand things about her, is a being totally uncongenial to our feelings from beginning to end. We acknowledge her firmness—we respect her determination—we feel for her struggles; but, for all that, and setting aside higher considerations, the impression she leaves on our mind is that of a decidedly vulgar-minded woman—one whom we should not care for as an acquaintance, whom we should not seek as a friend, whom we should not desire for a relation, and whom we should scrupulously avoid for a governess.

There seem to have arisen in the novel-reading world some doubts as to who really wrote this book; and various rumours, more or less romantic, have been current in Mayfair, the metropolis of gossip, as to the authorship. For example, *Jane Eyre* is sentimentally assumed to have proceeded from the pen of Mr. Thackeray's governess, whom he had himself chosen as his model of Becky, and who, in mingled love and revenge, personified him in return as Mr. Rochester. In this case, it is evident that the author of *Vanity Fair*, whose own pencil makes him grey-haired, has had the best of it, though his children may have had the worst, having, at all events, succeeded in hitting that vulnerable point in the Becky bosom, which it is our firm belief no man born of woman, from her Soho to her Ostend days, had ever so much as grazed. To this ingenious rumour the coincidence of the second edition of *Jane Eyre* being dedicated to Mr. Thackeray has probably given rise. For our parts, we see no great interest in the question at all. The first edition of *Jane Eyre* purports to be edited by Currer Bell, one of a trio of brothers, or sisters, or cousins, by names Currer, Acton, and Ellis Bell, already known as the joint-authors of a volume of poems. The second edition the same—dedicated, however, 'by the author,' to Mr. Thackeray; and the dedication (itself an indubitable *chip* of *Jane Eyre*) signed Currer Bell. Author and editor therefore are one, and we are as much satisfied to accept this double individual under the name of 'Currer Bell,' as under any other, more or less euphonious. Whoever it be, it is a person who, with great mental powers, combines a total ignorance of the habits of society, a great coarseness of taste, and a heathenish doctrine of religion. And as these characteristics appear more or less in the writings of all three, Currer, Acton, and Ellis alike, for their poems differ less in degree of power than in kind, we are ready to accept the fact of their identity or of their relationship with equal satisfaction. At all events there can be no interest attached to the writer of *Wuthering Heights*—a novel succeeding *Jane Eyre,* and purporting to be written by Ellis Bell—unless it were for the sake of more individual reprobation. For though there is a decided family likeness between the two, yet the aspect of the Jane and Rochester animals in their native state, as Catherine and Heathcliff, is too odiously and abominably pagan to be palatable even to the most vitiated class of English readers. With all the unscrupulousness of the French school of novels it combines that repulsive vulgarity in the choice of its vice which supplies its own antidote. The question of authorship, therefore, can deserve a moment's curiosity only as far as *Jane Eyre* is concerned, and though we cannot pronounce that it appertains to a real Mr. Currer Bell and to no other, yet that it appertains to a man, and not, as many assert, to a woman, we are strongly inclined to affirm. Without entering into the question whether the power of the writing be above her, or the vulgarity below her, there are, we believe, minutiae of circumstantial evidence which at once acquit the feminine hand. No woman—a lady friend, whom we are always happy to consult, assures us—makes mistakes in her own *metier*—no woman *trusses game* and garnishes dessert-dishes with the same hands, or talks of so doing in the same breath. Above all, no woman attires another in such fancy dresses as Jane's ladies assume—Miss Ingram coming down, irresistible, 'in a *morning* robe of sky-blue crape, a gauze azure scarf twisted in her hair!!' No lady, we understand, when suddenly roused in the night, would think of hurrying on 'a *frock.*' They have garments more convenient for such occasions, and more becoming too. This evidence seems incontrovertible. Even granting that these incongruities were purposely assumed, for the sake of disguising the female pen, there is nothing gained; for if we ascribe the book to a woman at all, we have no alternative but to ascribe it to one who has, for some sufficient reason, long forfeited the society of her own sex.

And if by no woman, it is certainly also by no artist. The Thackeray eye has had no part there. There is not more disparity between the art of drawing Jane assumes and her evident total ignorance of its first principles, than between the report she gives of her own character and the conclusions we form for ourselves. Not but what, in another sense, the author may be classed as an artist of very high grade. Let him describe the simplest things in nature—a rainy landscape, a cloudy sky, or a bare moorside, and he shows the hand of a master; but the moment he talks of the art itself, it is obvious that he is a complete ignoramus.

—Elizabeth Rigby, from *"Vanity Fair
and Jane Eyre," Quarterly Review,*
December 1848, pp. 165–176

GEORGE ELIOT (1848)

I have read *Jane Eyre,* mon ami, and shall be glad to know what you admire in it. All self-sacrifice is good—but one would like it to be in a somewhat nobler cause than that of a diabolical law which chains a man soul and body to a putrefying carcase. However the book *is* interesting—only I wish the characters would talk a little less like the heroes and heroines of police reports.

—George Eliot, letter to Charles Bray,
June 11, 1848

EDWIN P. WHIPPLE (1848)

Edwin Percy Whipple (1819–1886) was an immensely popular and influential American reviewer and lecturer whose works include *Essays and Review* (1848), *Lectures on Subjects Connected with Literature and Life* (1850), and *Character and Characteristic Men* (1866). His review of *Jane Eyre* extends many of Rigby's objections, noted in a previous excerpt, but it also admits that the ethical controversy associated with *Jane Eyre* only elevated its popularity.

Whipple draws attention to the curiosity surrounding Currer Bell's authorship as well, such as the early suspicion that *Jane Eyre* was a collaboration between Currer, Ellis, and Acton Bell, like their previously published book of poetry. *Jane Eyre* also reminds Whipple of Acton Bell's two novels—*Agnes Grey* (1847) and *The Tenant of Wildfell Hall* (1848)—and strikes him as the product of a "masculine" mind because of the clarity of its descriptions, its forceful tone, and its aggressive passions. Whipple finds these characteristics degrading and compromising of the novel's representation of life; the Bells, he writes, "seem to have a sense of the depravity of human nature peculiarly their own."

Not many months ago, the New England States were visited by a distressing mental epidemic, passing under the name of the "Jane Eyre fever," which defied all the usual nostrums of the established doctors of criticism. Its effects varied with different constitutions, in some producing a soft ethical sentimentality, which relaxed all the fibres of conscience, and in others exciting a general fever of moral and religious indignation. It was to no purpose that the public were solemnly assured, through the intelligent press, that the malady was not likely to have any permanent effect either on the intellectual or moral constitution. The book which caused the distemper would probably have been inoffensive, had not some sly manufacturer of mischief hinted that it was a book which no respectable man should bring into his family circle. Of course, every family soon had a copy of it, and one edition after another found eager purchasers. The hero, Mr. Rochester, (not the same person who comes to so edifying an end in the pages of Dr. Gilbert Burnet,) became a great favorite in the boarding-schools and in the worshipful society of governesses. That portion of Young America known as ladies' men began to swagger and swear in the presence of the gentler sex, and to allude darkly to events in their lives which excused impudence and profanity.

The novel of *Jane Eyre*, which caused this great excitement, purports to have been edited by Currer Bell, and the said Currer divides the authorship, if we are not misinformed, with a brother and sister. The work bears the marks of more than one mind and one sex, and has more variety than either of the novels which claim to have been written by Acton Bell. The family mind is strikingly peculiar, giving a strong impression of unity, but it is still male and female. From the masculine tone of *Jane Eyre*, it might pass altogether as the composition of a man, were it not for some unconscious feminine peculiarities, which the strongest-minded woman that ever aspired after manhood cannot suppress. These peculiarities refer not only to elaborate descriptions of dress, and the minutiae of the sick-chamber, but to various superficial refinements of feeling in regard to the external relations of the sex. It is true that the noblest and best representations of female character have been produced by men; but there are niceties of thought and emotion in a woman's mind which no man can delineate, but which often escape unawares from a female writer. There are numerous examples of these in *Jane Eyre*. The leading characteristic of the novel, however, and the secret of its charm, is the clear, distinct, decisive style of its representation of character, manners, and scenery; and this continually suggests a male mind. In the earlier chapters, there is little, perhaps, to break the impression that we are reading the autobiography of a powerful and peculiar female intellect; but when the admirable Mr. Rochester appears, and the profanity, brutality, and slang of the misanthropic profligate give their torpedo shocks to the nervous system,—and especially when we are favored with more than one scene given to the exhibition of mere animal appetite, and to courtship after the manner of kangaroos and the heroes of Dryden's plays,—we are gallant enough to detect the hand of a gentleman in the composition. There are also scenes of passion, so hot, emphatic, and condensed in expression, and so sternly masculine in feeling, that we are almost sure we observe the mind of the author of *Wuthering Heights* at work in the text.

The popularity of *Jane Eyre* was doubtless due in part to the freshness, raciness, and vigor of mind it evinced; but it was obtained not so much by these qualities as by frequent dealings in moral paradox, and by the hardihood of its assaults upon the prejudices of proper people. Nothing causes more delight, at least to one third of every community, than a successful attempt to wound the delicacy of their scrupulous neighbours, and a daring peep into regions which acknowledge the authority of no conventional rules. The authors of *Jane Eyre* have not accomplished this end without an occasional violation of probability and considerable confusion of plot and character, and they have made the capital mistake of supposing that an artistic representation of character and manners is a literal imitation of individual life. The consequence is, that in dealing with vicious personages they confound vulgarity with truth, and awaken too often a feeling of unmitigated disgust. The writer who colors too warmly the degrading scenes through which his immaculate hero passes is rightly held as an equivocal teacher of purity; it is not by the bold expression of blasphemy and ribaldry that a great novelist conveys the most truthful idea of the misanthropic and the dissolute. The truth is, that the whole firm of Bell & Co. seem to have a sense of the depravity of human nature peculiarly their own. It is the yahoo, not the demon, that they select for representation; their Pandemonium is of mud rather than fire.

—Edwin P. Whipple, "Novels of the Season,"
North American Review, October 1848,
pp. 355–357

Elizabeth Gaskell (1857)

Here Gaskell discusses the effect of Rigby's negative review of *Jane Eyre* on Brontë. Characteristically, Gaskell depicts Brontë's stoicism, in this case as she faces her adversarial critics. The numbing effects of death on Brontë that Gaskell refers to were the deaths of Emily and Anne in December 1848 and May 1849.

An article on 'Vanity Fair' and 'Jane Eyre' had appeared in the *Quarterly Review* of December, 1848. Some weeks after, Miss Brontë wrote to her publishers, asking why it had not been sent to her; and conjecturing that it was unfavourable, she repeated her previous request, that whatever was done with the laudatory, all critiques adverse to the novel might be forwarded to her without fail. The *Quarterly Review* was accordingly sent. I am not aware that Miss Brontë took any greater notice of the article than to place a few sentences out of it in the mouth of a hard and vulgar woman in 'Shirley,' where they are so much in character, that few have recognized them as a quotation. The time when the article was read was good for Miss Brontë; she was numbed to all petty annoyances by the grand severity of Death. Otherwise she might have felt more keenly that they deserved the criticisms which, while striving to be severe, failed in logic, owing to the misuse of prepositions; and have smarted under conjectures as to the authorship of 'Jane Eyre,' which, intended to be acute, were merely flippant. But flippancy takes a graver name when directed against an author by an anonymous writer. We call it then cowardly insolence.

Every one has a right to form his own conclusion respecting the merits and demerits of a book. I complain not of the judgment which the reviewer passes on 'Jane Eyre.' Opinions as to its tendency varied then, as they do now. While I write, I receive a letter from a clergyman in America in which he says: 'We have in our sacred of sacreds a special shelf, highly adorned, as a place we delight to honour, of novels which we recognize as having had a good influence on character, *our* character. Foremost is "Jane Eyre."

—Elizabeth Gaskell, *The Life of Charlotte Brontë*, p.359.

WILLIAM MAKEPEACE THACKERAY (1860)

How well I remember the delight, and wonder, and pleasure with which I read *Jane Eyre,* sent to me by an author whose name and sex were then alike unknown to me; the strange fascinations of the book; and how with my own work pressing upon me, I could not, having taken the volumes up, lay them down until they were read through! Hundreds of those who, like myself, recognized and admired that master-work of a great genius.

—William Makepeace Thackeray, "The Last Sketch," *Cornhill Magazine,* April 1860, p. 487

JAMES RUSSELL LOWELL (1867)

James Russell Lowell (1819–1891) was an American poet, critic, abolition-ist and diplomat, and the first editor of the *Atlantic Monthly*, to which he was also a regular contributor. The following letter excerpt was written to Charles Eliot Norton, a distinguished literary scholar and professor at Harvard University.

———— ———— ————

I have been reading novels—*Jane Eyre,* among the rest. It was very pleasant to me for its inexperience. It is a girl's dream of a world not yet known, or only glimpsed from afar. But there is real power in it, and the descriptions of scenery are the best I know, out of Ruskin.

—James Russell Lowell, letter to
Charles Eliot Norton, July 8, 1867

ALGERNON CHARLES SWINBURNE (1877)

Algernon Charles Swinburne (1837–1909) was a poet, affiliated with the decadent tradition, whose works generated much controversy for their sadomasochism, antireligious sentiment, violence, and sexuality. His most famous works are *Atalanta in Calydon* (1865), *Poems and Ballads I* (1866), *Poems and Ballads II* (1878), and *Poems and Ballads III* (1889).

Swinburne's impassioned praise of *Jane Eyre* takes a strike against Rigby's *Quarterly Review* article, characterizing its complaints as trivial in light of Brontë's more significant gifts. These, according to Swinburne, are her representations of "manly and womanly character," among which her portraits of Rochester and Paul Emmanuel in *Villette* are, for Swinburne, the most "wholly truthful" to ever be written by a woman.

———— ———— ————

Take the first work of her genius in its ripe fullness and freshness of new fruit; a twig or two is twisted or blighted of the noble tree, a bud or so has been nipped or cankered by adverse winds or frost; but root and branch and bole are all straight and strong and solid and sound in grain. Whatever in *Jane Eyre* is other than good is also less than important. The accident which brings a famished wanderer to the door of unknown kinsfolk might be a damning flaw in a novel of mere incident; but incident is not the keystone and commonplace is not the touchstone of this. The vulgar insolence and brutish malignity of the well-born guests at Thornfield Hall are grotesque and incredible in speakers of their imputed station; these are the natural properties of that class of persons which then supplied, as it yet supplies, the writers of such articles as one of memorable infamy and imbecility on *Jane Eyre* to the artistic and literary department of the *Quarterly Review.* So gross and grievous a blunder would entail no less than ruin on a mere novel of manners; but accuracy in the distinction and reproduction of social characteristics is not the test of capacity for such work as this. That test is only to be found in the grasp and manipulation of manly and womanly character. And, to my mind, the figure of Edward Rochester in this book remains, and seems like to remain, one of the only two male figures of wholly truthful workmanship and vitally heroic mould ever carved and coloured by a woman's hand. The other it is superfluous to mention; all possible readers will have uttered before I can transcribe the name of Paul Emanuel.

—Algernon Charles Swinburne,
A Note on Charlotte Brontë, 1877,
pp. 26–28

T. Wemyss Reid (1877)

Reid's dramatic description of the *"Jane Eyre* fever" that swept Great Britain and North America replays the characterization of Brontë as naïve to those worldly conventions that might have encouraged a more self-conscious author to tone down the raw passions of her novel. But the criticism she suffered at the hands of her early reviewers, writes Reid, tells us more about the prudishness of the day than the talents of the novelist.

Reid is one more critic to lambaste Rigby's ungenerous treatment of *Jane Eyre* in the *Quarterly Review.* He calls it "Pecksniffian," after Dickens's character Seth Pecksniff (*Martin Chuzzlewit,* 1844), a greedy opportunist wrongly convinced of his own moral rectitude.

In the late autumn of 1847 the reading public of London suddenly found itself called to admire and wonder at a novel which, without preliminary puff of any kind, had been placed in its hands. *Jane Eyre,* by Currer Bell, became the theme of every tongue, and society exhausted itself in conjectures as to the identity of the author, and the real meaning of the book. It was no ordinary book, and it produced no ordinary sensation. Disfigured here and there by certain crudities of thought and by a clumsiness of expression which betrayed the hand of a novice, it was nevertheless lit up from the first page to the last by the fire of a genius the depth and power of which none but the dullest could deny. The hand of its author seized upon the public mind whether it would or no, and society was led captive, in the main against its will, by one who had little of the prevailing spirit of the age, and who either knew nothing of conventionalism, or despised it with heart and soul. Fierce was the revolt against the influence of this new-comer in the wide arena of letters, who had stolen in, as it were in the night, and taken the citadel by surprise. But for the moment all opposition was beaten down by sheer force of genius, and *Jane Eyre* made her way, compelling recognition, wherever men and women were capable of seeing and admitting a rare and extraordinary intellectual supremacy. "How well I remember," says Mr. Thackeray, "the delight and wonder and pleasure with which I read *Jane Eyre,* sent to me by an author whose name and sex were then alike unknown to me; and how with my own work pressing upon me, I could not, having taken the volumes up, lay them down until they were read through." It was the same everywhere. Even those who saw nothing to commend in the story, those who revolted against its free employment of great passions and great griefs, and those who were elaborately critical upon its author's ignorance of the ways of polite society, had to confess themselves bound by the spell of the magician. *Jane Eyre* gathered admirers fast; and for every admirer she had a score of readers.

Those who remember that winter of nine-and-twenty years ago know how something like a *Jane Eyre* fever raged among us. The story which had suddenly discovered a glory in uncomeliness, a grandeur in overmastering passion, moulded the fashion of the hour, and "Rochester airs" and "Jane Eyre graces" became the rage. The book, and its fame and influence, traveled beyond the seas with a speed which in those days was marvelous. In sedate New England homes the history of the English governess was read with an avidity which was not surpassed in London itself, and within a few months of the publication of the novel it was famous throughout two continents. No such triumph has been achieved in our time by any other English author; nor can it be said, upon the whole, that many triumphs have been better merited. It happened that this anonymous story, bearing the unmistakable marks of an unpractised hand, was put before the world at the very moment when another great masterpiece of fiction was just beginning to gain the ear of the English public. But at the moment of publication *Jane Eyre* swept past *Vanity Fair* with a marvellous and impetuous speed which left Thackeray's work in the distant background; and its unknown author in a few weeks gained a wider reputation than that which one of the master minds of the century had been engaged for long years in building up. The reaction from this exaggerated fame, of course, set in, and it was sharp and severe. The blots in the book were easily hit; its author's unfamiliarity with the stage business of the play was evident enough—even to dunces; so it was a simple matter to write smart articles at the expense of a novelist who laid himself open to the whole battery of conventional criticism. In *Jane Eyre* there was much painting of souls in their naked reality; the writer had gauged depths which the plummet of the common story-teller could never have sounded, and conflicting passions were marshaled on the stage with a masterful daring which Shakespeare might have envied; but the costumes, the conventional by-play, the scenery, even the wording of the dialogue, were poor enough in all conscience. The merest playwright or reviewer could have done better in these matters—as the unknown author was soon made to understand. Additional piquancy was given to the attack by the appearance, at the very time when the *Jane Eyre* fever was at its height, of two other novels, written by persons whose sexless names proclaimed them the brothers or the sisters of Currer Bell. Human nature is not so much changed from what it was in 1847 that one need apologise for the readiness with which the reading world in general, and the critical world in particular, adopted the theory that *Wuthering Heights* and *Agnes Grey* were earlier works from the pen which had given them *Jane Eyre*. In *Wuthering Heights* some of the faults of the other book were carried to an extreme, and some of its conspicuous merits were distorted and exaggerated until they became positive blemishes; whilst *Agnes Grey* was a feeble and commonplace tale which it was easy to condemn. So the author of *Jane Eyre* was compelled to bear not only her own burden, but that of the two stories which had followed the successful novel; and the reviewers—ignorant of the fact that they were killing three birds at a single shot—rejoiced in the larger scope which was thus afforded to their critical energy.

Here and there, indeed, a manful fight on behalf of Currer Bell was made by writers who knew nothing but the name and the book. "It is soul speaking to soul," cried *Fraser's Magazine* in December, 1847; "it is not a book for prudes," added *Blackwood,* a few months later; "it is not a book for effeminate and tasteless men; it is for the enjoyment of a feeling heart and critical understanding." But in the main the verdict of the critics was adverse. It was discovered that the story was improper and immoral; it was said to be filled with descriptions of "courtship after the manner of kangaroos," and to be impregnated with a "heathenish doctrine of religion;" whilst there went up a perfect chorus of reprobation directed against its "coarseness of language," "laxity of tone," "horrid taste," and "sheer rudeness and vulgarity." From the book to the author was of course an easy transition. London had been bewildered, and its literary quidnuncs utterly puzzled, when such a story first came forth inscribed with an unknown name. Many had been the rumours eagerly passed from mouth to mouth as to the real identity of Currer Bell. Upon one point there had, indeed, been something like unanimity among the critics, and the story of *Jane Eyre* had been accepted as something more than a romance, as a genuine autobiography in which real and sorrowful experiences were related. Even the most hostile critic of the book had acknowledged that "it contained the story of struggles with such intense suffering and sorrow, as it was sufficient misery to know that any one had conceived, far less passed through." Where then was this wonderful governess to be found? In what obscure hiding-place could the forlorn soul, whose cry of agony had stirred the hearts of readers everywhere, be discovered? We may smile now, with more of sadness than of bitterness, at the base calumnies of the hour, put forth in mere wantonness and levity by a people ever seeking to know some new thing, and to taste some new sensation. The favourite theory of the day—a theory duly elaborated and discussed in the most orthodox and respectable of the reviews—was that Jane Eyre and Becky Sharp were merely different portraits of the same character; and that their original was to be found in the person of a discarded mistress of Mr. Thackeray, who had furnished the great author with a model for the heroine of *Vanity Fair,* and had revenged herself upon him by painting him as the Rochester of *Jane Eyre!* It was after dwelling upon this marvellous theory of the authorship of the story that the *Quarterly Review,* with Pecksniffian charity, calmly summed up its conclusions in these memorable words: "If we ascribe the book to a woman at all, we have no alternative but to ascribe it to one who has for some sufficient reason long forfeited the society of her own sex."

The world knows the truth now. It knows that these bitter and shameful words were applied to one of the truest and purest of women; to a woman who from her birth had led a life of self-sacrifice and patient endurance; to a woman whose affections dwelt only in the sacred shelter of her home, or with companions as pure and worthy as herself; to one of those few women who can pour out all their hearts in converse with their friends, happy in the assurance that years hence the stranger into whose hands their frank confessions may pass will find nothing there that is not loyal, true, and blameless. There was wonder among the critics, wonder too in the gay world of London, when the secret was revealed, and men were told that the author of *Jane Eyre* was no passionate light-o'-love who had merely transcribed the sad experiences of her own life; but "an austere little Joan of Arc," pure, gentle, and high-minded, of whom Thackeray himself could say that "a great and holy reverence of right and truth seemed to be with her always." The quidnuncs had searched far and wide for the author of *Jane Eyre*; but we may well doubt whether, when the truth came out at last, they were not more than ever mystified by the discovery that Currer Bell was Charlotte Brontë, the young daughter of a country parson in a remote moorland parish of Yorkshire.

—T. Wemyss Reid, *Charlotte Brontë:*
A Monograph, 1877

QUEEN VICTORIA (1880)

Victoria (1819–1901), queen of the United Kingdom of Great Britain and Ireland and later (in 1876) empress of India, was a woman of tremendous power and deeply conventional taste. Somewhat surprisingly, given the tide of objections to *Jane Eyre*'s portrayal of religious hypocrisy, the queen approved of the novel's religious tone and especially enjoyed its romance between Jane and Rochester.

Finished *Jane Eyre*, which is really a wonderful book, very peculiar in parts, but so powerfully and admirably written, such a fine tone in it, such fine religious feeling, and such beautiful writings. The description of the mysterious maniac's nightly appearances awfully thrilling. Mr. Rochester's character a very remarkable one, and Jane Eyre's herself a beautiful one. The end is very touching, when Jane Eyre returns to him and finds him blind, with one hand gone from injuries during the fire in his house, which was caused by his mad wife.

—Queen Victoria, *Journal*,
November 23, 1880

AUGUSTINE BIRRELL (1887)

Augustine Birrell (1850–1933) was a literary critic who later entered politics and was most famous for co-engineering the British response to the Easter Rising in Ireland. His 1887 biography of Charlotte Brontë agrees with Reid's in its relatively positive description of Brontë's life—and so contradicts Gaskell's overwhelmingly dour version of the novelist's experience. This emphasis is visible in Birrell's discussion of *Jane Eyre*, which he finds energetic, "alive," and refreshingly unhampered by propriety.

The crowning merit of *Jane Eyre* is its energy—a delightful quality at any time, but perhaps especially so just now. Some of our novelists make their characters walk through their parts after the languid fashions lately prevailing in the ball-room, and this proving irritating to some others of robuster frame of mind, has caused these latter, out of sheer temper, to make their heroines skip about like so many Kitty Clovers on the village green. But Jane Eyre neither languishes in drawing-rooms nor sits dangling her ankles upon gates, but is always interesting, eloquent, vehement. . . .

Miss Brontë's errors lie on the surface, and can be easily removed. Half-a-dozen deletions and as many wisely-tempered alterations, and the work of correction would be done in any one of her novels. I am far from saying they would then be faultless, but at least they would be free from those faults which make the fortunes of small critics and jokes for the evening papers.

A novel like *Jane Eyre*, fresh from the hands of its creator—unmistakably alive—speaking a bold, unconventional language, recognizing love even in a woman's heart as something which does not always wait to be asked before springing into being, was sure to disturb those who worship the goddess Propriety. Prim women, living hardly on the interest of "a little hoard of maxims," men judiciously anxious to confine their own female folk to a diet of literary lentils, read *Jane Eyre* with undisguised alarm. There was an outrageous frankness about the book—a brushing away of phrases and formulas calculated to horrify those who, to do them justice, generally recognize an enemy when they see him.

—Augustine Birrell, *Life of Charlotte Brontë*, 1887, pp. 105–108

LOUIS E. GATES (1900)

Gates here goes against the critical consensus and praises the "reason" of *Jane Eyre* instead of its zeal, vigor, or fancifulness. Or rather, he combines some of these more common descriptions with his admiration for the structural logic of Brontë's novel, thus lauding the book's ability to combine an "organizing force of reason" with "the visions of a passionate imagination." Still, he criticizes Brontë's reliance on coincidence, her hyperbolic portrait of Rochester, and the romance between Jane and Rochester.

Charlotte Brontë . . . is never completely the victim of her hallucinations. Contemptuous as she may be of "common sense" in conventional matters, she is never really false to reason or careless of its dictates in the regions either of conduct or of art. When all is said, *Jane Eyre,* the wildest of her stories, is a shining example of the infinite importance, both in life and in art, of reason. As a story, it is from beginning to end admirably wrought. It moves forward with an inevitableness, a logic of passion, an undeviating aim, that become more and more impressive, the more familiar one is with the novel, and that mark it as the work of a soundly intellectual artist—of an artist who is instinctively true to the organizing force of reason as well as to the visions of a passionate imagination. In spite of its length and wealth of detail, *Jane Eyre* is an admirably unified work of art. Every moment prepares for, or reinforces, or heightens by way of subsequent contrast, the effect of the tragic complication in the lives of Rochester and Jane Eyre,—the complication in that passion which seeming for the moment about to bring perfect happiness to the dreary existence of the little green-eyed, desolate waif of a woman, finally overwhelms her and seems to have wrecked her life. The steady march of destiny may be heard if one will listen for it; the fate-motif sounds almost as plainly as in *Tristan und Isolde.* To give us now and then this sense that we are watching the working out of fate, is the great triumph of the imaginative artist.

To some, this praise of *Jane Eyre* may sound like droll hyperbole, for there are undoubtedly sadly distracting defects in the story which for certain readers, particularly on a first reading, mar irretrievably its essential greatness. The most important of these have already been noted. "The long arm of coincidence" stretches out absurdly in one or two places, and makes all thought of fate for the moment grotesque. The vices and the ugliness of Rochester are dwelt upon with a fervour that suggests an old maid's belated infatuation for a monstrosity. The sempiternally solemn love-making of Jane and Rochester drones its pitilessly slow length along, with no slightest ironical consciousness or comment on the part of the author. These faults and these lapses of taste are undeniably exasperating, but they grow less prominent as one comes to know the story intimately and to feel its strenuous movement and sincerity; and they finally sink, for any reader who has an instinct for essentials, into their true place, as superficial blemishes on a powerfully original work of art.

—Lewis E. Gates, from "Charlotte Brontë,"
Studies and Appreciations, 1900

Sir George Murray Smith (1901)

Sir George Murray Smith (1824–1901) was the publisher of Brontë's novels and her close friend and advocate as well. Their friendship suffered an estrangement in 1853, when Brontë found out that Smith was engaged to be married to another woman, and many critics and biographers have speculated on her romantic attachment to her handsome publisher. Smith is thought to be the inspiration for Dr. John Graham Bretton, the dashing doctor in *Villette*. He also published famous authors including John Ruskin, Leigh Hunt, Harriet Martineau, William Makepeace Thackeray, and Elizabeth Gaskell.

Here Smith recalls his first encounter with the manuscript of *Jane Eyre*, which consumed him from start to finish. He claims to have known that "Currer Bell" was a woman based on the author's "qualities of style" and "turns of expression."

After breakfast on Sunday morning I took the MS. of *Jane Eyre* to my little study, and began to read it. The story quickly took me captive. Before twelve o'clock my horse came to the door, but I could not put the book down. I scribbled two or three lines to my friend, saying I was very sorry circumstances had arisen to prevent my meeting him, sent the note off by my groom, and went on reading the MS. Presently the servant came to tell me that luncheon was ready; I asked him to bring me a sandwich and a glass of wine, and still went on with *Jane Eyre*. Dinner came; for me the meal was a very hasty one, and before I went to bed that night I had finished reading the manuscript.

The next day we wrote to "Currer Bell" accepting the book for publication. I need say nothing about the success which the book achieved, and the speculations as to whether it was written by a man or a woman. For my own part, I never had much doubt on the subject of the writer's sex; but then I had the advantage over the general public of having the handwriting of the author before me. There were qualities of style, too, and turns of expression, which satisfied me that "Currer Bell" was a woman.

—Sir George Murray Smith,
"In the Early Forties," *Critic*,
January 1901, p. 52

SHIRLEY: A TALE

Brontë's second novel bears few obvious similarities with *Jane Eyre*. To begin with, *Shirley* has a historical subtext: the Luddite riots of 1812, named for General Ned Ludd, the imaginary leader of members of the Lancashire textile trade who destroyed the mills and machinery that replaced their manual labor. Against this backdrop of unrest, *Shirley* features parallel romantic plots between young Caroline Helstone and Robert Moore, an industrialist, and heiress Shirley Keeldar and Louis Gérard, Robert's younger brother.

Brontë wrote *Shirley* between February 1848 and September 1849, and the novel was published in October 1849. This period also marked the most traumatic time of her life with the sequential deaths of Branwell, Emily, and Anne. Some biographers (notably Gaskell) use this personal tragedy to explain *Shirley's* grim tone. Whatever its source, the novel failed to resonate with readers the way that *Jane Eyre* had. Critics routinely found the novel didactic and even unnatural, a sentiment made especially clear in Lewes's harsh review that follows.

GEORGE HENRY LEWES (1850)

Especially after his strong praise of *Jane Eyre*, Brontë was stung by Lewes's negative critique of *Shirley*. His review makes several important points: First, it refers to the now common knowledge that "Currer Bell" is indeed a woman, setting to rest one of the main controversies of *Jane Eyre* criticism. Second, Lewes registers his admiration for *Jane Eyre* as an unfavorable comparison to *Shirley*, which to him extends the faults of the first novel (its coarseness) without the mitigating strengths of its remarkably realistic representation and exciting plot. Third, he finds *Shirley's* weakness to extend from its lack of coherence. Where *Jane Eyre* was organized around the "autobiography" of its central character, *Shirley's* expanded point of view attenuates the novel's objective and compromises its focus. But most damning in this review is Lewes's claim that *Shirley's* faults eradicate its status as a work of art. Too much roughness and idiosyncrasy, he believes, color the novel's characterizations and, rather than portray human qualities that others can identify with, they only succeed in creating crude caricature.

———⟨⟨⟨⟩⟩⟩——— ———⟨⟨⟨⟩⟩⟩——— ———⟨⟨⟨⟩⟩⟩———

We take Currer Bell to be one of the most remarkable of *female* writers; and believe it is now scarcely a secret that Currer Bell is the pseudonyme of a woman. An eminent contemporary, indeed, has employed the sharp vivacity of a female pen to prove 'upon irresistible evidence' that *Jane Eyre must be* the work of a man! But all that 'irresistible evidence' is set aside by the simple fact that Currer Bell *is* a woman. We never, for our own parts, had a moment's doubt on the subject. That Jane herself was drawn by a woman's delicate hand,

and that Rochester equally betrayed the sex of the artist, was to our minds so obvious, as absolutely to shut our ears to all the evidence which could be adduced by the erudition even of a *marchande des modes;* and that simply because we knew that there were women profoundly ignorant of the mysteries of the toilette, and the terminology of fashion (independent of the obvious solution, that such ignorance might be counterfeited, to mislead), and felt that there was no man who *could so* have delineated a woman—or *would so* have delineated a man. The fair and ingenious critic was misled by her own acuteness in the perception of details; and misled also in some other way, and more uncharitably, in concluding that the *author* of *Jane Eyre* was a heathen educated among heathens,—the *fact* being, that the *authoress* is the daughter of a clergyman!

This question of authorship, which was somewhat hotly debated a little while ago, helped to keep up the excitement about *Jane Eyre;* but, independently of that title to notoriety, it is certain that, for many years, there had been no work of such power, piquancy, and originality. Its very faults were faults on the side of vigour; and its beauties were all original. The grand secret of its success, however,—as of all genuine and lasting success,—was its *reality.* From out the depths of a sorrowing experience, here was a voice speaking to the experience of thousands. The aspects of external nature, too, were painted with equal fidelity,—the long cheerless winter days, chilled with rolling mists occasionally gathering into the strength of rains,—the bright spring mornings,—the clear solemn nights,—were all painted to your *soul* as well as to your eye, by a pencil dipped into a soul's experience for its colours. Faults enough the book has undoubtedly: faults of conception, faults of taste, faults of ignorance, but in spite of all, it remains a book of singular fascination. A more masculine book, in the sense of vigour, was never written. Indeed that vigour often amounts to coarseness,—and is certainly the very antipode to 'lady like.'

This same over-masculine vigour is even more prominent in *Shirley,* and does not increase the pleasantness of the book. A pleasant book, indeed, we are not sure that we can style it. Power it has unquestionably, and interest too, of a peculiar sort; but not the agreeableness of a work of art. Through its pages we are carried as over a wild and desolate heath, with a sharp east wind blowing the hair into our eyes, and making the blood tingle in our veins: There is health perhaps in the drive; but not much pleasantness. Nature speaks to us distinctly enough, but she does not speak sweetly. She is in her stern and sombre mood, and we see only her dreary aspects.

Shirley is inferior to *Jane Eyre* in several important points. It is not quite so true; and it is not so fascinating. It does not so rivet the reader's attention, nor hurry him through all obstacles of improbability, with so keen a sympathy in its reality. It is even coarser in texture, too, and not unfrequently flippant; while the characters are almost all disagreeable, and exhibit intolerable rudeness of manner. In *Jane Eyre* life was viewed from the standing point of individual experience; in *Shirley* that standing point is frequently abandoned, and the artist paints only a panorama of which she, as well as you, are but spectators. Hence the unity of *Jane Eyre* in spite of its clumsy and improbable contrivances was great and effective: the fire of one passion fused the discordant materials into one mould. But in *Shirley* all unity, in consequence of defective art, is wanting. There is no passionate link; nor is there any artistic fusion, or intergrowth, by which one part evolves itself from another. Hence its falling-off in interest, coherent movement, and life. The book may be laid down at any chapter, and almost any chapter might be omitted. The various scenes are gathered up into three volumes,—they have not grown into a work. The characters often need a justification for their introduction; as in the case of the three Curates, who are offensive, uninstructive, and unamusing. That they are not *inventions,* however, we feel persuaded. For nothing but a strong sense of their reality could have seduced the authoress into such a mistake as admitting them at all. We are confident she has seen them, known them, despised them; and *therefore* she paints them! although they have no relation with the story, have no interest in themselves, and cannot be accepted as types of a class,—for they are not *Curates* but *boors:* and although not inventions, we must be permitted to say that they are *not true.* Some such objection the authoress seems indeed to have anticipated; and thus towards the close of her work defends herself against it. 'Note well! wherever you present *the actual simple truth, it is somehow always denounced as a lie:* they disown it, cast it off, throw it on the parish; whereas the product of your imagination, the mere figment, the sheer fiction, is adopted, petted, termed pretty, proper, sweetly natural.' Now Currer Bell, we fear, has here fallen into a vulgar error. It is one, indeed, into which even Miss Edgeworth has also fallen: who conceived that she justified the introduction of an improbable anecdote in her text, by averring in a note that it was a 'fact.' But, the intrusion is not less an error for all that. Truth is never rejected, unless it be truth so exceptional as to stagger our belief; and in that case the artist is wrong to employ it, without so *preparing* our minds that we might receive it unquestioned. The coinage of imagination, on the other hand, is not accepted *because* it departs from the actual truth, but only because it presents the recognised attributes of our nature in new and striking combinations. If it falsify these attributes, or the known laws of their associations, the fiction is at once pronounced to be *monstrous,* and is rejected. Art, in short, deals with the broad principles of human nature, not with idiosyncracies: and, although it requires an experience of life both comprehensive and profound, to enable us to say with confidence, that 'this motive is unnatural,' or 'that passion is untrue,' it requires no great experience to say 'this character has not the air of reality; it may be copied from nature, but it does not *look* so.' Were Currer Bell's defence allowable, all criticism must be silenced at once. An author has only to say that his characters *are copied from nature,* and the discussion is closed. But though the portraits may be like the oddities from whom they are copied, they are faulty as works of art, if they strike all who never met with these oddities, as unnatural. The curious anomalies of life, which find their proper niches in Southey's *Omniana, or Commonplace Book,* are not suitable to a novel. It is the same with incidents.

Again we say that *Shirley* cannot be received as a work of art. It is not a picture; but a portfolio of random sketches for one or more pictures. The authoress never seems distinctly to have made up her mind as to what she was to do; whether to describe the habits and manners of Yorkshire and its social aspects in the days of King Lud, or to paint character, or to tell a love story. All are by turns attempted and abandoned; and the book consequently moves slowly, and by starts—leaving behind it no distinct or satisfactory impression. Power is stamped on various parts of it; power unmistakeable, but often misapplied. Currer Bell has much yet to learn,—and, especially, the discipline of her own tumultuous energies. She must learn also to sacrifice a little of her Yorkshire roughness to the demands of good taste: neither saturating her writings with such rudeness and offensive harshness, nor suffering her style to wander into such vulgarities as would be inexcusable—even in a man. No good critic will object to the homeliness of natural diction, or to the racy flavour of conversational idiom; but every one must object to such phrases as 'Miss Mary, *getting up the steam* in her turn, now asked,' &c, or as 'making hard-handed worsted spinners *cash up to the tune of* four or five hundred per cent.,' or as 'Malone much chagrined at hearing him *pipe up in most superior style;'* all which phrases occur within the space of about a dozen pages, and that not in dialogue, but in the authoress's own narrative. And while touching on this minor, yet not trivial point, we may also venture a word of quiet remonstrance against a most inappropriate obtrusion of French phrases. When Gerard Moore and his sister talk in French, *which the authoress translates,* it surely is not allowable to leave scraps of French in the translation. A French word or two may be introduced now and then on account of some peculiar fitness, but Currer Bell's use of the language is little better than that of the 'fashionable' novelists. To speak of a grandmother as *une grand'mere,* and of treacle as *melasse,* or of a young lady being angry as *courroucee,* gives an air of affectation to the style strangely at variance with the frankness of its general tone.

—George Henry Lewes, *Edinburgh Review,*
January 1850, pp. 158–161

Elizabeth Barrett Browning (1850)

Elizabeth Barrett Browning (1806–1861) is the most important female poet of the Victorian age. Her privileged and isolated childhood was marred by illness, which she suffered from her entire life. Her correspondence with the poet Robert Browning led to their scandalous elopement to Italy in 1846; her father had forbidden her to marry. The Brownings lived in Florence for the rest of her life and had one son, Robert Wiedemann Browning, in 1849.

Barrett Browning's publications include the youthful *The Seraphin, and Other Poems* (1838), *Poems* (1844), which won great acclaim, as did *Sonnets from the Portuguese* (1850), *Casa Guidi Windows*, and perhaps her greatest work, the epic poem *Aurora Leigh* (1857).

1 have read *Shirley* lately; it is not equal to *Jane Eyre* in spontaneousness and earnestness. I found it heavy, I confess, though in the mechanical part of the writing—the compositional *savoirfaire*—there is an advance.

—Elizabeth Barrett Browning,
letter to Mrs. Jameson, April 2, 1850

Charles Kingsley (1857)

Charles Kingsley (1819–1875) was a rector, Cambridge historian, and novelist whose strongly didactic novels of social reform—such as *Yeast* (1850), *Alton Locke* (1850), and *Two Years Ago* (1857)—have largely gone out of fashion today. His (deferred) enthusiasm for *Shirley* described here marks his advocacy of working-class issues.

Shirley disgusted me at the opening: and I gave up the writer and her books with the notion that she was a person who liked coarseness. How I misjudged her! and how thankful I am that I never put a word of my misconceptions into print, or recorded my misjudgments of one who is a whole heaven above me.

—Charles Kingsley, letter to
Elizabeth Gaskell, May 14, 1857

ELIZABETH GASKELL (1857)

Gaskell usefully outlines the historical research Brontë undertook in writing *Shirley*, which was based on labor unrest in the neighborhood of Roe Head. While the work is imaginative, Gaskell confirms that Brontë offended certain people with the accuracy of her portraiture; the three boorish curates in *Shirley* were easily identified in Haworth originals. More famously, Emily Brontë was the prototype of the heroine Shirley.

Once again, Gaskell's object in describing one of Brontë's achievements is to rescue the novelist and her work from her harsher critics. To this end, she emphasizes the pall of loss that was hanging over Brontë while she finished the novel: the successive deaths of Branwell, Emily, and Anne.

The tale of *Shirley* had been begun soon after the publication of *Jane Eyre*. If the reader will refer to the account I have given of Miss Brontë's school-days at Roe Head, he will there see how every place surrounding that house was connected with the Luddite riots, and will learn how stories and anecdotes of that time were rife among the inhabitants of the neighboring villages; how Miss W___ [Wooler] herself, and the elder relations of most of her schoolfellows, must have known the actors in those grim disturbances. What Charlotte had heard there as a girl came up in her mind when, as a woman, she sought a subject for her next work; and she sent to Leeds for a file of the "Mercuries" of 1812, '13, and '14, in order to understand the spirit of those eventful times. She was anxious to write of things she had known and seen; and among the number was the West Yorkshire character, for which any tale laid among the Luddites would afford full scope. In *Shirley* she took the idea of most of her characters from life, although the incidents and situations were, of course, fictitious. She thought that if these last were purely imaginary, she might draw from the real without detection; but in this she was mistaken: her studies were too closely accurate. This occasionally led her into difficulties. People recognized themselves, or were recognized by others, in her graphic descriptions of their personal appearances, and modes of action and turns of thought, though they were placed in new positions, and figured away in scenes far different to those in which their actual life had been passed. . . . The "three curates" were real living men, haunting Haworth and the neighboring district; and so obtuse in perception that, after the first burst of anger at having their ways and habits chronicled was over, they rather enjoyed calling each other by the names she had given them. "Mrs. Pryor" was well known to many who loved the original dearly. The whole family of the Yorkes were, I have been assured, almost daguerreotypes. . . .

The character of Shirley herself is Charlotte's representation of Emily. I mention this because all that I, a stranger, have been able to learn about her has not tended to give either me, or my readers, a pleasant impression of her. But we must remember how little we are acquainted with her, compared to that sister, who, out of her more intimate knowledge, says that she "was genuinely good, and truly great," and who tried to depict her character in Shirley Keeldar, as what Emily Brontë would have been, had she placed in health and prosperity.

Down into the very midst of her writing came the bolts of death. She had nearly finished the second volume of her tale when Branwell died—after him Emily—after her Anne; the pen, laid down where there were three sisters living and loving, were taken up when one alone remained. Well might she call the first chapter that she wrote after this, "The Valley of the Shadow of Death."

—Elizabeth Gaskell,
Life of Charlotte Brontë, 1857

WILBUR L. CROSS (1899)

Wilber Lucius Cross (1862–1948) was an American professor of English and a politician. He taught at Yale from 1894 until 1930 and also served as dean before going on to be the Democratic governor of Connecticut from 1931 to 1939. His literary criticism includes *The Life and Times of Laurence Sterne* (1909) and *The History of Henry Fielding* (1918), as well as broader studies of the English novel in general.

Cross's analysis of *Shirley* takes issue with the liberties she took in historical representation and describes the novel's "historical allegory" rather than realism. He follows the lead of many of the Brontë critics who precede him (most notably or influentially, Elizabeth Gaskell, as we see in the previous excerpt) in claiming that Shirley is a "minute study" of Emily Brontë.

———

Shirley (1849) is milder in tone (than *Jane Eyre*); in it Charlotte Brontë is not quite herself. Much disturbed by criticism of *Jane Eyre*, she undertook to profit by it, particularly by the advice of George Henry Lewes, who told her to avoid poetry, sentiment, and melodrama, and to read Jane Austen. She now sought to daguerreotype Yorkshire life and scenes; and this is the way she did it. For an enveloping plot of exciting incident, she went back some forty years to the commercial troubles with the United States, and to the contest between mill-owners and operatives over the introduction of labor-saving machinery. She thus made for herself an opportunity to describe the battering of a woollen mill by starlight, and the shooting of the manager. In this setting she placed Yorkshire men and women with whom she was acquainted,—her sister Emily, her father, her school friends, one of her lovers, and the neighboring curates. Incident, too, she reproduced from life, with varying degrees of modification. The novel is thus an historical allegory. It is hardly necessary to observe that it is constructed on false notions of art and on a complete misunderstanding of Jane Austen. It is, however, as a description of externals the most careful and most sympathetic of all Charlotte Brontë's work, and is still the novel of hers most liked by Yorkshiremen, who see themselves there. The portrait which has the most unusual interest is the minute study of Emily Brontë under the name of Shirley Keeldar. In all her moods and loves and changes of feature under excitement, Charlotte represents her,—her indolence, her passion for fierce dogs and the moors; the quivering lip, the trembling voice, the eye flashing dark, the dilating nostrils, the sarcastic laugh, the expansion of the frail body in indignation, and her wild picturesque beauty when visited by one of her rare dreams, such, for example, as the vision of Nature, the Titanic mother.

Shirley failed to please Lewes, who was expecting another *Pride and Prejudice*. To his flippant criticism Charlotte Brontë replied cavalierly (with *Villette)*, and became herself once more.

—Wilbur L. Cross, *The Development of
the English Novel,* 1899, pp. 231–232

LOUIS E. GATES (1900)

Here Gates refers to the Victorian propensity to depict sociological life in great detail, which he exemplifies by George Eliot's *Middlemarch*, and to which standard *Shirley* comes up short. His description of *Shirley* as histori-cally and socially shallow also represents a truism about Brontë's work that was not challenged until very recently: the tendency to view Brontë as an alienated and isolated figure, working on the outskirts of society, and thus not adequately attentive to the nuances of social experience.

Shirley takes in, too, more of the light miscellaneousness of life than *Jane Eyre,*—more of its variegated surface. *Jane Eyre* concentrates all the interest on the struggle of two hearts with fate; *Shirley,* while loyal to the fortunes of a few principal characters, suggests the whole little world of the country-side, through conflict and cooperation with which these characters gain their strength and quality. At least it tries to suggest this world,—a world of curates, rectors, squires, and even labourers. Tea-drinkings and church festivals and labour riots are conscientiously set forth, and in the midst of their bustle and confusion the wooings of Robert Moore and Louis Moore go on.

Yet one has after all but to think of *Middlemarch* to feel how superficial in Charlotte Brontë's novels is the treatment of sociological detail. In *Shirley* the labourers and their riotous attacks on the mill are plainly enough simply used to heighten the effect of the plot; the rioters come in almost as perfunctorily as the mob in a melodrama, and they pass out of view the moment they have served the purpose of giving the reader an exciting scene in which Moore may act heroically, and over which Shirley and Charlotte may feel intensely. The genius of Charlotte Brontë lay not in the power to realize minutely and thoroughly the dependence of character on social environment, but in her power to portray with lyrical intensity the fates of a few important characters. *Shirley* isolates its characters far less than *Jane Eyre,*—tries to see them and portray them as more intimately and complexly acted upon by a great many forces. It is therefore a wiser, saner, and more modern book than *Jane Eyre.* But in proportion it loses in intensity, passionate colour, and in subduing singleness of aim. The interest is divided; the dreamlike involvement of the reader in the mist of a single temperament's fancies and feelings disappears; the peculiar, half-hypnotizing effect of Jane Eyre's murmurous, monotonous recital vanishes; and in the place of all this we have a brilliant, often powerful, and undeniably picturesque and entertaining criticism of various aspects of Yorkshire life, written somewhat after the method that George Eliot later used much more skilfully.

—Lewis E. Gates, from "Charlotte Brontë,"
Studies and Appreciations, 1900

VILLETTE

Brontë's last and darkest novel is set almost entirely in Belgium. The novel's introspective study of Lucy Snowe, a lonely British schoolteacher in the village of Villette, revives many experiences of Brontë's own time in Belgium, including a thinly veiled portrait of her Belgian schoolmaster Constantin Héger in the novel's hero, Paul Emmanuel.

Brontë wrote the novel slowly and painstakingly between January 1850 and October 1852. It was published in January 1853 to mixed reviews, most of which praised the novel's intricate psychological portraiture but also found it gloomy and its ending frustratingly vague. At worst, Lucy Snowe is considered unappealing and morbid (see Matthew Arnold's review), but some readers found the novel superior to *Jane Eyre* in its maturity and depth.

Charlotte Brontë (1852)

In this letter to W.S. Williams, Brontë discusses *Villette* in response to Williams's request for her "statement of impressions" about the novel. Brontë acknowledges aspects of *Villette* that many readers would subsequently critique, such as Lucy Snowe's "morbid" nature and "coldness," but defends these characterizations as realistic to Lucy's experience.

———

'My dear Sir, I must not delay thanking you for your kind letter, with its candid and able commentary on "Villette." With many of your strictures I concur. The third volume may, perhaps, do away with some of the objections; others still remain in force. I do not think the interest culminates anywhere to the degree you would wish. What climax there is does not come on till near the conclusion; and even then, I doubt whether the regular novel-reader will consider the "agony piled sufficiently high" (as the Americans say), or the colours dashed on to the canvass with the proper amount of daring. Still, I fear, they must be satisfied with what is offered: my palette affords no brighter tints; were I to attempt to deepen the reds, or burnish the yellows, I should but botch.

'Unless I am mistaken, the emotion of the book will be found to be kept throughout in tolerable subjection. As to the name of the heroine, I can hardly express what subtlety of thought made me decide upon giving her a cold name; but, at first, I called her "Lucy Snowe" (spelt with an "e"); which Snowe I afterwards changed to "Frost." Subsequently, I rather regretted the change, and wished it "Snowe" again. If not too late, I should like the alteration to be made now throughout the MS. A cold name she must have; partly, perhaps, on the "lucus a non lucendo" principle—partly on that of the "fitness of things," for she has about her an external coldness.

'You say that she may be thought morbid and weak, unless the history of her life be more fully given. I consider that she is both morbid and weak at times; her character sets up no pretensions to unmixed strength, and anybody living her life would necessarily become morbid. It was no impetus of healthy feeling which urged her to the confessional, for instance; it was the semi-delirium of solitary grief and sickness. If, however, the book does not express all this, there must be a great fault somewhere. I might explain away a few other points, but it would be too much like drawing a picture and then writing underneath the name of the object intended to be represented. We know what sort of a pencil that is which needs an ally in the pen.

'Thanking you again for the clearness and fullness with which you have responded to my request for a statement of impressions, I am, my dear Sir, yours very sincerely,

—Charlotte Brontë, letter to W.S. Williams,
November 6, 1852, quoted in Gaskell,
pp. 392–393

HARRIET MARTINEAU (1853)

The following review of *Villette* by Martineau was hurtful to Brontë, who respected Martineau's judgment and sought her approval. Martineau's primary complaint is that Brontë's heroines are consumed by romantic love, and this near-obsessive quality impairs the realism of their portrayal. Martineau, a keen advocate of women's rights (particularly in the area of employment and education), frequently despaired of the representation of women as narrowly romantic, which she believed restricted their ability to be taken seriously in professional and public domains.

Everything written by 'Currer Bell' is remarkable. She can touch nothing without leaving on it the stamp of originality. Of her three books, this is perhaps the strangest, the most astonishing, though not the best. The sustained ability is perhaps greater in *Villette* than in its two predecessors, there being no intervals of weakness, except in the form of a few passages, chiefly episodical, of over-wrought writing, which, though evidently a sincere endeavour to express real feeling, are not felt to be congenial, or very intelligible, in the midst of so much that is strong and clear. In regard to interest, we think that this book will be pronounced inferior to *Jane Eyre* and superior to *Shirley*. In point of construction it is superior to both; and this is a vast gain and a great encouragement to hope for future benefits from the same hand which shall surpass any yet given. The whole three volumes are crowded with beauties—with the good things for which we look to the clear sight, deep feeling and singular, though not extensive, experience of life which we associate with the name of 'Currer Bell'. But under all, through all, over all, is felt a drawback, of which we were anxious before, but which is terribly aggravated here—the book is almost intolerably painful. We are wont to say, when we read narratives which are made up of the external woes of life, such as may and do happen every day, but are never congregated in one experience—that the author has no right to make readers so miserable. We do not know whether the right will be admitted in the present case, on the ground of the woes not being external; but certainly we ourselves have felt inclined to rebel against the pain, and, perhaps on account of protraction, are disposed to deny its necessity and truth. With all her objectivity, 'Currer Bell' here afflicts us with an amount of subjective misery which we may fairly remonstrate against; and she allows us no respite—even while treating us with humour, with charming description and the presence of those whom she herself regards as the good and gay. In truth, there is scarcely anybody that is good—serenely and cheerfully good, and the gaiety has pain in it. An atmosphere of pain hangs about the whole, forbidding that repose which we hold to be essential to the true presentment of any large portion of life and experience. In this pervading pain, the book reminds us of Balzac; and so it does in the prevalence of one tendency, or one idea, throughout the whole conception and action. All the female characters, in all their thoughts and lives, are full of one thing, or are regarded by the reader in the light of that one thought—love. It begins with the child of six years old, at the opening—a charming picture—and it closes with it at the last page; and, so dominant is this idea—so incessant is the writer's tendency to describe the need of being loved, that the heroine, who tells her own story, leaves the reader at last under the uncomfortable impression of her having either entertained a double love, or allowed one to supersede another without notification of the transition. It is not thus in real life. There are substantial, heartfelt interests for women of all ages, and under ordinary circumstances, quite apart from love: there is an absence of introspection, an unconsciousness, a repose in women's lives—unless under peculiarly unfortunate circumstances—of which we find no admission in this book; and to the absence of it, may be attributed some of the criticism which the book will meet from readers who are not prudes, but whose reason and taste will reject the assumption that events and characters are to be regarded through the medium of one passion only.

And here ends all demur. We have thought it right to indicate clearly the two faults in the book, which it is scarcely probable that anyone will deny.

Abstractions made of these, all else is power, skill and interest. The freshness will be complete to readers who know none but English novels. Those who are familiar with Balzac may be reminded, by the sharp distinction of the pictured life, place and circumstance, of some of the best of his tales: but there is nothing borrowed; nothing that we might not as well have had if 'Currer Bell' had never read a line of Balzac—which may very likely be the case. As far as we know, the life of a foreign *pension* (Belgian, evidently) and of a third-rate capital, with its half provincial population and proceedings, is new in purely English literature; and most lifelike and spirited it is. The humour which peeps out in the names— the court of Labassecour, with its heir-apparent, the Duc of Dindoneau—the Professors Boissec and Rochemorte—and so forth—is felt throughout, though there is not a touch of lightheartedness from end to end. The presence of the heroine in that capital and *pension* is strangely managed; and so is the gathering of her British friends around her there; but, that strangeness surmounted, the picture of their lives is admirable. The reader must go to the book for it; for it fills two volumes and a half out of the three. The heroine, Lucy Snowe, tells her own story. Every reader *of Jane Eyre* will be glad to see the autobiographical form returned to. Lucy may be thought a younger, feebler sister of Jane. There is just enough resemblance for that—but she has not Jane's charm of mental and moral health, and consequent repose. She is in a state of chronic nervous fever for the most part; is usually silent and suffering; when she speaks, speaks in enigmas or in raillery, and now and then breaks out under the torture of passion; but she acts admirably—with readiness, sense, conscience and kindliness. Still we do not wonder that she loved more than she was beloved, and the love at last would be surprising enough, if love could ever be so. Perhaps Pauline and her father are the best-drawn characters in the book, where all are more or less admirably delineated. We are not aware that there is one failure.

A striking peculiarity comes out in the third volume, striking from one so large and liberal, so removed from ordinary social prejudices as we have been accustomed to think 'Currer Bell'. She goes out of her way to express a passionate hatred of Romanism. It is not the calm disapproval of a ritual religion, such as we should have expected from her, ensuing upon a presentment of her own better faith. The religion she envokes is itself but a dark and doubtful refuge from the pain which impels the invocation; while the Catholicism on which she enlarges is even virulently reprobated. We do not exactly see the moral necessity for this (there is no artistical necessity) and we are rather sorry for it, occurring as it does at a time when catholics and protestants hate each other quite sufficiently; and in a mode which will not affect conversion. A better advocacy of protestantism would have been to show that it can give rest to the weary and heavy laden; whereas it seems to yield no comfort in return for every variety of sorrowful invocation.

—Harriet Martineau, *Daily News,*
February 3, 1853, p. 2

GEORGE ELIOT (1853)

Eliot was one critic who found *Villette* superior to the much more commercially successful *Jane Eyre.*

I am only just returned to a sense of the real world about me for I have been reading *Villette,* a still more wonderful book than *Jane Eyre.* There is something almost preternatural in its power.

—George Eliot, letter to Mrs. Charles Bray,
February 15, 1853

MATTHEW ARNOLD (1853)

Arnold cites *Villette's* intensity as evidence of Brontë's own anger, once again showing a critical tendency to conflate the writer with her characters.

Why is *Villette* disagreeable? Because the writer's mind contains nothing but hunger, rebellion, and rage, and therefore that is all she can, in fact, put into her book. No fine writing can hide this thoroughly, and it will be fatal to her in the long run.

—Matthew Arnold, letter to
Mrs. Forster, April 14, 1853

GEORGE HENRY LEWES (1853)

Lewes's review contrasts *Villette* to Elizabeth Gaskell's novel of the same year, *Ruth,* which is the story of a young woman who is seduced by a wealthy man and bears his illegitimate child. The "moral" in *Ruth* that Lewes refers to here is of a more dogmatic nature than that which he finds in *Villette,* which far exceeds the often preachy *Ruth* in its abstraction and what Lewes calls the "feelings of a strong, struggling soul."

There is a moral too in *Villette,* or rather many morals, but not so distinctly a *morale en action.* It is a work of astonishing power and passion. From its pages there issues an influence of truth as healthful as a mountain breeze. Contempt of conventions in all things, in style, in thought, even in the art of story-telling, here visibly springs from the independent originality of a strong mind nurtured in solitude. As a novel, in the ordinary sense of the word, *Villette* has few claims; as a *book,* it is one which, having read, you will not easily forget. It is quite true that the episode of Miss Marchmont, early in the first volume, is unnecessary, having no obvious connexion with the plot or the characters; but with what wonderful imagination is it painted! Where shall we find such writing as in that description of her last night, wherein the memories of bygone years come trooping in upon her with a vividness partaking of the last energy of life? It is true also that the visit to London is unnecessary, and has many unreal details. Much of the book seems to be brought in merely that the writer may express something which is in her mind; but at any rate she *has* something in her mind, and expresses it as no other can. . . .

In this world, as Goethe tells us, "there are so few voices, and so many echoes;" there are so few books, and so many volumes—so few persons thinking and speaking for themselves, so many reverberating the vague noises of others. Among the few stands *Villette.* In it we read the actual thoughts and feelings of a strong, struggling soul; we hear the cry of pain from one who has loved passionately, and who has sorrowed sorely. Indeed, no more distinct characteristic of Currer Bell's genius can be named, than the depth of her capacity for all passionate emotions.

—George Henry Lewes, *"Ruth* and *Villette,"*
Westminster Review, April 1853,
pp. 485–490

Catharine M. Sedgwick (1853)

Catharine Maria Sedgwick (1789–1867) was a well-known and respected American writer who published novels, religious tracts, children's literature, and nonfiction. Among her primary literary interests were the autonomy of women and the relations between Native Americans and white settlers. Here she takes a fairly well-established path in conflating Brontë with her heroines, Jane Eyre and Lucy Snowe, which is Sedgwick's compliment to the realism with which these characters are drawn.

Have you all read *Villette?* and do you not admire the book, and own it as one of the great books of the time? I confess that I have seldom been more impressed with the genius of the writer, and seldom less drawn to her personally. She has nerves of such delicate fineness of edge that the least touch turns them, or she has had an exasperating experience. Whether she calls herself Jane Eyre, or Lucy Snowe, it does not matter—it is Miss Brontë. She has the intensity of Byron—of our own Fanny Kemble. She unconsciously infuses herself into her heroine. It is an egotism whose fires are fed by the inferior vitality of others; and how well she conceives others! how she daguerreotypes them!

> —Catharine M. Sedgwick, letter to
> Dr. Dewey, April 1853, cited in
> Mary E. Dewey, *Life and Letters of
> Catharine M. Sedgwick*, 1871, p. 349

T. Wemyss Reid (1877)

While Reid's biography of Charlotte Brontë takes issue with the gloomy tone of Elizabeth Gaskell's portrait of the author, in this analysis of *Villette,* he acknowledges the novel's tragic aura and attributes it to the "almost absolute hopelessness" that struck Brontë after the deaths of her siblings.

[*Villette*] was written years after the period when *The Professor* was composed, when the hard realities of life had ceased to be veiled under tender mists of sentiment or imagination, and when the lonely present, the future, "which often appals me," made the writer too painfully aware that she had drunk the cup of existence almost to the dregs. As a piece of workmanship there is no comparison between it and the earlier story. On every page we see traces of the artist's hand. Genius flashes forth from both works it is true, but in *Villette* it is genius chastened and restrained by a cultivated taste, or working under that high pressure which only the trained writer can bring to bear upon it. Yet, whilst we must admit the immense superiority of the later over the earlier work, we cannot turn from the one to the other without being painfully touched by the sad, strange difference in the spirit which animates them. The stories, as I have said, are nearly the same. With some curious transformations, in fact, they are practically identical. But they are only the same in the sense in which the portrait of the fair and hopeful girl, with life's romance shining before her eyes, is the same as the portrait of the worn and solitary woman for whom the romance is at an end. A whole world of suffering, of sorrow, of patient endurance, lies between the two. I have spoken of the mood in which *The Professor* was written—Hope still lingered at that time in the heart, breathing its merciful though illusory suggestions of something brighter and better in the future. All who have passed through the ordeal of a life's sorrow will be able to understand the distinction between the temperament of the author at that period in her life, and her temperament when she composed *Villette*. For such suffering ones know, how, in the first and bitterest moment of sorrow, the heart cannot shut out the blessed belief that a time of release from the pain will come—a time far off, perhaps, but in which a day bright as that which has suddenly been eclipsed will shine again. It is only as the years go by, and as the first ache of intolerable anguish has been lulled into a dreary rest by habit, that the faith which gave them strength to bear the keenest smart, takes flight, and leaves them to the pale monotony of a twilight which can know no dawn. It was in this later and saddest stage of endurance that *Villette* was written. The sharpest pangs of the heart-experiences at Brussels had vanished. The author, no longer full of the self-consciousness of the girl, could even treat her own story, her own sorrows of that period, with a lighter hand, a more artistic touch, than when she first wrote of them; but through all her work there ran the dreary conviction that in those days of mingled joy and suffering she had tasted life at its best, and that in the future which lay before her there could be nothing which should renew either the strong delights or keen anguish of that time. So the book is pitched, as we know, in a key of almost absolute hopelessness. Nothing but the genius of Charlotte Brontë could have saved such a work from sinking under its own burden of gloom. That this intense and tragic study of a soul should have had power to fascinate, not the psychologist alone, but the vast masses of the reading world, is a triumph which can hardly be paralleled in recent literary efforts. In *The Professor* we move among the same scenes, almost among the same characters and incidents, but the whole atmosphere is a different one. It is a dull, cold atmosphere, if you will, but one feels that behind the clouds the sun is shining, and that sooner or later the hero and heroine will be allowed to bask in his reviving rays. Set the two stories together, and read them in the light of all that passed between the years in which they were written—the death of Branwell, of Emily, and of Anne, the utter shattering of some fair illusions which buoyed up Charlotte's heart in the first years of her literary triumph, the apparent extinction of all hope as to future happiness—and you will get from them a truer knowledge of the author's soul than any critic or biographer could convey to you.

—T. Wemyss Reid, *Charlotte Brontë:*
A Monograph, 1877, pp. 7–13, 219–225,
The Story of Jane Eyre

MARGARET OLIPHANT (1892)

Margaret Oliphant (1828–1897) wrote novels, short stories, biographies, and journalism. Her fiction, of which *Miss Marjoribanks* (1866) is the best-known novel, focuses on domestic relations in provincial settings. She was a prolific critic of Victorian fiction and was known for her exacting moral standards.

The third of Miss Brontë's works, *Villette*, published 1853, returned in a great measure to the atmosphere of *Jane Eyre*, the scene being chiefly laid in Brussels, and in a school there; and the real hero—after one or two failures—being found in the person of a French master, the fiery, vivacious, undignified and altogether delightful M. Paul Emmanuel, who plays upon the heroine's heart and nerves something after the manner of Rochester, but who is so absolutely real in his fantastic peculiarities and admirable, tender, manly character, that the pranks he plays and the confusion he produces are all forgiven him. Lucy Snowe, the heroine, the cool little proper Englishwoman with the well-concealed volcano under her primness, is by no means so captivating as Jane Eyre, but every detail is so astonishingly true to life, and the force and vigour of the romance—occasionally reaching to fever-heat, and all the more startling from its contrast with the cold white Brussels house, the school atmosphere, and the chill exterior of Miss Snowe—so absorbing, that the book made a still greater impression than *Jane Eyre*, and the ultimate fate of M. Paul, left uncertain at the conclusion, was debated in a hundred circles with greater vehemence than many a national problem.

—Margaret Oliphant, *The Victorian Age of*
English Literature, 1892, vol. 1, pp. 307–308

LEWIS E. GATES (1900)

Gates faults *Villette* for its morbidity, like many critics here, and relates that perspective to Brontë's gender and her particular intellect: an

intense and somber self-consciousness. Again we see the Romantic portrait of the suffering genius in Gates's description of Brontë.

—⁓⁓— —⁓⁓— —⁓⁓—

In *Villette* Charlotte Brontë returns to the personal point of view and the
more lyrical tone. Lucy Snowe, who is merely a reincarnation of Jane Eyre,
though somewhat less energetic and less ugly, puts upon us in this story,
as Jane Eyre had put upon us before, the spell of her dream, and imposes
on us the sad or happy hallucinations that made up her life. In some
respects, *Villette* is the most of a *tour de force* of Charlotte Brontë's novels.
She takes for heroine a plain, shy, colourless school-teacher; she puts her
in the midst of a girl's boarding-school, and keeps her there pitilessly from
almost the start to the finish of the story; she makes use of hardly any
exciting incident—the Spectral Nun is a mere picturesque hoax, though
her repeated introduction illustrates the weakness for sensationalism in
plots that Charlotte Brontë could never quite rid herself of; there are,
however, this time no mad wives, no hollow mysterious laughter, no men
or women with suspicious pasts. Yet in spite of the commonplace characters
and the seemingly dull situations, the story that results holds the reader's
interest firmly with its alternate gayety, pathos, and passion. In places it is
as poignant as *Jane Eyre*. After all, we mortals are ridiculously sympathetic
creatures; it is the fluttering of the human heart that captures us; and Lucy
Snowe's heart finds enough excitement in her Belgian boarding-school to
justify a great deal of passionate beating.

Villette suffers, however, from a divided allegiance on the part of the
author. Her method in the story is plainly a compromise between the
egoistic self-concentration of *Jane Eyre* and the professional detachment
of *Shirley*. Lucy Snowe is made more speculative, less acridly self-assertive,
than Jane Eyre, to the very end that she may note more of the ordinary
happenings of life, and set down a more reflective and inclusive record
of what goes on about her than the impassioned Jane would have had
patience for. As a consequence, *Villette* gains in range but loses in intensity.
The fortunes of the Bassompierres, which, in spite of Lucy's loyalty to the
charm of these worthy folk, fail to perturb the reader very deeply, fill far
too much space. In a letter written about the time of the publication of the
novel, Charlotte Brontë laments the weakness of the character of Paulina,
and the apparent *non-sequitur* that results in the story from the early
importance of the Bassompierres and of Dr. John, and from their later
obscuration by Lucy's love for the Professor. This flickering purpose is

perhaps the sign of the difficulty the author met in trying to be objective. The power to portray the world with passionate truth as seen through a woman's temperament,—a narrowly exacting and somewhat morbidly self-centred temperament,—this was the peculiar power of Charlotte Brontë; and in *Jane Eyre* this power found its perfect expression. In her other novels, though she wins a greater range, she sacrifices her peculiar coign of vantage.

—Lewis E. Gates, from "Charlotte Brontë,"
Studies and Appreciations, 1900

THE PROFESSOR: A TALE

Brontë's first novel was rejected by publishers as many as eight times and only came out posthumously in 1857, in part because of the renewal of interest in Brontë generated by Gaskell's biography of the same year. Most of the publishers who refused it found the beginning weak and the plot thin. As the reviewers below attest, the characters of William Crimsworth and Frances Henri show some promise but fail to impress many as fully realized.

It is thought that Brontë began *The Professor* as early as 1844 and worked on the manuscript in collaboration with Emily and Anne as they wrote *Wuthering Heights* and *Agnes Grey,* respectively. *The Professor* was completed in August 1846 and started making the publishers' rounds shortly thereafter.

CHARLOTTE BRONTË (1847)

In this letter to W.S. Williams, Brontë draws a somewhat surprising comparison between the unpublished *The Professor* and *Jane Eyre,* one that few critics and readers would agree with.

[*The Professor* was] deficient in incident and in general attractiveness; yet the middle and latter portions of the work, all that relates to Brussels, the Belgian school, &c. is as good as I can write; it contains more pith, more substance, more reality, in my judgment, than much of *Jane Eyre.*

—Charlotte Brontë, letter to
W.S. Williams, December 14, 1847

Elizabeth Gaskell (1857)

As Gaskell explains, Brontë wrote *The Professor* alongside Emily and Anne as they wrote their first novels, *Wuthering Heights* and *Agnes Grey*. Gaskell's treatment of Brontë's first novel is lukewarm, but she does praise *The Professor* for its restraint and some of its characterizations. Nevertheless, when Gaskell was invited to edit *The Professor* for publication after Brontë's death, she refused, citing its "coarseness."

Each of them had written a prose tale, hoping that the three might be published together. 'Wuthering Heights' and 'Agnes Grey' are before the world. The third—Charlotte's contribution—is yet in manuscript, but will be published shortly after the appearance of this memoir. The plot in itself is of no great interest; but it is a poor kind of interest that depends upon startling incidents rather than upon dramatic development of character; and Charlotte Brontë never excelled one or two sketches of portraits which she has given in 'The Professor,' nor, in grace of womanhood, ever surpassed one of the female characters there described. By the time she wrote this tale, her taste and judgment had revolted against the exaggerated idealisms of her early girlhood, and she went to the extreme of reality, closely depicting characters as they had shown themselves to her in actual life: if there they were strong even to coarseness,—as was the case with some that she had met with in flesh and blood existence,—she 'wrote them down an ass;' if the scenery of such life as she saw was for the most part wild and grotesque, instead of pleasant or picturesque, she described it line for line. The grace of the one or two scenes and characters, which are drawn rather from her own imagination than from absolute fact, stand out in exquisite relief from the deep shadows and wayward lines of others, which call to mind some of the portraits of Rembrandt.

—Elizabeth Gaskell, *The Life of
Charlotte Brontë*, 1857, p. 304–305

Margaret Sweat (1857)

Margaret Jane Sweat was a reviewer and minor novelist (*Ethel's Love Life*, 1859) and travel writer (*Highways of Travel, or a Summer in Europe*, 1859). Her tepid analysis of *The Professor* is excerpted from a longer piece about the tone and style of Brontë's novels collectively.

From [*Jane Eyre, Shirley*, and *Villette*] we must make up our estimate of Currer Bell's genius; for *The Professor*, written first, but not published till the halo of assured reputation surrounded the name of its author, hardly influences our judgment either way. Its faults, which are many, were redeemed in her subsequent works; its crudeness, which is great, gave place to exquisite finish both of plot and of character; and its choice of material, which reminds us of her sisters rather more than of herself as we now know her, was replaced by more genial and more natural specimens of humanity. Its best portions were developed in *Villette* with more power and richer charm, and, so far as Currer Bell is concerned, the publication of *The Professor* might still have been omitted; but viewed by itself, and compared with most of the romance issuing from the prolific and not over-fastidious press of the day, we confess some surprise that the occasional flashes of talent in its details, and the unquestionable strength of its conception, should not have won the attention of some one of the publishers to whose inspection it was submitted.

—Margaret Sweat, *The North American Review*,
October 1857, lxxxv, pp. 293–329

T. WEMYSS REID (1877)

In his generous assessment of *The Professor*, Reid calls attention to an important nineteenth-century reading convention: the idea that fiction should offer an escape from the ordinary cares of life. This expectation, he believes, is what doomed *The Professor* when Brontë first distributed it to publishers. Its portraiture is too bleak and realistic to appeal to readers in hope of lighter entertainment. This judgment, he goes on to say, prompted Brontë to write her next novel, *Jane Eyre*, in a more suspenseful and diverting tone.

But even as a mere novel *The Professor* has striking merits, and would well repay perusal from that point of view alone; whilst as a means of gaining fresh light with regard to the character of the writer, it is not less valuable than *Wuthering Heights* itself. True, *The Professor* is not really a first attempt. "A first attempt it certainly was not," says Charlotte in reference to it, "as the pen which wrote it had previously been worn a good deal in a practice of some years." But the previous writings, of which hardly a trace now remains—those early MSS. having been carefully destroyed, with the exception of the few which Mrs. Gaskell was permitted to see—were in no respect finished productions, nor had they been written with a view to publication. The first occasion on which Charlotte Brontë really began a prose work which she proposed to commit to the press was on that day when, seated by her two sisters, she joined them in penning the first page of a new novel.

To all practical intents, therefore, *The Professor* is entitled to be regarded as a first work; and certainly nothing can show Charlotte's peculiar views on the subject of novel-writing more clearly or strikingly than this book does. The world knows how resolutely in all her writings she strove to be true to life as she saw it. In *Jane Eyre* there are, indeed, romantic incidents and situations, but even in that work there is no trespassing beyond the limits always allowed to the writer of fiction; whilst it must not be forgotten that *Jane Eyre* was in part a response to the direct appeal from the publishers for something different in character from *The Professor*. In that first story she determined that she would write a man's life as men's lives usually are. Her hero was "never to get a shilling he had not earned;" no sudden turns of fortune were "to lift him in a moment to wealth and high station;" and he was not even to marry "a beautiful girl or a lady of rank." "As Adam's son he should share Adam's doom, and drain throughout life a mixed and moderate cup of enjoyment."

Very few novel-readers will share this conception of what a novel ought to be. The writer of fiction is an artist whose accepted duty it is to lift men and women out of the cares of ordinary life, out of the sordid surroundings which belong to every lot in this world, and to show us life under different, perhaps under fantastic, conditions: a life which by its contrast to that we ourselves are leading shall furnish some relief to our mental vision, wearied and jaded by its constant contemplation of the fevers and disappointments, the crosses and long years of weary monotony, which belong to life as it is. We know how a great living writer has ventured to protest against this theory, and how in her finest works of fiction she has shown us life as it is, under the sad and bitter conditions of pain, sorrow, and hopelessness. But Charlotte Brontë wrote *The Professor* long before "George Eliot" took up her pen; and she must at least receive credit for having been in the field as a reformer of fiction before her fellow-labourer was heard of. She was true to the conditions she had laid down for herself in writing *The Professor*. Nothing more sober and matter-of-fact than that story is to be found in English literature. And yet, though the landscape one is invited to view is but a vast plain, without even a hillock to give variety to the prospect, it has beauties of its own which commend it to our admiration. The story, as everybody knows, deals with Brussels, from which she had just returned when she began to write it. But it is sad to note the difference between the spirit of *The Professor* and that which is exhibited in *Villette*. Dealing with the same circumstances, and substantially with the same story, the author has nevertheless cast each in a mould of its own. Nor is the cause of this any secret to those who know Charlotte Brontë. When she wrote *The Professor*, disillusioned though she was, she was still young, and still blessed with that fervent belief in a better future which the youthful heart can never quite cast out, even under the heaviest blows of fate. She had come home restless and miserable, feeling Haworth to be far too small and quiet a place for her; and her mind could not take in the reality that under that modest roof the remainder of her life was destined to be spent. Suffering and unhappy as she was, she could not shut out the hope that brighter days lay before her. The fever of life racked her; but in the very fact that it burnt so high there was proof that love and hope, the capacity for a large enjoyment of existence, still lived within her. So *The Professor*, though a sad, monotonous book, has life and hope, and a fair faith in the ultimate blessedness of all sorrowful ones, shining through all its pages; and it closes in a scene of rest and peace.

—T. Wemyss Reid, *Charlotte Brontë:*
A Monograph, 1877, pp. 219–222

Peter Bayne (1881)

The Belgian settings in *The Professor* and *Villette* invite Bayne's comparison of the two novels, and he acknowledges that his preference for *The
Professor* is unusual.

Of her experience in Brussels, Charlotte Brontë availed herself in the composition of two novels, her first and last—*The Professor* and *Villette*. Critics have loudly praised *Villette*, and I do not recollect seeing anything said in commendation of *The Professor*; but I own to finding it a stiffer business to read the later than the earlier book. *The Professor*, I make bold to say, has not received due appreciation. It is by no means a wonderful book, but it has signal merits. Nothing could be more sharp than the chiseling of the characters, which are neither uninteresting nor commonplace, and the story is full of life. Hunsden is unmistakeably a first sketch of the Yorke of *Shirley*, and the school scenes, though not so carefully elaborated as in *Villette*, are, to my thinking, more fresh, and, in general respects, about as good. Frances, of *The Professor*, is perhaps somewhat too commonplace for a heroine: but not

even a critic has, to my knowledge, been found who could care for the Lucy
Snowe of *Villette*.

—Peter Bayne, "Charlotte Brontë
and Her Sisters," 1881, p. 239

MARY A. WARD (1900)

Mary Augusta Ward (1851–1920) was a novelist who published under
the name Mrs. Humphrey Ward. She was the granddaughter of Thomas
Arnold and the niece of Matthew Arnold, and, in addition to being a
novelist, she was well known in her day as a philanthropist, an advocate
for social reform, and an opponent of the women's suffrage movement.
While Ward published well into the twentieth century, she remained
associated with the values of the nineteenth. Her best-known novel,
Robert Elsemere (1888), which explores religious doubt and a civic com-
mitment to the poor, was one of the best-selling novels of the Victorian
age. Other well-known novels by Ward, though seldom read today, were
Marcella (1894) and *Helbeck of Bannisdale* (1898).

In 1899–1900, Ward wrote introductions to the seven-volume Haworth
editions of the Brontë sisters' novels, including the introduction to *The
Professor*, excerpted below. She considers *The Professor* in the context of
Brontë's other work, rather than discussing the novel's achievement in
its own right, and determines that its lasting importance is as a record of
artistic development.

'The Professor' indeed is grey and featureless compared with any of
Charlotte Brontë's other work. The final impression is that she was working
under restraint when writing it, and that her proper gifts were consciously
denied full play in it. In the preface of 1851, she says, as an explanation
of the sobriety of the story—'In many a crude effort destroyed almost as
soon as composed, I had got over any such taste as I might once have had
for ornamented and redundant composition, and come to prefer what was
plain and homely.' In other words, she was putting herself under discipline
in 'The Professor'; trying to subdue the poetical impulse; to work as a realist
and an observer only. . . . In truth, the method of 'The Professor' represents
a mere temporary reaction,—an experiment—in Charlotte Brontë's literary
development. When she returned to that exuberance of imagination and
expression which was her natural utterance, she was not merely writing to
please her publishers and the public. Rather it was like Emily's passionate

return to the moorland. . . . The strong native bent reasserted itself, and with the happiest effects.

But because of what came after, and because the mental history of a great and delightful artist will always appeal to the affectionate curiosity of later generations, 'The Professor' will continue to be read both by those who love Charlotte Brontë, and by those who find pleasure in tracking the processes of literature. It needs no apology as a separate entity; but from its relation to 'Villette' it gains an interest and importance the world would not otherwise have granted it. It is the first revelation of a genius which from each added throb of happiness or sorrow, from each short after-year of strenuous living . . . was to gain fresh wealth, and steadily advancing power.

—Mary A. Ward, introduction to
the Haworth edition of *The Professor*, 1900

THEODORE WATTS-DUNTON (1906)

Theodore Watts-Dunton (1832–1914) achieved fame as a critic and poet but is also known for his friendships with Algernon Charles Swinburne (whom he rescued from alcoholism) and Dante Gabriel Rossetti. Watts-Dunton was trained as a solicitor but turned to literature in the 1870s, writing for the *Examiner* and the *Atheneum*, for which he was the main poetry critic in the last decades of the nineteenth century. Watts-Dunton published his own volume of poetry in 1897, *The Coming of Love*, and other books including *Studies of Shakespeare* (1910).

In this excerpt from his 1906 introduction to *The Professor*, Watts-Dunton begins by expanding on Gaskell's biographical treatment of Charlotte, arguing for more individuality among the sisters. He also disagrees with Gaskell's astonishment at the Brontë sisters' precociousness and artistry, arguing that their intellectual talent and productivity were not as unusual as Gaskell infers. Watts-Dunton considers *The Professor* important as a precursor to *Villette* and also praises a few specific points, including the characterization of Frances and Brontë's "softness of touch."

The Professor, which was afterwards recast and enlarged into *Villette*, is the novel which Charlotte Brontë wrote when her sisters Emily and Anne were writing *Wuthering Heights* and *Agnes Grey*. To picture to one's mind the three wonderful girls at work upon three novels so very unlike each other as these, is to realize how irresistible are the working of individual character, and how comparatively weak is the effect of companionship, and, indeed, of all environment, in directing the course of those workings. If Mrs. Gaskell's own imagination has thrown too strong a light of romance from her own magic lens upon the life-drama which went on when those novels were being evolved at the Haworth Parsonage, that is to the reader's gain. I am not of those, however, who share her astonishment at the kind of literary studies and activities for which the Brontë children have become famous. Even the precocious interest they took in politics does not surprise me as much as it surprises their noble-hearted biographer. . . .

That *The Professor* was rejected by publisher after publisher was a stroke of good fortune for English literature, partly because that rejection caused *Jane Eyre* to be completed, and partly because Charlotte Brontë afterwards took *The Professor* up and converted it into *Villette*—the writer's masterpiece from the literary point of view, if from none other. *Jane Eyre* and *The Professor* were both written about the same time. If it is true, as that admirable critic of Charlotte Brontë, Dr. Robertson Nicoll, affirms, that 'she is one great example of the truth that style is not the result of reading, but of thinking,' this is seen in *The Professor* as much as in any theory of her stories. There is no such failure in *Jane Eyre*, or *Shirley*, or *Villette* as Hunsden: Crimsworth is a poor creature, as he might well be, seeing that he speaks through the voice of a woman whose experiences had been those of a school-girl and nursery governess. But what about the heroine, Frances? Surely Charlotte Brontë never drew a more natural or a more interesting portrait than this of the Brussels lace-worker. As a rule, the drawing of Charlotte Brontë's characters is too intense, they are too much the opposite of Jane Austen's characters—they are bitten into the texture of the story as though by *aqua fortis*. In other words, they lack that softness of touch which, as I have often remarked, is displayed by the great masters of prose fiction, and those only. Now, in the character of the heroine of *The Professor* there is seen a softness of touch such as is perhaps scarcely excelled in any other of Charlotte Brontë's portraits.

—Theodore Watts Dunton, introduction
to *The Professor*, 1906, pp. v, x–xi

EMILY BRONTË

BIOGRAPHY

EMILY BRONTË
(1818–1848)

Emily Jane Brontë was born on July 30, 1818, in Thornton, the fifth of six children. Her elder sisters Maria and Elizabeth died as children. Her surviving siblings, Anne (1820–1849), Charlotte (1816–1855), and brother Branwell (1817–1848), were also writers. Emily briefly attended school at Cowan Bridge in 1824–25, but after the deaths of Maria and Elizabeth from tuberculosis contacted at the school, she was largely educated at home. During 1837 she served as governess at Law Hill, near Halifax, and in 1842 she went to Brussels with Charlotte to study languages; but the greater part of her life was spent at Haworth, where she lived a private existence, with no close friends and little correspondence. In 1846 a collection of verse by Charlotte, Emily, and Anne was published as *Poems by Currer, Ellis, and Acton Bell* (their respective pseudonyms); Emily's contributions, many of them set in the imaginary world of Gondal, which she had created with Anne, reveal an intensely inward-turning imagination.

Emily Brontë's one novel, *Wuthering Heights,* was written between October 1845 and June 1846 and published in 1847 under the name Ellis Bell. The book was not well received, being regarded as excessively morbid and violent, and it was only after Brontë's death that its reputation began to grow. By the twentieth century it was generally considered a masterpiece, in which gothic and Romantic elements were handled with great originality and poetic force. Emily Brontë died of tuberculosis at the age of thirty on December 19, 1848.

PERSONAL

The fascination with Emily Brontë's life and character that her early critics attest to follows Charlotte's lead, who characterized her sister as a true eccentric, happier in nature than society. Other critics, notably Elizabeth Gaskell and T. Wemyss Reid, extend this representation with a variety of anecdotes about Emily's strange affinity for animals and her almost complete withdrawal from the world. While we have to question the degree to which such treatments of Emily embellish her reputation as a Romantic loner and to what degree they represent the real person, the relatively scant information we have about Emily's personal life has certainly augmented their stature and mythological reach.

EMILY BRONTË (1841)

Emily and Anne Brontë each wrote a number of "diary papers," journal-like descriptions of their lives at a specific point that mandate a future date on which they will read the account and then write an updated one. These documents offer rare forays into Emily's own voice, and while her fiction and poetry have been routinely mined for their biographical information, these diary papers do not require a generic translation.

Emily's account of her life—reproduced with original spelling and punctuation errors—is curious for many reasons. First, she gives the locations of her family members and animals as if they were on an equal footing. Second, Emily focuses on her optimistic vision of the future, in which she hopes and imagines she and her sisters will run a flourishing school and be living together in busy harmony. The school was never to open; Emily left Haworth only briefly, and their short adulthood was to be dedicated to writing rather than teaching.

<hr>

A Paper to be opened
when Anne is
25 years old
or my next birthday after
if
-all be well-

It is Friday evening—near 9 o'clock—wild rainy weather. I am seated in the dining room alone—having just concluded tidying our desk-boxes—writing this document—Papa is in the parlour. Aunt up stairs in her room—she has been reading Blackwood's Magazine to papa—Victoria and Adelaide are ensconced in the peat-house—Keeper is in the kitchen—Nero in his cage—We are all stout and hearty as I hope is the case with Charlotte, Branwell, and Anne, of whom the first is at John White Esqre upperwood House, Rawden The second is at Luddendon foot and the third is I believe at—Scarborough—enditing perhaps a paper corresponding to this—A scheme is at present in agitation for setting up a school of our own as yet nothing is determined but I hope and trust it may go on and prosper and answer our highest expectations. This day 4—years I wonder whether we shall still be dragging on in our present condition or established to our heart's content. Time will show—

I guess that at the time appointed for the opening of this paper—we (i.e.) Charlotte, Anne and I—shall be all merrily seated in our own sitting-room

in our pleasant and flourishing seminary having just gathered in for the midsummer holydays our debts will be paid off and we shall have cash in hand to a considerable amount. papa Aunt and Branwell will either have been—or be coming—to visit us—it will be a fine warm summery evening. very different from this bleak look-out Anne and I will perchance slip out into the garden a minutes to peruse our papers. I hope either this [o]r something better will be the case—

—Emily Brontë, July 30, 1841

EMILY BRONTË (1845)

This second diary paper brings the one from 1841 up to date and starts with a similar accounting of her family. She next writes about the imaginative world of Gondal that she and Anne continued to invent. "The Gondals still flourish bright as ever," Emily explains, and indicates a measure of her (and Anne's) involvement in this fantasy world by mentioning that they "were" some of the characters while on a brief trip from home.

Meanwhile, the "school-scheme" that had so inspired her hopes in 1841 has been abandoned, after some considerable efforts made. Her interest in teaching had waned from 1841, though, as she says that "now I dont desire a school at all." Emily seems content and absorbed by life at Haworth and with a routine that revolves around her many animals, household tasks, and, of course, her constant excursions outside.

My birthday–showery–breezy–cool–I am twenty seven years old today–this morning Anne and I opened the papers we wrote 4 years since on my twenty third birthday–this paper we intend, if all be well, to open on my 30th three years hence in 1848–since the 1841 paper, the following events have taken place

Our school-scheme has been abandoned and instead Charlotte and I went to Brussels on the 8th of Febrary 1842 Branwell left his place at Luddenden Foot C and I returned from Brussels November 8th 1842 in consequence of Aunt's death–Branwell went to Thorp Green as a tutor where Anne still continued–January 1843 Charlotte returned to Brussels the same month and after staying a year came back again on new years day 1844 Anne left her situation at Thorp Green of her own accord–June 1845 Branwell left–July 1845

Anne and I went our first long journey by ourselves together–leaving Home on the 30th of June–monday sleeping at York–returning to Keighley Tuesday evening sleeping there and walking home on Wednesday morning–

though the weather was broken, we enjoyed ourselves very much except during a few hours at Bradford and during our excursion we were Ronald Macelgin, Henry Angora, Juliet Augusteena, Rosobelle Esualdar, Ella and Julian Egramont Catherine Navarre and Cordelia Fitzaphnold escaping from the palaces of Instruction to join the Royalists who are hard driven at present by the victorious Republicans–The Gondals still flourish bright as ever I am at present writing a work on the First Wars–Anne has been writing some articles on this and a book by Henry Sophona–We intend sticking firm by the rascals as long as they delight us which I am glad to say they do at present–I should have mentioned that last summer the school scheme was revived in full vigor–We had prospectuses printed, despatched letters to all aquaintances imparting our plans and did our little all–but it was found no go–now I dont desire a school at all and none of us have any great longing for it. We have cash enough for our present wants with a prospect of accumulation–we are all in decent health–only that papa has a complaint in his eyes and with the exception of B who I hope will be better and do better, hereafter. I am quite contented for myself–not as idle as formerly, altogether as hearty and having learnt to make the most of the present and hope for the future with less fidgetiness that I cannot do all I wish–seldom or ever troubled with nothing to do, and merely desiring that every body could be as comfortable as myself and as undesponding and then we should have a very tolerable world of it

By mistake I find we have opened the paper on the 31st instead of the 30th Yesterday was much such a day as this but the morning was devine–

Tabby who was gone in our last paper is come back and has lived with us–two years and a half and is in good health–Martha who also departed is here too. We have got Flossey, got and lost Tiger–lost the Hawk. Hero which with the geese was given away and is doubtless dead for when I came back from Brussels I enquired on all hands and could hear nothing of him–Tiger died early last year–Keeper and Flossey are well also the canary acquired 4 years since

We are now all at home and likely to be there some time–Branwell went to Liverpool on 'Tuesday' to stay a week. Tabby has just been teasing me to turn as formerly to 'pilloputate'. Anne and I should have picked the black currants if it had been fine and sunshiny. I must hurry off now to my taming and ironing I have plenty of work on hands and writing and am altogether full of buisness with best wishes for the whole House till 1848 July 3oth and as much longer as may be I conclude

E J Brontë

—Emily Brontë, July 30, 1845

Matthew Arnold (1855)

Matthew Arnold (1822–1888) was one of the great critics and poets of the Victorian age. The son of Thomas Arnold, headmaster at Rugby School and educational reformer, Matthew Arnold's scholarly career began early. His poetry was recognized while he was still an undergraduate, and, after a brief tenure in the diplomatic field, he became a highly respected inspector of schools.

Arnold's most important works of poetry are *Poems: A New Edition* (1853) and *Poems: Second Series* (1855) and, in literary criticism, he is best known for *Culture and Anarchy* (1869), which urges England to retain its classical and liberal values in an age of increasing materialism.

While most of Arnold's poem "Haworth Churchyard" was inspired by the death of Charlotte Brontë, these lines commemorate a particular vision of Emily as heiress to Byron's tradition of boldness and passion. Arnold was one of many nineteenth-century critics to compare Emily's work to Byron's, though others (see the Robinson extract, for example) often find Byronic overtones in *Wuthering Heights*'s Heathcliff. As Arnold implies here, the resemblance between the two poets is based on a common emotional intensity rather than actual themes or subjects.

———

and she
(How shall I sing her?) whose soul
Knew no fellow for might,
Passion, vehemence, grief,
Daring, since Byron died,
That world-famed son of fire—she, who sank
Baffled, unknown, self-consumed;
Whose too bold dying song
Stirr'd, like a clarion-blast, my soul.

—Matthew Arnold,
"Haworth Churchyard," 1855

Elizabeth Gaskell (1857)

Gaskell's riveting description of a domestic scene in which Emily punishes her beloved dog, Keeper, by punching him in the eyes with her bare hands, transfers what Gaskell calls Keeper's "ferocity of nature" to Emily herself. Such accounts, conveyed to Gaskell by Charlotte, helped mythologize Emily as a fierce and almost otherworldly creature, closer to animals and nature than to people. This characterization is bolstered by the raw power of *Wuthering Heights,* as so many critics have noted.

The feeling, which in Charlotte partook of something of the nature of an affection, was, with Emily, more of a passion. Some one speaking of her to me, in a careless kind of strength of expression, said, "she never showed regard to any human creature; all her love was reserved for animals." The helplessness of an animal was its passport to Charlotte's heart; the fierce, wild, intractability of its nature was what often recommended it to Emily. Speaking of her dead sister, the former told me that from her many traits in Shirley's character were taken; her way of sitting on the rug reading, with her arm round her rough bull-dog's neck; her calling to a strange dog, running past, with hanging head and lolling tongue, to give it a merciful draught of water, its maddened snap at her, her nobly stern presence of mind, going right into the kitchen, and taking up one of Tabby's red-hot Italian irons to sear the bitten place, and telling no one, till the danger was well-nigh over, for fear of the terrors that might beset their weaker minds. All this, looked upon as a well-invented fiction in *Shirley,* was written down by Charlotte with streaming eyes; it was the literal true account of what Emily had done. The same tawny bull-dog (with his "strangled whistle"), called "Tartar" in *Shirley,* was "Keeper" in Haworth parsonage; a gift to Emily. With the gift came a warning. Keeper was faithful to the depths of his nature as long as he was with friends; but he who struck him with a stick or whip, roused the relentless nature of the brute, who flew at his throat forthwith, and held him there till one or the other was at the point of death. Now Keeper's household fault was this. He loved to steal up-stairs, and stretch his square, tawny limbs, on the comfortable beds, covered over with delicate white counterpanes. But the cleanliness of the parsonage arrangements was perfect; and this habit of Keeper's was so objectionable, that Emily, in reply to Tabby's remonstrances, declared that, if he was found again transgressing, she herself, in defiance of warning and his well-known ferocity of nature, would beat him so severely that he would never offend again. In the gathering dusk of an autumn evening, Tabby came, half triumphantly, half tremblingly, but in great wrath, to tell Emily that Keeper was lying on the best bed, in drowsy voluptuousness. Charlotte saw Emily's whitening face, and set mouth, but dared not speak to interfere; no one dared when Emily's eyes glowed in that manner out of the paleness of her face, and when her lips were so compressed into stone. She went up-stairs, and Tabby and Charlotte stood in the gloomy passage below, full of the dark shadows of coming night. Down-stairs came Emily, dragging after her the unwilling Keeper, his hind legs set in a heavy attitude of resistance, held by the "scruff of his neck," but growling low and savagely all the time. The watchers would fain have spoken, but durst not, for fear of taking off Emily's attention, and causing her to avert her head for a moment from the enraged brute. She let him go, planted in a dark corner at the bottom of the stairs; no time was there to fetch stick or rod, for fear of the strangling clutch at her throat—her bare clenched fist struck against his red fierce eyes, before he had time to make his spring, and in the language of the turf, she "punished him" till his eyes were swelled up, and the half-blind, stupefied beast was led to his accustomed lair, to have his swelled head fomented and cared for by the very Emily herself.

—Elizabeth Gaskell, *The Life of Charlotte Brontë*, 1857, pp. 268–269

CHARLOTTE BRONTË (1857)

Charlotte's account of Emily's brief tenure in Belgium was included in Gaskell's *Life*. The suffering that Charlotte refers to here recalls Emily's similar, and similarly brief, experiences living away from Haworth as a student at Miss Wooler's school in Roe Head (July–October 1835) and as a governess at Miss Patchett's school in Halifax in 1837.

At the age of twenty, having meantime studied alone with diligence and perseverance, [Emily] went with me to an establishment on the Continent. The same suffering and conflict ensued, heightened by the strong recoil of her upright heretic and English spirit from the gentle Jesuitry of the foreign and Romish system. Once more she seemed sinking, but this time she rallied through the mere force of resolution: with inward remorse and shame she looked back on her former failure, and resolved to conquer, but the victory cost her dear. She was never happy till she carried her hard-won knowledge back to the remote English village, the old parsonage-house, and desolate Yorkshire hills.

—Charlotte Brontë, quoted by Elizabeth Gaskell, *The Life of Charlotte Brontë*, 1857, p. 225

T. Wemyss Reid (1877)

Reid's description of Emily must be attributed indirectly to Ellen Nussey, Charlotte's close school friend, who worked with Reid while he wrote his biography of Charlotte. Ellen Nussey is the "Miss N____" referred to in this excerpt. Still, we have to question the near omniscience Reid claims here in describing Emily's behavior in all of her interactions with the world beyond the parsonage.

Emily . . . had, like Charlotte, a bad complexion; but she was tall and well-formed, whilst her eyes were of remarkable beauty. All through her life her temperament was more than merely peculiar. She inherited not a little of her father's eccentricity, untempered by her father's *savoir faire*. Her aversion to strangers has been already mentioned. When the curates, who formed the only society of Haworth, found their way to the parsonage, she avoided them as though they had brought pestilence in their train. On the rare occasions when she went out into the world, she would sit absolutely silent in the company of those who were unfamiliar to her. So intense was this reserve that even in her own family, where alone she was at ease, something like dread was mingled with the affection felt towards her. On one occasion, whilst Charlotte's friend was visiting the parsonage, Charlotte herself was unable through illness to take any walks with her. To the amazement of the household, Emily volunteered to accompany Miss N____ on a ramble over the moors. They set off together, and the girl threw aside her reserve, and talked with a freedom and vigour which gave evidence of the real strength of her character. Her companion was charmed with her intelligence and geniality. But on returning to the parsonage Charlotte was found awaiting them, and, as soon as she had a chance of doing so, she anxiously put to Miss N____ the question, "How did Emily behave herself?" It was the first time she had ever been known to invite the company of any one outside the narrow limits of the family circle. Her chief delight was to roam on the moors, followed by her dogs, to whom she would whistle in masculine fashion.

—T. Wemyss Reid, *Charlotte Brontë:*
A Monograph, 1877, pp. 42–43

James Ashcroft Noble (1883)

James Ashcroft Noble (1844–1896) was an English critic, essayist, and poet. He wrote on a variety of literary figures and topics, including

Robert Louis Stevenson and Edgar Allan Poe, and his works include *The Sonnet in England and Other Essays* (1893). Here Noble takes a familiar approach to understanding Emily by using nature as a metonym for her somewhat uncultivated character.

Though Emily Brontë's life was not an eventful one in the usual sense of the word, it may certainly be called a crowded life. That twenty-nine years was not a large demesne, but it was fertile enough, though only with rue and rosemary and nightshade and the poppy that bloomed before the harvest.

—James Ashcroft Noble, "Emily Brontë,"
Academy, May 19, 1883, p. 340

GENERAL

The critical reception of Emily Brontë in the nineteenth century hinges on the reception of *Wuthering Heights*. While many critics admired her poetry, it was *Wuthering Heights* that made her name and, in lieu of other fiction (except for the juvenilia, which was not published until much later), it was the primary record of her writing talent.

Aside from discussion of the novel, however, critics were consistent in some of their appraisals of Emily's style, strengths, and shortcomings. Most critics admire the vigor of her prose, and many compare her tragic vision to Shakespeare's (see Smith, Swinburne, and Ward, for instance). Emily Brontë's ability to describe nature, too, repeatedly invokes critical praise. Finally, her unconventionality and the boldness of her language inspire both critical awe and, in some cases, censure.

George Barnett Smith (1873)

English author, journalist, editor, and etcher George Barnett Smith (1841–1909) wrote biographies of William Gladstone and Queen Victoria, critical works on authors including Jane Austen, and the two-volume *Illustrated British Ballads, Old and New* (1886).

Smith's treatment of Emily as "the most extraordinary of the three sisters" follows a period, roughly from the time of Emily's life until the 1860s, when Emily's work was out of critical favor and her critical acclaim dwarfed by Charlotte's. But increasingly in the 1860s and 1870s, critics including Smith reassessed *Wuthering Heights* and Emily's poetry and argued that earlier dismissals of her art neglected its rarity and originality. And while Smith allows that *Wuthering Heights* was "perhaps one of the most unpleasant books ever written," he maintains that its ugliness does not obviate its genius.

In his reading of Emily, Smith compares her style and force to Shakespeare's and Goethe's and makes some important points about her previously compromised reputation. It was Charlotte's handling of Emily's reputation after Emily's death, he writes, that augmented the sense of *Wuthering Heights* and its author as crude and anomalous.

Emily Brontë—for it is now time that we should say something of the two other persons in this remarkable trio—was, in certain respects, the most extraordinary of the three sisters. She has this distinction at any rate, that she has written a book which stands as completely alone in the language as does the *Paradise Lost* or the *Pilgrim's Progress*. This of itself, setting aside subject and construction, is no mean eminence. Emily Jane Brontë, as is well known, was the youngest but one of the Rev. Mr. Brontë's children, and died before she was thirty years of age. Early in life she displayed a singularly masculine bent of intellect, and astonished those with whom she came in contact by her penetration, and that settlement of character which generally only comes with age. She went from home twice, once to school and once to Brussels, but it was like the caging of a lioness, and her soul yearned for the liberty of home. When in Brussels she attracted and impressed deeply all those who came across her, and M. Heger declared she should have been a man, for 'her powerful reason would have deduced new spheres of discovery from the knowledge of the old, and her strong, imperious will would never have been daunted by opposition or difficulty: never have given way but with life.' On her return to Haworth she began to lose in beauty but to gain in impressiveness of feature, and she divided her time between homely domestic duties, studies, and rambles. Shrinking entirely from contact with the life which surrounded her, she gave herself up to nature, the result being apparent in her works, which reveal a most intimate acquaintance with the great Mother in all her moods. Her mind was absolutely free to all the lessons which she should teach, and she embraced them with the most passionate longing. 'Her native hills were far more to her than a spectacle; they were what she lived in, and by, as much as the wild birds, their tenants, or as the heather, their produce.' Her descriptions, then, of natural scenery, are what they should be, and all they should be. Any reader of her works must perforce acknowledge the accuracy of these observations. Her life, however, seemed to be an unprized one, except by that sister who loved her profoundly, and who keenly appreciated her genius as it essayed to unfold its wings in the sun. But whilst she lived the world made no sign of recognition of her strangely weird powers. When illness came her indomitable will still enabled her to present an unflinching front to sympathising friends. She refused to see the doctor, and would not have it that she was ill. To the last she retained an independent spirit, and on the day of her death she arose and dressed herself as usual. Her end reminds us of that of her brother Branwell whose will was so strong that he insisted on standing up to die and did actually so die. Emily did everything for herself on that last day, but as the hours drew on got manifestly worse, and could only whisper in gasps. The end came when it was too late to profit by human skill. *Wuthering Heights,* the principal work she has left behind her, shows a massive strength which is of the rarest description. Its power is absolutely Titanic: from the first page to the last it reads like the intellectual throes of a giant. It is fearful, it is true, and perhaps one of the most unpleasant books ever written: but we stand in amaze at the almost incredible fact that it was written by a slim country girl who would have passed in a crowd as an insignificant person, and who had had little or no experience of the ways of the world. In Heathcliff, Emily Brontë has drawn the greatest villain extant, after Iago. He has no match out of Shakspeare. The Mephistopheles of Goethe's *Faust* is a person of gentlemanly proclivities compared with Heathcliff. There is not a redeeming quality in him; his coarseness is very repellent; he is a unique specimen of the human tiger. Charlotte Brontë in her digest of this character finds one ameliorating circumstance in his favour, one link which connects him with humanity—viz., his regard for one of his victims, Hareton Earnshaw. But we cannot agree with her: his feeling towards Earnshaw is excessively like that feline affection which sometimes destroys its own offspring. As to his alleged esteem for Nelly Dean, perhaps also the less said about that the

better. But *Wuthering Heights* is a marvellous curiosity in letters. We challenge
the world to produce another work in which the whole atmosphere seems so
surcharged with suppressed electricity, and bound in with the blackness of
tempest and desolation. From the time when young Heathcliff is introduced
to us, 'as dark almost as if he came from the devil,' to the last page of the story,
there is nothing but savagery and ferocity, except when we are taken away from
the persons to the scenes of the narratives, and treated to those pictures in
which the author excels. The Heights itself, the old north-country manor-
house, is made intensely real to us, but not more so than the central figure
of the story, who, believing himself alone one night, throws open the lattice,
and cries with terrible anguish—'Cathy! oh, my heart's darling. Hear me
this once. Catherine, at last!' Then his history is recapitulated, by one who
witnessed his life in all its stages; and in the passage where Catherine informs
her nurse that she has promised to marry Edgar Linton, but ought not to have
done so, we get the following example of concentrated force:—

I have no more business to marry Edgar Linton than I have to be in Heaven.
But it would degrade me to marry Heathcliff now; so he shall never know how
I love him, and that not because he's handsome, Nelly, but because he's more
myself than I am. Whatever our souls are made of, his and mine are the
same; and Linton's is as different as moonbeams from lightning, or frost from
fire. . . . Who is to separate us? they'll meet the fate of Milo. I cannot express
it; but surely you and everybody have a notion that there is, or should be,
an existence of yours beyond you. What were the use of my creation if I were
entirely contained here? My great miseries in this world have been Heathcliff's
miseries, and I watched and felt each from the beginning; my great thought in
living is himself. If all else perished and he remained, I should continue to be;
and if all else remained and he were annihilated, the universe would turn to
a mighty stranger; I should not seem a part of it. My love for Linton is like the
foliage in the woods: time will change it, I'm well aware, as winter changes the
trees. My love for Heathcliff resembles the eternal rocks beneath: a source of
little visible delight, but necessary. Nelly, I *am* Heathcliff! He's always, always in
my mind; not as a pleasure any more than I am always a pleasure to myself,
but as my own being.

Then comes Catherine's death—when she asks forgiveness for having
wronged him, and Heathcliff answers, 'Kiss me again; and don't let me see your
eyes! I forgive what you have done to me. I love *my* murderer—but *yours!* How
can I?' The tale of woe proceeds; the despairing man longing for the dead, until
at last he faces death, and being asked if he will have the minister, replies—'I tell
you I have nearly attained *my* Heaven; and that of others is altogether unvalued

and uncoveted by me.' He then sleeps beside her: the tragedy of eighteen years is complete. A great deal has been said on the question whether such a book as *Wuthering Heights* ought to be written, and Charlotte Brontë herself felt impelled to utter some words of defence for it. Where the mind is healthy it can do no harm; but there are, possibly, organisations upon whom it might exercise a baleful influence. With regard to the drawing of Heathcliff, Currer Bell scarcely thought the creation of such beings justifiable, but she goes on to say that 'the writer who possesses the creative gift owns something of which he is not always master—something that, at times, strangely wills and works for itself.' We are afraid that if this opinion were pushed to its logical issues it would be found incapable of being supported. A multiplication of such books as *Wuthering Heights* without corresponding genius would be a lamentable thing, no doubt; yet, while we cannot defend it altogether possibly as it stands, we should regret never having seen it, as one of the most extraordinary and powerful productions in the whole range of English literature.

—George Barnett Smith, from
"The Brontës," 1873, *Poets and
Novelists*, 1876, pp. 236–242

Algernon Charles Swinburne "Emily Brontë" (1883)

Swinburne's important analysis of Emily Brontë follows the reassessment of her work in the later nineteenth century, aided in large part by the 1883 publication of A. Mary Francis Robinson's biography, *Emily Brontë*, to which Swinburne here refers.

By considering the role of and expectations for the novel in Victorian England, Swinburne significantly helps to contextualize the uneven and often negative reception of *Wuthering Heights*. While the age of Shakespeare was the age of drama, he explains, that of Queen Victoria is the era of the novel. Moreover, the novels that were popular and identifiable welcome not tragedy but comedy, romance, and sociological detail. They also follow the laws of probability, which *Wuthering Heights* and its gothic flights of reason do not. Nevertheless, despite the novel's inconsistency with its times, Swinburne praises its internal consistency, which is "as perfectly and triumphantly attained as in *King Lear* or *The Duchess of Malfy*, in *The Bride of Lammermoor* or *Notre-Dame de Paris*."

Swinburne lauds Robinson's biography of Emily Brontë for its willing embrace of its subject's singularity. Previous biographers had been unable or unwilling to comprehend Emily's oddity: "The sweet and noble genius of Mrs. Gaskell," he claims, "did not enable her to see far into so strange and so sublime a problem." He does fault Robinson, however, for making "a little too much" of the influence of Branwell Brontë on Emily's work. Only Anne Brontë's *The Tenant of Wildfell Hall*, a novel Swinburne considers "ludicrously weak," deals with Branwell's disgrace directly, while he believes that *Wuthering Heights* is "a tragedy simply because it is the work of a writer whose genius is essentially tragic."

Swinburne's defense of Emily's sometimes brutal vision is based on his sense that, as an artist, she was utterly true to her sense of the world. This transcendence of convention may not have made her more popular, he explains, but it certainly makes her more authentic.

To the England of our own time, it has often enough been remarked, the novel is what the drama was to the England of Shakespeare's. The same general interest produces the same incessant demand for the same inexhaustible supply of imaginative produce, in a shape more suited to the genius of a later day and the conditions of a changed society. Assuming this simple explanation to be sufficient for the obvious fact that in the modern world of English letters the novel is everywhere and the drama is nowhere, we may remark one radical point of difference between the taste of playgoers in the age of Shakespeare and the taste of novel-readers in our own. Tragedy was then at least as popular as either romantic or realistic comedy; whereas nothing would seem to be more unpopular with the run of modern readers than the threatening shadow of tragedy projected across the whole length of a story, inevitable and unmistakable from the lurid harshness of its dawn to the fiery softness of its sunset. The objection to a novel in which the tragic element has an air of incongruity and caprice—in which a tragic surprise is, as it were, sprung upon the reader, with a jarring shock such as might be given by the actual news of some unforeseen and grievous accident—this objection seems to me thoroughly reasonable, grounded on a true critical sense of fitness and unfitness; but the distaste for high and pure tragedy, where the close is in perfect and simple harmony with the opening, seems not less thoroughly pitiable and irrational.

A later work of indisputable power, in which the freshness of humour is as real and vital as the fervour of passion, was at once on its appearance compared with Emily Brontë's now famous story. And certainly not without good cause; for in point of local colour *Mehalah* is, as far as I know, the one other book which can bear and may challenge the comparison. Its pages, for one thing, reflect the sterile glitter and desolate fascination of the salt marshes, their minute splendours and barren beauties and multitudinous monotony of measureless expanse, with the same instinctive and unlaborious accuracy which brings all the moorland before us in a breath when we open any chapter of *Wuthering Heights*. But the accumulated horrors of the close, however possible in fact, are wanting in the one quality which justifies and ennobles all admissible horror in fiction: they hardly seem inevitable; they lack the impression of logical and moral certitude. All the realism in the world will not suffice to convey this impression: and a work of art which wants it wants the one final and irreplaceable requisite of inner harmony. Now in *Wuthering Heights* this one thing needful is as perfectly and triumphantly attained as in *King Lear* or *The Duchess of Malfy*, in *The Bride of Lammermoor* or *Notre-Dame de Paris*. From the first we breathe the fresh dark air of tragic passion and presage; and to the last the changing wind and flying sunlight are in keeping with the stormy promise of the dawn. There is no monotony, there is no repetition, but there is no discord. This is the first and last necessity, the foundation of all labour and the crown of all success, for a poem worthy of the name; and this it is that distinguishes the hand of Emily from the hand of Charlotte Brontë. All the works of the elder sister are rich in poetic spirit, poetic feeling, and poetic detail; but the younger sister's work is essentially and definitely a poem in the fullest and most positive sense of the term. It was therefore all the more proper that the honour of raising a biographical and critical monument to the author of *Wuthering Heights* should have been reserved for a poetess of the next generation to her own. And those who had already in their mind's eye the clearest and most definite conception of Emily Brontë will be the readiest to acknowledge their obligation and express their gratitude to Miss Robinson for the additional light which she has been enabled to throw upon a great and singular character. It is true that when all has been said the main features of that character stand out before us unchanged. The sweet and noble genius of Mrs. Gaskell did not enable her to see far into so strange and sublime a problem; but, after all, the main difference between the biographer of Emily and the biographer of Charlotte is that Miss Robinson has been interested and attracted where Mrs. Gaskell was scared and perplexed. On one point, however, the new light afforded us is of the very utmost value and interest. We all knew how great was Emily Brontë's tenderness for the lower animals; we find, with surprise as well as admiration, that the range of this charity was so vast as to include even her own miserable brother. Of that lamentable and contemptible caitiff—contemptible not so much for his commonplace debauchery as for his abject selfishness, his lying pretention, and his nerveless cowardice—there is

far too much in this memoir: it is inconceivable how any one can have put into
a lady's hand such a letter as one which defaces two pages of the volume, and
it may be permissible to regret that a lady should have made it public; but this
error is almost atoned for by the revelation that of all the three sisters in that
silent home 'it was the silent Emily who had ever a cheering word for Branwell;
it was Emily who still remembered that he was her brother, without that
remembrance freezing her heart to numbness.' That she saved his life from
fire, and hid from their father the knowledge of her heroism, no one who
knows anything of Emily Brontë will learn with any mixture of surprise in
his sense of admiration; but it gives a new tone and colour to our sympathetic
and reverent regard for her noble memory when we find in the depth of that
self-reliant and stoic nature a fountain so inexhaustible of such Christlike
longsuffering and compassion.

I cannot however but think that Miss Robinson makes a little too much of
the influence exercised on Emily Brontë's work by the bitter, narrow, and ignoble
misery of the life which she had watched burn down into such pitiful ruin
that its memory is hardly redeemed by the last strange and inconsistent flash
of expiring manhood which forbids us to regard with unmixed contempt the
sufferer who had resolution enough to die standing if he had lived prostrate,
and so make at the very last a manful end of an abject history. The impression
of this miserable experience is visible only in Anne Brontë's second work,
The Tenant of Wildfell Hall; which deserves perhaps a little more notice and
recognition than it has ever received. It is ludicrously weak, palpably unreal,
and apparently imitative, whenever it reminds the reader that it was written
by a sister of Charlotte and Emily Brontë; but as a study of utterly flaccid
and invertebrate immorality it bears signs of more faithful transcription from
life than anything in *Jane Eyre* or *Wuthering Heights.* On the other hand, the
intelligent reader of *Wuthering Heights* cannot fail to recognize that what he
is reading is a tragedy simply because it is the work of a writer whose genius is
essentially tragic. Those who believe that Heathcliff was called into existence
by the accident that his creator had witnessed the agonies of a violent
weakling in love and in disgrace might believe that Shakespeare wrote *King
Lear* because he had witnessed the bad effects of parental indulgence, and that
Aeschylus wrote the *Eumenides* because he had witnessed the uncomfortable
results of matricide. The book is what it is because the author was what she
was; this is the main and central fact to be remembered. Circumstances have
modified the details; they have not implanted the conception. If there were
any need for explanation there would be no room for apology. As it is, the few
faults of design or execution leap to sight at a first glance, and vanish in the

final effect and unimpaired impression of the whole; while those who object to the violent illegalities of conduct with regard to real or personal property on which the progress of the story does undeniably depend—'a senseless piece of glaring folly,' it was once called by some critic learned in the law—might as well complain, in Carlylesque phrase, that the manners are quite other than Belgravian.

It is a fine and accurate instinct that has inevitably led Miss Robinson to cite in chosen illustration of the book's quality at its highest those two incomparable pictures of dreamland and delirium which no poet that ever lived has ever surpassed for passionate and life-like beauty of imaginative truth. But it is even somewhat less than exact to say that the latter scene 'is given with a masterly pathos that Webster need not have made more strong, nor Fletcher more lovely and appealing.' Fletcher could not have made it as lovely and appealing as it is; he would have made it exquisitely pretty and effectively theatrical; but the depth, the force, the sincerity, recalling here so vividly the 'several forms of distraction' through which Webster's Cornelia passes after the murder of her son by his brother, excel everything else of the kind in imaginative art; not excepting, if truth may be spoken on such a subject, the madness of Ophelia or even of Madge Wildfire. It is hardly ever safe to say dogmatically what can or cannot be done by the rarest and highest genius; yet it must surely be borne in upon us all that these two crowning passages could never have been written by any one to whom the motherhood of earth was less than the brotherhood of man—to whom the anguish, the intolerable and mortal yearning, of insatiate and insuppressible homesickness, was less than the bitterest of all other sufferings endurable or conceivable in youth. But in Emily Brontë this passion was twin-born with the passion for truth and rectitude. The stale and futile epithet of Titaness has in this instance a deeper meaning than appears; her goddess mother was in both senses the same who gave birth to the divine martyr of Æschylean legend: Earth under one aspect and one name, but under the other Righteousness. And therefore was the first and last word uttered out of the depth of her nature a cry for that one thing needful without which all virtue is as worthless as all pleasure is vile, all hope as shameful as all faith is abject—a cry for liberty.

And therefore too, perhaps we may say, it is that any seeming confusion or incoherence in her work is merely external and accidental, not inward and spiritual. Belief in the personal or positive immortality of the individual and indivisible spirit was not apparently, in her case, swallowed up or nullified or made nebulous by any doctrine or dream of simple reabsorption into some indefinite infinity of eternal life. So at least it seems to me that her last ardent confession of dauntless and triumphant faith should properly be read, however capable certain phrases in it may seem of the vaguer and more impersonal interpretation. For surely no scornfuller or stronger comment on the 'unutterable' vanity of creeds could pass more naturally into a chant expressive of more profound and potent faith; a song of spiritual trust more grave and deep and passionate in the solemn ardour of its appeal than the Hymn to God of Cleanthes. Her infrangible self-reliance and lonely sublimity of spirit she had in common with him and his fellows of the Porch; it was much more than 'some shy ostrich prompting' which bade her assign to an old Stoic the most personal and characteristic utterance in all her previous poems; but the double current of imaginative passion and practical compassion which made her a tragic poet and proved her a perfect woman gives as it were a living warmth and sweetness to her memory, such as might well have seemed incompatible with that sterner and colder veneration so long reserved for her spiritual kinsmen of the past. As a woman we never knew her so well as now that we have to welcome this worthy record of her life, with deeper thanks and warmer congratulations to the writer than can often be due even to the best of biographers and critics. As an author she has not perhaps even yet received her full due or taken her final place. Again and again has the same obvious objection been taken to that awkwardness of construction or presentation which no reader of *Wuthering Heights* can undertake to deny. But, to judge by the vigour with which this objection is urged, it might be supposed that the rules of narrative observed by all great novelists were of an almost legal or logical strictness and exactitude with regard to probability of detail. Now most assuredly the indirect method of relation through which the story of Heathcliff is conveyed, however unlikely or clumsy it may seem from the realistic point of view, does not make this narrative more liable to the charge of actual impossibility than others of the kind. Defoe still remains the one writer of narrative in the first person who has always kept the stringent law of possibilities before the eye of his invention. Even the admirable ingenuity and the singular painstaking which distinguish the method of Mr. Wilkie Collins can only give external and transient plausibility to the record of long conversations overheard or shared in by the narrator only a few hours before the supposed date of the report drawn up from memory. The very greatest masters in their kind, Walter Scott and Charles Dickens, are of all narrators the most superbly regardless of this objection. From *Rob Roy* and *Redgauntlet*, from *David Copperfield* and *Bleak House,* we might select at almost any stage of the autobiographic record some instance of detail in which the violation of plausibility, probability, or even possibility, is at least as daring and as glaring as any to be found in the narrative of Nelly Dean. Even when that narrative is removed, so to speak, yet one degree further back—even when we are supposed to be reading a minute detail of incident and dialogue transcribed by the hand of the lay figure Mr. Lockwood from Nelly Dean's report of the account conveyed to her years ago by Heathcliff's fugitive wife or gadding servant, each invested for the nonce with the peculiar force and distinctive style of the author—even then we are not asked to put such an overwhelming strain on our faculty of imaginative belief as is exacted by the great writer who invites us to accept the report drawn up by Mr. Pendennis of everything that takes place—down even to the minutest points of dialogue, accent, and gesture—in the household of the Newcomes or the Firmins during the absence no less than in the presence of their friend the reporter. Yet all this we gladly and gratefully admit, without demur or cavil, to be thoroughly authentic and credible, because the whole matter of the report, however we get at it, is found when we do get at it to be vivid and lifelike as an actual experience of living fact. Here, if ever anywhere, the attainment of the end justifies the employment of the means. If we are to enjoy imaginative work at all, we must 'assume the virtue' of imagination, even if we have it not; we must, as children say, 'pretend' or make believe a little as a very condition of the game.

A graver and perhaps a somewhat more plausible charge is brought against the author of *Wuthering Heights* by those who find here and there in her book the savage note or the sickly symptom of a morbid ferocity. Twice or thrice especially the details of deliberate or passionate brutality in Heathcliff's treatment of his victims make the reader feel for a moment as though he were reading a police report or even a novel by some French 'naturalist' of the latest and brutallest order. But the pervading atmosphere of the book is so high and healthy that the effect even of those 'vivid and fearful scenes' which impaired the rest of Charlotte Brontë is almost at once neutralized—we may hardly say softened, but sweetened, dispersed, and transfigured—by the general impression of noble purity and passionate straightforwardness, which removes it at once and for ever from any such ugly possibility of association or comparison. The whole work is not more incomparable in the effect of its atmosphere or landscape than in the peculiar note of its wild and bitter pathos; but most of all is it unique in the special and distinctive character of its passion. The love which devours life itself, which devastates the present and desolates the future with unquenchable and raging fire, has nothing less pure in it than flame or sunlight. And this passionate and ardent chastity is utterly and unmistakably spontaneous and unconscious. Not till the story is ended, not till the effect of it has been thoroughly absorbed and digested, does the reader even perceive the simple and natural absence of any grosser element, any hint or suggestion of a baser alloy in the ingredients of its human emotion than in the splendour of lightning or the roll of a gathered wave. Then, as on issuing sometimes from the tumult of charging waters, he finds with something of wonder how absolutely pure and sweet was the element of living storm with which his own nature has been for awhile made one; not a grain in it of soiling sand, not a waif of clogging weed. As was the author's life, so is her book in all things: troubled and taintless, with little of rest in it, and nothing of reproach. It may be true that not many will ever take it to their hearts; it is certain that those who do like it will like nothing very much better in the whole world of poetry or prose.

—Algernon Charles Swinburne,
"Emily Brontë," 1883, *Miscellanies*,
1886, pp. 260–270

RICHARD GARNETT (1892)

Richard Garnett (1835–1906) was a Victorian man of letters who worked as a librarian, a scholar, a biographer, and a poet. His most important professional post was as keeper of printed books (a librarian's position) at the British Museum, from 1890 until 1899. His scholarship included works of poetry and fiction; translations of Greek, German, Italian, and Spanish works; biographies of Blake, Carlyle, and Milton; and reviews of national literatures including *History of Italian Literature* (1897) and *English Literature: An Illustrated Record,* with Edmund Gosse (1903–1904).

Garnett's poetic evocation of Emily Brontë as "the laureate of the moors" is generally positive, but he regrets her portrait of Heathcliff as the evidence of mental and moral "unsoundness." His evaluation of Emily's poetry is less qualified, and he writes that on the basis of "supreme inspiration" she can be placed "above every other female lyrist since Sappho."

Few persons of whom so little has been or can be recorded as Emily Brontë have made so deep an impression upon the popular mind, or are so distinctly present to the imagination. There is nothing to be said except that she was born in August 1818, and died of consumption in December 1848; that she was first a teacher without pupils, and then an authoress without readers; that her life was harassed by an impracticable father, and infected by a base, profligate brother; and that nevertheless she was visited by such noble inspirations, and was such a piece of her own moorland, that one hardly accounts her unfortunate. She was the laureate of the moors, and no fanciful analogy might be drawn between her and these scenes of her residence, and objects of her affections. Like them she was free, rough, wild; in a certain sense barren and limited; in another sense rich and expansive; from one point of view mournful, from another joyous. In one respect only is she false to the teaching of the nature that environed her: the moor is ever healthy, but it is impossible to acquit the creator of "Heathcliffe" of a taint of unsoundness. The hero of *Wuthering Heights* is indeed by no means untrue to nature; what is unnatural is the authoress's evident sympathy with the most repulsive traits in his character. By over-much insistence on these, she all but destroys our interest in her hero, who has after all found the pearl of great price. Her poetry, in general less powerful, is more pleasing than her fiction; harsh and forbidding as her view of life seems at first, it gains upon us as we realise her proud superiority to external circumstances, and the passionate affection for those she really loves, which redeems her unamiability towards the rest. . . .

Not until nigh to death did she compose a strain of quite another sort, which, if it were just to judge her solely by one supreme inspiration, would place her above every other female lyrist since Sappho. The grandeur and eloquence of her last verses have in our judgment never been rivalled by any English poetess: the question whether she could have maintained herself at such an elevation, were it capable of an answer, would help to elucidate the deeper problem how far poetical inspiration is the result of favourable conditions, and how far it is a visitation from above. It must remain for ever unanswered.

—Richard Garnett, "Emily Brontë,"
The Poets and the Poetry of the Century,
ed. Alfred H. Miles, 1892, vol. 8, pp. 283–285

ARTHUR L. SALMON (1892)

Like so many critics, Salmon emphasizes the raw passion in Emily's poetry and fiction and considers the many ways in which *Wuthering Heights* was out of step with the fashions and tastes of the times. He differs with some critics, however, and notably Swinburne, in his attribution of the brutal scenes in *Wuthering Heights* to the crises she witnessed in Branwell. The sins and tragedies of the novel, he believes, were "merely

transcripts from [her] life" as Branwell's sister. Salmon's heavily biographical reading of Emily's art also delves into her love of home and
nature, her dislike of society, her capacity for bravery and selflessness,
and her communion with animals, especially her dog, Keeper. We can
infer that the scenes from life that he includes here are heavily indebted
to biographies, most probably Gaskell's and Robinson's.

Some of the most powerful poetry and prose ever written by woman was
written by Emily Brontë. The range of her genius was possibly narrow, but it
was supreme. Best known by her novel *Wuthering Heights,* she was yet preeminently a poet. That novel is really a prose-poem. She wrote this tale and
a few verses,—wrote them with unflinching touch; wrote without a public,
without admirers, without a hearing. Faith, the faith of a definite creed, she
voluntarily renounced; yet her soul remained untroubled by any of the
mysteries of the unseen. Her foot seemed placed upon absolute certainty with
regard to her immortal and glorious future. In the last poem that she ever
wrote she expressed this boundless confidence,—

> No coward soul is mine,
> No trembler in the world's storm-troubled sphere;
> I see heaven's glories shine,
> And faith shines equal, arming me from fear.

Her prayer was not for spiritual peace, for comfort or consolation; she would
have deemed it almost unworthy to need such supports. When she wrote of
the 'Old Stoic,' it was of herself that she was really writing,—

> Yes, as my swift days near their goal,
> 'Tis all that I implore;
> In life and death a chainless soul,
> With courage to endure.

The world never recognized Emily Brontë's genius as it did that of her
sister. It is true that when the little volume of poems was published by Messrs.
Aylott and Jones, Ellis Bell's verse received most of the very scanty recognition.
But in fiction Charlotte easily outstripped Emily; nor can we altogether
wonder that such should be the case. Even *Jane Eyre,* it seems, startled some
old-fashioned people when first published, and was branded by a few as an
immoral book. We smile at this now. But if readers looked askance at *Jane Eyre,*
what could be expected for *Wuthering Heights?* The story, it is true, presents

no such problem as that contained in *Jane Eyre*,—whether a man with a mad wife may marry again; but it none the less seethes and surges with moral turmoil. Emily's genius revealed itself in uncouth, untamed, almost repulsive force, though it could sometimes be as gentle as an infant's lullaby. It needs a hardy reader to thoroughly appreciate her book; yet the power displayed is not that of French realism. No laws of decency are infringed; no social sewers are opened. The characters are few, the scene almost unvaried. It is a wild, rugged book, heaving and uptorn with primitive passions; frankly displaying much that is usually concealed; unveiling depths of the human heart, just when those depths were most stirred and sullied with tempest.

Wuthering Heights is not like a common sensational novel; there is nothing of the vulgar or conventional about it. The latest 'shilling shocker,' containing the narrative of strange murders or hypnotic marvels, may circulate by the thousand; no such popularity could be expected for *Wuthering Heights*. Nor is it like an ordinary ghost-story. There is nothing distinctly supernatural in its pages, although its characters—even the wicked Heathcliff—have an intense faith in the spiritual world. But, though no ghost-story, persons of excitable fancies should avoid reading it near bedtime. Even the author's sister spoke of the tale as "terrible and goblinlike." This woman—one might almost say this girl—had witnessed little enough of the ordinary every-day world; but the little that she had seen was well utilized, and was supplemented by stern spiritual experience. Her eye had observed and her heart pondered. Many a scene of tempestuous passion had been enacted in that lonely parsonage on the Yorkshire moors. Some of these live again in *Wuthering Heights*. The brother Branwell, clever, good-for-nothing,—we may hope insane,—raised many a storm, by reason of his intoxication and worse errors. He madly loved a woman who could never be his,—a woman whom he had brought low into sin and disgrace; and some of his wild paroxysms are reproduced for us in the pages of this book. For a solitary girl to have invented such scenes and such language would have been impossible; but with Emily Brontë they are merely transcripts from life. There had been an antetype for it all at Haworth; and the girl's experience was almost entirely limited to her home. She painted the life that she knew; it was her misfortune, not her fault, that this life contained such terrible scenes.

As a child Emily was the prettiest of the Haworth children. It was a childhood without toys, without sweetmeats, without petting; but a childhood of almost unlimited freedom. The baby-eyes soon learned to drink in the fascination of the moors, the baby-ears soon loved their wild music. All the sisters felt the charm of their home-scenery, but Emily more especially.

Charlotte was quite capable of enjoying herself elsewhere, as she proved in their stay at Brussels; Emily only really *lived* when at home. When Catharine, in *Wuthering Heights*, dreams that she is in heaven, and is not happy there, she is simply expressing Emily's deep love of her home. "Heaven did not seem to be any home; and I broke my heart with weeping to come back to earth; and the angels were so angry that they flung me out into the middle of the heath on the top of Wuthering Heights, where I woke sobbing for joy." Without doubt, that was also Emily's dream.

It seems difficult to realize how helpful, how gentle and unselfish she was in her domestic life; how she excelled in ironing linen and in baking bread. Would-be geniuses are apt to regard such offices as though unworthy of attention; but the really gifted soul can find happiness in any useful labor,—can feel the blessedness of all ministry for others. To some slight extent, Charlotte Brontë's Shirley is a picture of Emily. Shirley is Emily as she might have been under different circumstances. But the real Emily was not so easily drawn, and was an even finer character. She seems to have known no petty spite or jealousy. She was patient under the neglect with which her masterpiece was received; patient, also, under the trial of illness, even unto death. There are two incidents in Charlotte's novels which specially claim notice, as being drawn from the life. On one occasion, in the stupor of drunkenness, Branwell set fire to his bed. The other sisters were terrified and helpless; he would undoubtedly have been burned to death but for Emily's prompt bravery. She saved him, as Jane Eyre saved Mr. Rochester. At another time Emily was bitten by a mad dog, whom she had approached with indiscreet kindness; she went into the kitchen and boldly cauterized the wound with her own hand. Here we have Shirley, who did the same under similar circumstances. At that strange, sad death-bed, when Branwell Brontë stood up to die, Emily was watching by his side with repressed anguish; the terror of the moment had been too much for Charlotte.

Emily was five years old when she went with her sisters to the school at Cowan's Bridge. This school is familiar to all readers of *Jane Eyre*. It has been the unenviable fate of Yorkshire schools to be immortalized by Charlotte Brontë and by Dickens. Emily is said to have been a great favorite with scholars and teachers at Cowan's Bridge. In later years she went with Charlotte to Brussels. The Belgian professor, Monsieur Heger, who won so much of the elder sister's affection, thought that Emily showed the greater genius. "She should have been a man, a great navigator," he exclaimed. "Her powerful reason would have deduced new spheres of discovery from the knowledge of the old, and her strong, imperious will would never have been daunted by opposition or difficulty, never have given way but with life." The proof of this inflexible will was shown by her fighting with the giant powers of consumption, to the very day of her death.

The stay at Brussels, so fruitful in Charlotte's case, was useless to Emily. It seems to have left no trace upon her, except the knowledge of French acquired there, and an acquaintance with German literature, which may have slightly affected *Wuthering Heights*. She was homesick the whole time, longing for the wild freedom of the moors. One of her poems, written in the twilight after school-work had been put aside, utters this ardent and unquenchable yearning. Her fancy called up the features of a well-known scene:

> A little and a lone green lane
>   That opened on a common wide;
> A distant, dreary, dim blue chain
>   Of mountains circling every side:
> A heaven so dear, an earth so calm,
>   So sweet, so soft, so hushed an air;
> And, deepening still the dream-like charm,
>   Wild moor-sheep feeding everywhere.
> *That* was the scene; I knew it well.
>   I knew the turfy pathway's sweep,
> That, winding o'er each billowy swell,
>   Marked out the tracks of wandering sheep.

All the life and varied interests of Brussels had no charm for her; she was thoroughly miserable. Returning to Haworth, to find their aunt dead, their father almost blind, their brother fallen into irretrievable ruin,—still it was returning home, and home meant happiness. It was at this time that *Wuthering Heights* was conceived.

Many would have regarded Emily as little likely to die young. If indomitable will could have preserved life, hers would have done it. Not improbably, this unbending will may have hastened her end. She declined to take care of herself, and would let no one else take care of her. In spite of her tall and energetic figure, the taint of consumption lurked in her breast; and, in spite of the breezy moorland air, the Haworth parsonage may not have been altogether sanitary. The decline came slowly but surely. It was possibly hastened by Branwell's death; he had been closer to Emily than to the other sisters. A cold and cough led to a pain in the chest and to troubled breathing. She grew pale and thin, but would spare herself no pains in caring for others, and would take no pains for herself. She refused to see any "poisoning doctor." With the chill waters of death creeping round, she still persisted in her household labors. Even a passing reference to her condition fretted her; she tried to ignore and rise above it, and wished others to do the same. Charlotte was greatly troubled, but could do nothing to combat this stoical madness; as for Anne, she was already sickening with the disease that led her gentle steps after Emily's. On the very morning of her death, Emily rose and dressed herself as usual. At noon she was hardly able to gasp, "If you will send for a doctor, I will see him now;" and at two o'clock she died, in a vain effort to raise herself from the sofa. Probably she wished to die standing, as Branwell had done.

The dog Keeper led the small procession of mourners to the grave. They laid her in the vault under the church, whither so many had preceded her. When the mourning party had returned, the dog went up to her bedroom and lay before the door. He remained there, howling dismally, for many days, and refused to be comforted. So died the writer of *Wuthering Heights,* in her thirtieth year.

Undoubtedly, Emily Brontë's genius was unique and masterful, and her book will always charm individual readers. It has been compared with Shelley's *Cenci* and with Webster's *Duchess of Malfi.* All such comparisons, of course, only go to indicate a generic likeness, but they sufficiently explain the tale's little popularity. It might not be altogether a good sign for such works to be popular; they are for a "fit audience, though few,"—not for the many. They would not be wholesome food for all, and might cause a mental indigestion. Not every reader can assimilate such strong food, or turn it to good purpose. Those who can, will find it attract them irresistibly. Faulty as a narrative, *Wuthering Heights* burns with energy and pulses with life-blood. It is a poem without the accompaniment of rhyme. After all its strife and passion, it closes with an image of deep peace: "I lingered round the graves under that benign sky, watched the moths fluttering among the heath and harebells, listened to the soft wind breathing through the grass; and wondered how any one could ever imagine unquiet slumbers for the sleepers in that quiet earth."

—Arthur L. Salmon, "A Modern Stoic:
Emily Brontë," *Poet-Lore,* January 1892,
pp. 64–70

Margaret Oliphant (1897)

Oliphant's quixotic description of Emily Brontë treats her as simultaneously more raw and more humane than Charlotte.

—◦◦◦— —◦◦◦— —◦◦◦—

To me Emily Brontë is chiefly interesting as the double of her sister, exaggerating at once and softening her character and genius as showing those limits of superior sense and judgment which restrained her, and the softer lights which a better developed humanity threw over the landscape common to them both.

—Margaret Oliphant, *Women Novelists*
of Queen Victoria's Reign, 1897, p. 28

MARY A. WARD (1900)

Ward's conviction that Emily's artistry was superior to Charlotte's marks a shift in late-century taste to a formalist appreciation of literature. In this vein, Ward confidently praises the structural coherency of *Wuthering Heights* and can dismiss its brutal themes and language as more incidental features of plot. Ward also finds evidence of Charlotte's own personality in her novels, whereas *Wuthering Heights* transcends the experience and vision of Emily and achieves an artistic objectivity that Charlotte's works do not. While both sisters reflect strong Romantic loyalties, Emily's are "German" in their forcefulness and Charlotte's display a comparatively Gallic tone and self-consciousness.

But for all of her claims about Emily's dispassionate relationship to her own art, Ward treads familiar ground in relating the violence of *Wuthering Heights* to the example of Branwell Brontë. She goes on to say, however, that Heathcliff's inhumanity bears "no relation to any life of men and women that the true world knows." In this portrait, she infers, Emily Brontë has gone too far. The child Heathcliff, however, is more satisfying to Ward, as is the novel's evocations of nature as a backdrop and parallel to the tempestuous relations of the family at the center of the story.

Wuthering Heights's final volume earns Ward's comparison to "all that is best in Romantic literature." This praise refers to both the homely but wrenching details of the domestic scenes and to the haunting death of Heathcliff himself. At her final count, Ward places Emily with the strain of Romantic literature that embraces life rather than with those practitioners seemingly consumed by it; "[f]or all her crudity and inexperience, she is in the end with Goethe, rather than with Hoffmann, and thereby with all that is sane, strong, and living in literature."

'Stronger than a man, simpler than a child:'—these words are Emily Brontë's true epitaph, both as an artist and as a human being. Her strength of will and imagination struck those who knew her and those who read her as often inhuman or terrible; and with this was combined a simplicity partly of genius partly of a strange innocence and spirituality, which gives her a place apart in English letters. It is important to realise that of the three books written simultaneously by the three sisters, Emily's alone shows genius already matured and master of its tools. Charlotte had a steady development before her, especially in matters of method and style; the comparative dulness of *The Professor,* and the crudities of *Jane Eyre* made way for the accomplished variety and brilliance of *Villette.* But though Emily, had she lived, might have chosen many happier subjects, treated with a more flowing unity than she achieved in *Wuthering Heights,* the full competence of genius is already present in her book. The common, hasty, didactic note that Charlotte often strikes is never heard in *Wuthering Heights.* The artist remains hidden and self-contained; the work, however morbid and violent may be the scenes and creatures it presents, has always that distinction which belongs to high talent working solely for its own joy and satisfaction, with no thought of a spectator, or any aim but that of an ideal and imaginative whole. Charlotte stops to think of objectors, to teach and argue, to avenge her own personal grievances, or cheat her own personal longings. For pages together, she often is little more than the clever clergyman's daughter, with a sharp tongue, a dislike to Ritualism and Romanism, a shrewd memory for persecutions and affronts, and a weakness for that masterful lover of whom most young women dream. But Emily is pure mind and passion; no one, from the pages of *Wuthering Heights* can guess at the small likes and dislikes, the religious or critical antipathies, the personal weaknesses of the artist who wrote it. She has that highest power—which was typically Shakespeare's power, and which in our day is typically the power of such an artist as Turgueniev—the power which gives life, intensest life, to the creatures of imagination, and, in doing so, endows them with an independence behind which the maker is forgotten. The puppet show is everything; and, till it is over, the manager—nothing. And it is his delight and triumph to have it so.

Yet, at the same time, *Wuthering Heights* is a book of the later Romantic movement, betraying the influences of German Romantic imagination, as Charlotte's work betrays the influences of Victor Hugo and George Sand. The Romantic tendency to invent and delight in monsters, the *exaltation du moi,* which has been said to be the secret of the whole Romantic revolt against classical models and restraints; the love of violence in speech and action, the preference for the hideous in character and the abnormal in situation—of all these there are abundant examples in *Wuthering Heights.*

The dream of Mr. Lockwood in Catherine's box bed, when in the terror of nightmare he pulled the wrist of the little wailing ghost outside on to the broken glass of the window, 'and rubbed it to and fro till the blood ran down and soaked the bed-clothes'—one of the most gruesome fancies of literature!—Heathcliff's long and fiendish revenge on Hindley Earnshaw; the ghastly quarrel between Linton and Heathcliff in Catherine's presence after Heathcliff's return; Catherine's three days' fast, and her delirium when she 'tore the pillow with her teeth;' Heathcliff dashing his head against the trees of her garden, leaving his blood upon their bark, and 'howling, not like a man, but like a savage beast being goaded to death with knives and spears;' the fight between Heathcliff and Earnshaw after Heathcliff's marriage to Isabella; the kidnapping of the younger Catherine, and the horror rather suggested than described of Heathcliff's brutality towards his sickly son:—all these things would not have been written precisely as they were written, but for the 'Germanism' of the thirties and forties, but for the translations of *Blackwood* and *Fraser,* and but for those German tales, whether of Hoffmann or others, which there is evidence that Emily Brontë read both at Brussels and after her return.

As to the 'exaltation of the Self,' its claims, sensibilities and passions, in defiance of all social law and duty, there is no more vivid expression of it throughout Romantic literature than is contained in the conversation between the elder Catherine and Nelly Dean before Catherine marries Edgar Linton. And the violent, clashing egotisms of Heathcliff and Catherine in the last scene of passion before Catherine's death, are as it were an epitome of a whole *genre* in literature, and a whole phase of European feeling.

Nevertheless, horror and extravagance are not really the characteristic mark and quality of *Wuthering Heights.* If they were, it would have no more claim upon us than a hundred other forgotten books—Lady Caroline Lamb's *Glenarvon* amongst them—which represent the dregs and refuse of a great literary movement. As in the case of Charlotte Brontë, the peculiar force of Emily's work lies in the fact that it represents the grafting of a European tradition upon a mind already richly stored with English and local reality, possessing at command a style at once strong and simple, capable both of homeliness and magnificence. The form of Romantic imagination which influenced Emily was not the same as that which influenced Charlotte; whether from a secret stubbornness and desire of difference, or no, there is not a mention of the French language, or of French books, in Emily's work, while Charlotte's abounds in a kind of display of French affinities, and French scholarship. The dithyrambs of *Shirley* and *Villette,* the 'Vision of Eve' of *Shirley,* and the description of Rachel in *Villette,* would have been impossible to Emily; they come to a great extent from the reading of Victor Hugo and George Sand. But in both sisters there is a similar *fonds* of stern and simple realism; a similar faculty of observation at once shrewd, and passionate; and it is by these that they produce their ultimate literary effect. The difference between them is almost wholly in Emily's favour. The uneven, amateurish manner of so many pages in *Jane Eyre* and *Shirley;* the lack of literary reticence which is responsible for Charlotte's frequent intrusion of her own personality, and for her occasional temptations to scream and preach, which are not wholly resisted even in her masterpiece *Villette;* the ugly tawdry sentences which disfigure some of her noblest passages, and make quotation from her so difficult:—you will find none of these things in *Wuthering Heights.* Emily is never flurried, never self-conscious; she is master of herself at the most rushing moments of feeling or narrative; her style is simple, sensuous, adequate and varied from first to last; she has fewer purple patches than Charlotte, but at its best, her insight no less than her power of phrase, is of a diviner and more exquisite quality.

III

Wuthering Heights then is the product of romantic imagination, working probably under influences from German literature, and marvellously fused with local knowledge and a realistic power which, within its own range, has seldom been surpassed. Its few great faults are soon enumerated. The tendency to extravagance and monstrosity may, as we have seen, be taken to some extent as belonging more to a literary fashion than to the artist. Tieck and Hoffmann are full of raving and lunatic beings who sob, shout, tear out their hair by the roots, and live in a perpetual state of personal violence both towards themselves and their neighbours. Emily Brontë probably received from them an additional impulse towards a certain wildness of manner and conception which was already natural to her Irish blood, to a woman brought up amid the solitudes of the moors and the ruggedness of Yorkshire life fifty years ago, and natural also, alas! to the sister of the opium-eater and drunkard Branwell Brontë.

To this let us add a certain awkwardness and confusion of structure; a strain of ruthless exaggeration in the character of Heathcliff; and some absurdities and contradictions in the character of Nelly Dean. The latter criticism indeed is bound up with the first. Nelly Dean is presented as the faithful and affectionate nurse, the only good angel both of the elder and the younger Catherine. But Nelly Dean does the most treacherous, cruel, and indefensible things, simply that the story may move. She becomes the go-between for Catherine and Heathcliff; she knowingly allows her charge Catherine, on the eve of her confinement, to fast in solitude and delirium for three days and nights, without saying a word to Edgar Linton, Catherine's affectionate husband, and her master, who was in the house all the time. It is her breach of trust which brings about Catherine's dying scene with Heathcliff, just as it is her disobedience and unfaith which really betray Catherine's child into the hands of her enemies. Without these lapses and indiscretions indeed the story could not maintain itself; but the clumsiness or carelessness of them is hardly to be denied. In the case of Heathcliff, the blemish lies rather in a certain deliberate and passionate defiance of the reader's sense of humanity and possibility; partly also in the innocence of the writer, who, in a world of sex and passion, has invented a situation charged with the full forces of both, without any true realisation of what she has done. Heathcliff's murderous language to Catherine about the husband whom she loves with an affection only second to that which she cherishes for his hateful self; his sordid and incredible courtship of Isabella under Catherine's eyes; the long horror of his pursuit and capture of the younger Catherine, his dead love's child; the total incompatibility between his passion for the mother and his mean ruffianism towards the daughter; the utter absence of any touch of kindness even in his love for Catherine, whom he scolds and rates on the very threshold of death; the mingling in him of high passion with the vilest arts of the sharper and the thief:—these things o'erleap themselves, so that again and again the sense of tragedy is lost in mere violence and excess, and what might have been a man becomes a monster. There are speeches and actions of Catherine's, moreover, contained in these central pages which have no relation to any life of men and women that the true world knows. It may be said indeed that the writer's very ignorance of certain facts and relations of life, combined with the force of imaginative passion which she throws into her conceptions, produces a special poetic effect—a strange and bodiless tragedy—unique in literature. And there is much truth in this; but not enough to vindicate these scenes of the book, from radical weakness and falsity, nor to preserve in the reader that illusion, that inner consent, which is the final test of all imaginative effort.

IV

Nevertheless there are whole sections of the story during which the character of Heathcliff is presented to us with a marvellous and essential truth. The scenes of childhood and youth; the up-growing of the two desolate children, drawn to each other by some strange primal sympathy, Heathcliff 'the little black thing, harboured by a good man to his bane,' Catherine who 'was never so happy as when we were all scolding her at once, and she defying us with her bold saucy look, and her ready words;' the gradual development of the natural distance between them, he the ill-mannered ruffianly no-man's-child, she the young lady of the house; his pride and jealous pain; her young fondness for Edgar Linton, as inevitable as a girl's yearning for pretty finery, and a new frock with the spring; Heathcliff's boyish vow of vengeance on the brutal Hindley and his race; Cathy's passionate discrimination, in the scene with Nelly Dean which ends as it were the first act of the play, between her affection for Linton and her identity with Heathcliff's life and being;—for the mingling of daring poetry with the easiest and most masterly command of local truth, for sharpness and felicity of phrase, for exuberance of creative force, for invention and freshness of detail, there are few things in English fiction to match it. One might almost say that the first volume of *Adam Bede* is false and mannered beside it,—the first volumes of *Waverley* or *Guy Mannering* flat and diffuse. Certainly, the first volume of *Jane Eyre*, admirable as it is, can hardly be set on the same level with the careless ease and effortless power of these first nine chapters. There is almost nothing in them but shares in the force and the effect of all true 'vision'—Joseph, 'the wearisomest self-righteous Pharisee that ever ransacked a Bible to rake the promises to himself, and fling the curses to his neighbours;' old Earnshaw himself, stupid, obstinate and kindly; the bullying Hindley with his lackadaisical consumptive wife; the delicate nurture and superior wealth of the Lintons; the very animals of the farm, the very rain- and snow-storms of the moors,—all live, all grow together, like the tangled heather itself, harsh and gnarled and ugly in one aspect, in another beautiful by its mere unfettered life and freedom, capable too of wild moments of colour and blossoming.

And as far as the lesser elements of style, the mere technique of writing are concerned, one may notice the short elastic vigour of the sentences, the tightness of epithet and detail, the absence of any care for effect, and the flashes of beauty which suddenly emerge like the cistus upon the rock.

V

Of what we may call the third and last act of *Wuthering Heights*, which extends from the childhood of the younger Catherine to the death of Heathcliff, much might be said. It is no less masterly than the first section of the book and much more complex in plan. The key to it lies in two earlier passages—in Heathcliff's boyish vow of vengence on Hindley Earnshaw, and in his fierce appeal to his lost love to haunt him, rather than leave him 'in this abyss where I cannot find her.' The conduct of the whole 'act' is intricate and difficult; the initial awkwardness implied in Nelly Dean's function as narrator is felt now and then; but as a whole, the strength of the intention is no less clear than the deliberate and triumphant power with which the artist achieves it. These chapters are not always easy to read, but they repay the closest attention. Not an incident, not a fragment of conversation is thrown away, and in the end the effect is complete. It is gained by that fusion of terror and beauty, of ugliness and a flying magic—'settling unawares'—which is the characteristic note of the Brontë's, and of all that is best in Romantic literature. Never for a moment do you lose hold upon the Yorkshire landscape and the Yorkshire folk—look at the picture of Isabella's wasteful porridge-making and of Joseph's grumbling rage, amid her gruesome experience as a bride; never are you allowed to forget a single sordid element in Heathcliff's ruffianism; and yet through it all the inevitable end developes, the double end which only a master could have conceived. Life and love rebel and reassert themselves in the wild slight love-story of Hareton and Cathy, which break the final darkness like a gleam of dawn upon the moors; and death tames and silences for ever all that remains of Heathcliff's futile cruelties and wasted fury.

But what a death! Heathcliff has tormented and oppressed Catherine's daughter; and it is Catherine's shadow that lures him to his doom, through every stage and degree of haunting feverish ecstasy, of reunion promised and delayed, of joy for ever offered and for ever withdrawn. And yet how simple the method, how true the 'vision' to the end! Around Heathcliff's last hours the farm-life flows on as usual. There is no hurry in the sentences; no blurring of the scene. Catherine's haunting presence closes upon the man who murdered her happiness and youth, interposes between him and all bodily needs, deprives him of food and drink and sleep, till the madman is dead of his 'strange happiness,' straining after the phantom that slays him, dying of the love whereby alone he remains human, through which fate strikes at last—and strikes home.

'Is he a ghoul or vampire?' I mused. 'I had read of such hideous incarnate demons.' So says Nelly Dean just before Heathcliff's death. The remark is not hers in truth, but Emily Brontë's, and where it stands it is of great significance. It points to the world of German horror and romance, to which we know that she had access. That world was congenial to her, as it was congenial to Southey, Scott, and Coleridge; and it has left some ugly and disfiguring traces upon the detail of *Wuthering Heights*. But *essentially* her imagination escaped from it and mastered it. As the haunting of Heathcliff is to the coarser horrors of Tieck and Hoffmann, so is her place to theirs. For all her crudity and inexperience, she is in the end with Goethe, rather than with Hoffmann, and thereby with all that is sane, strong, and living in literature. 'A great work requires many-sidedness, and on this rock the young author splits,' said Goethe to Eckermann, praising at the same time the art which starts from the simplest realities and the subject nearest at hand, to reach at last by a natural expansion the loftiest heights of poetry. But this was the art of Emily Brontë. It started from her own heart and life; it was nourished by the sights and sounds of a lonely yet sheltering nature; it was responsive to the art of others, yet always independent; and in the rich and tangled truth of *Wuthering Heights* it showed promise at least of a many-sidedness to which only the greatest attain.

—Mary A. Ward, from "Introduction,"
Wuthering Heights, 1900, pp. xxiii–xxxviii

CHARLOTTE M. MEW (1904)

Charlotte Mary Mew (1869–1929) was a well-regarded English poet who led a somewhat tragic life. Members of her family suffered from mental illness, and in fear of passing on these genes, Mew did not marry or have children, and she did eventually seem to succumb to the family illness, as her suicide suggests. Professionally, however, Mew enjoyed considerable success in the early modern era. Her first collection of poetry, *The Farmer's Bride* (1916), published in the United States as *Saturday Market* in 1921, earned her the respect of Thomas Hardy, Virginia Woolf, and Siegfried Sassoon.

Mew's focus on Emily Brontë's "appalling personality" perhaps reflects her own (and familial) preoccupation with unstable psychologies. The characterization of Emily as "a great artist and a repulsive woman" is memorable for its stridency and boldness but perhaps infers more about Emily's individual personality than others would comfortably draw from her art.

Mew continues, however, by noting that the rashness of *Wuthering Heights* yields in Emily's poems (those written after the novel) to a more mature voice that, had she lived, would have been further developed.

To those who, holding dear, have formed for themselves any conception of that great genius who died "between the finishing of labour and the award of praise" the works of Emily Brontë must be chiefly interesting as the record of a unique and in some senses, an appalling personality: and it is undeniable that to the majority of those readers to whom she is but casually known, this personality—one of the most remarkable in the history of modern literature—presents itself as repugnant and distasteful.

"Mind," says Mr. Pater, "we cannot choose but approve when we recognise it: soul may repel us and not because we misunderstand it." But it is possible that here is a soul which has most repelled where least it has been understood.

It is mainly upon *Wuthering Heights* that Emily Brontë's reputation as a great artist and a repulsive woman has been built: her poems—which in part supply its key and commentary—are a truer revelation of her veritable self than that grim and matchless tragedy, by which she is too exclusively known and upon which, perforce, her fame must rest. The note of violence which in a measure disfigures, and yet in a measure enhances and always triumphantly fails to weaken, the passion of *Wuthering Heights* is absent from the author's poems—as it would probably have been absent from her later work. In that dreadful and incomparable story she was testing her powers, she had not altogether gauged them. They were, at the outset, perhaps too much for her, and overwhelmed a mind, which young in waking, could not confine and comprehend itself. Swept forward by the oncoming and strong current of her genius, she was, in the first rush of it, somewhat borne away; so strongly that we too are borne along with it, forgiving the impetuosity and turbid tumult of that stream.

Charlotte has urged, in vindication of a violence she might not dismiss and could not altogether explain, that "the writer who possesses the creative gift owns something of which he is not always master." But that ultimately Emily must have been master of any gift she did possess, it is hardly possible to doubt. The evidence of her poems goes far to show that, in time, she would have discarded the unchecked vehemence of immaturity for a vigour more intrinsic and appealing. Her last lines—the dignity and grandeur of which it is hardly possible to overestimate—remind us that she was out-growing her mighty childhood—that within sight of eternity the fruit of time was ripening fast.

—Charlotte M. Mew, "The Poems of
Emily Brontë," *Temple Bar,* August 1904,
pp. 153–154

WORKS

WUTHERING HEIGHTS

Emily Brontë's masterpiece, the novel *Wuthering Heights*, is the tragic love story, set on the Yorkshire moors, of Heathcliff and Cathy Earnshaw, who are not related but are raised as siblings. The love story continues into the next generation, centering on Cathy's daughter, also named Catherine. A dominant part of the story is nature, which with violent storms and dramatic changes in the weather is less of a backdrop to the human story than a tempestuous player in its own right. The starkness of the novel's language, setting, and especially Heathcliff's brutality shocked and disconcerted many critics, and the novel was not considered important by critical consensus until decades after Emily's death.

It is unknown when Emily wrote *Wuthering Heights*, and no original copy of the manuscript exists. It was first published with Anne's *Agnes Grey* in December 1847 by the publisher Thomas Cautley Newby. Newby's production of the novels was poor, rife with typographical and grammatical errors. Charlotte corrected many of these mistakes in her 1850 edition of the novels, which she published (after Emily's and Anne's deaths) with Smith, Elder & Company.

The history of *Wuthering Heights*'s reception is uneven. While some early critics recognized its power and significance (see Dobell), many deemed it offensive. One of the challenges that the novel presented to readers was its refusal to fit into Victorian convention. The novel is a strange mix of Romantic ideology (seen especially in the power accorded to nature, and in the Byronic nature of Heathcliff) and protomodern narrative features, such as its shifting and unreliable viewpoints. Its critical treatment was also complicated by the public fascination with Emily whose uncompromising gifts and personal eccentricity were often used to corroborate interpretations of the novel (see especially Robinson).

CATHARINE M. SEDGWICK (1848)

Sedgwick's turgid dismissal of *Wuthering Heights* only allows for a certain resemblance to *Jane Eyre*, in its directness and forcefulness, and determines that its author must be a brother to Currer Bell, as *Wuthering Heights* recasts the family voice in a "masculine" mode.

───────────

I trust you have not, as we have, wasted your time on "that little family in Hell," living and dying at *Wuthering Heights*. It is a most signal waste of talent.

There is a certain resemblance to *Jane Eyre*, like a family look; the energy of thought and style, the northern mind as well as air that breathes through it, the intimate and masterly acquaintance with a location and coterie, and exclusion from the world, the remarkable directness of style, are all qualities peculiar, and marvelously like *Jane Eyre*, so that I think the author must be her brother, the masculine of her masculine mind.

—Catharine M. Sedgwick, letter to
Mrs. K.S. Minot, May 27, 1848, cited in
Mary E. Dewey, *Life and Letters of
Catharine M. Sedgwick*, 1871, p. 307

EDWIN P. WHIPPLE (1848)

Whipple's erroneous (but confident) judgment that Acton Bell is the author of *Wuthering Heights*, *The Tenant of Wildfell Hall*, and "certain offensive but powerful portions of *Jane Eyre*" tries to attribute the violence of these works to one aberrant mind. The brutality of which "Acton" is capable, thinks Whipple, reaches its apex in *Wuthering Heights*, which he goes on to describe with a variety of colorful and passionate insults that emphasize the novel's crudeness, especially in its despicable portrait of Heathcliff.

In addition to bemoaning the offensiveness of *Wuthering Heights* itself, Whipple also laments the waste of talent it represents, noting its author's formidable, if poorly directed, power.

The truth is, that the whole firm of Bell & Co. seem to have a sense of the depravity of human nature peculiarly their own. It is the yahoo, not the demon, that they select for representation; their Pandemonium is of mud rather than fire.

This is especially the case with Acton Bell, the author of *Wuthering Heights*, *The Tenant of Wildfell Hall*, and, if we mistake not, of certain offensive but powerful portions *of Jane Eyre*. Acton, when left altogether to his own imaginations, seems to take a morose satisfaction in developing a full and complete science of human brutality. In *Wuthering Heights* he has succeeded in reaching the summit of this laudable ambition. He appears to think that spiritual wickedness is a combination of animal ferocities, and has accordingly made a compendium of the most striking qualities of tiger, wolf, cur, and wild-cat, in the hope of framing out of such elements a suitable brute-demon to serve as the hero of his novel. Compared with Heathcliff, Squeers is considerate and Quilp humane. He is a deformed monster, whom the Mephistopheles of Goethe would have nothing to say to, whom the Satan of Milton would consider as an object of simple disgust, and to whom Dante would hesitate in awarding the honor of a place among those whom he has consigned to the burning pitch. This epitome of brutality, disavowed by man and devil, Mr. Acton Bell attempts in two whole volumes to delineate, and certainly he is to be congratulated on his success. As he is a man of uncommon talents, it is needless to say that it is to his subject and his dogged manner of handling it that we are to refer the burst of dislike with which the novel was received. His mode of delineating a bad character is to narrate every offensive act and repeat every vile expression which are characteristic. Hence, in *Wuthering Heights,* he details all the ingenuities of animal malignity, and exhausts the whole rhetoric of stupid blasphemy, in order that there may be no mistake as to the kind of person he intends to hold up to the popular gaze. Like all spendthrifts of malice and profanity, however, he overdoes the business. Though he scatters oaths as plentifully as sentimental writers do interjections, the comparative parsimony of the great novelists in this respect is productive of infinitely more effect. It must be confessed that this coarseness, though the prominent, is not the only characteristic of the writer. His attempt at originality does not stop with the conception of Heathcliff, but he aims further to exhibit the action of the sentiment of love on the nature of the being whom his morbid imagination has created. This is by far the ablest and most subtle portion of his labors, and indicates that strong hold upon the elements of character, and that decision of touch in the delineation of the most evanescent qualities of emotion, which distinguish the mind of the whole family. For all practical purposes, however, the power evinced in *Wuthering Heights* is power thrown away. Nightmares and dreams, through which devils dance and wolves howl, make bad novels.

—Edwin P. Whipple, "Novels of the Season," *North American Review,* October 1848, pp. 357–359

Charlotte Brontë ("Currer Bell") (1850)

Charlotte Brontë wrote the preface to the second edition (and first single-volume edition) of *Wuthering Heights* and *Agnes Grey* after the deaths of Emily and Anne as part of an effort to respond to the many complaints about the novel's violence and brutality. After a more pedestrian purpose, Charlotte also wanted to revise parts of the novel for readers' ease, altering punctuation and "translating" the thick Yorkshire dialect of certain characters into more phonetic and intelligible prose.

It was the subtext of Charlotte's preface, however, that influenced the novel's reception. At a time when *Wuthering Heights* was generally found suspect and unpleasant, Charlotte tried to explain and defend the novel—but only to a point. She begins by explaining that Yorkshire (and the moors) accounts for much of the novel's rudeness and for the untamed and impolite language that was shocking to many readers. But Charlotte also holds Emily accountable for aspects of the novel's unpleasantness and regrets Emily's habit of representing expletives with a first letter of the word, followed by a dash ("a proceeding which, however well meant, is weak and futile").

Of *Wuthering Heights* itself, Charlotte calls the novel "moorish, and wild, and knotty as a root of heath. Nor was it natural that it should be otherwise; the author being herself a native and nursling of the moors." Maybe this was intended to explain Emily's "wild" work, but it had the effect of feeding into the mythologized picture of Emily as a remote and uncivilized character, oblivious to the ways and means of "polite" society. Charlotte does, however, offer unqualified praise of her sister's accurate representation of nature.

More complex is Charlotte's representation of Emily's characters and their particular relations. Here her motives are difficult to read, for in her effort to facilitate the reception of *Wuthering Heights*, she mainly succeeds in portraying her sister as exceptional and, even to a sibling, hard to understand. Charlotte muses that Emily "had scarcely more practical knowledge of the peasantry amongst whom she lived, than a nun has of the country people who sometimes pass her convent gates." Such explanations seem more effective in making Emily a figure of speculation and mystery than in easing the reception of her novel into the public taste. And while Charlotte makes some effort to detect humanity and affection in the book's characters, including the homely Nelly Dean, her reading of Heathcliff as an "evil" presence could be seen to encourage readers' aversions to the novel. Charlotte's final ambivalence toward the novel is both admirable and puzzling. When she questions "[w]hether it is right or advisable to create beings like Heathcliff, I do not know: I scarcely think it is," we are at once interested in her own ethical stance and baffled by the effect she sought in her representation of her sister's work.

I have just read over *Wuthering Heights,* and, for the first time, have obtained a clear glimpse of what are termed (and, perhaps, really are) its faults; have gained a definite notion of how it appears to other people—to strangers who knew nothing of the author; who are unacquainted with the locality where the scenes of the story are laid; to whom the inhabitants, the customs, the natural characteristics of the outlying hills and hamlets in the West Riding of Yorkshire are things alien and unfamiliar.

To all such *Wuthering Heights* must appear a rude and strange production. The wild moors of the North of England can for them have no interest: the language, the manners, the very dwellings and household customs of the scattered inhabitants of those districts must be to such readers in a great measure unintelligible, and—where intelligible—repulsive. Men and women who, perhaps, naturally very calm, and with feelings moderate in degree, and little marked in kind, have been trained from their cradle to observe the utmost evenness of manner and guardedness of language, will hardly know what to make of the rough, strong utterance, the harshly manifested passions, the unbridled aversions, and headlong partialities of unlettered moorland hinds and rugged moorland squires, who have grown up untaught and unchecked, except by Mentors as harsh as themselves. A large class of readers, likewise, will suffer greatly from the introduction into the pages of this work of words printed with all their letters, which it has become the custom to represent by the initial and final letter only—a blank line filling the interval. I may as well say at once that, for this circumstance, it is out of my power to apologize; deeming it, myself, a rational plan to write words at full length. The practice of hinting by single letters those expletives with which profane and violent persons are wont to garnish their discourse, strikes me as a proceeding which, however well meant, is weak and futile. I cannot tell what good it does—what feeling it spares—what horror it conceals.

With regard to the rusticity of *Wuthering Heights,* I admit the charge, for I feel the quality. It is rustic all through. It is moorish, and wild, and knotty as a root of heath. Nor was it natural that it should be otherwise; the author being herself a native and nursling of the moors. Doubtless, had her lot been cast in a town, her writings, if she had written at all, would have possessed another character. Even had chance or taste led her to choose a similar subject, she would have treated it otherwise. Had Ellis Bell been a lady or a gentleman accustomed to what is called "the world," her view of a remote and unreclaimed region, as well as of the dwellers therein, would have differed greatly from that actually taken by the home-bred country girl. Doubtless it would have been wider—more comprehensive: whether it would have been more original or more truthful is not so certain. As far as the scenery and locality are concerned, it could scarcely have been so sympathetic: Ellis Bell did not describe as one whose eye and taste alone found pleasure in the prospect; her native hills were far more to her than a spectacle; they were what she lived in, and by, as much as the wild birds, their tenants, or as the heather, their produce. Her descriptions, then, of natural scenery, are what they should be, and all they should be.

Where delineation of human character is concerned, the case is different. I am bound to avow that she had scarcely more practical knowledge of the peasantry amongst whom she lived, than a nun has of the country people who sometimes pass her convent gates. My sister's disposition was not naturally gregarious; circumstances favoured and fostered her tendency to seclusion; except to go to church or take a walk on the hills, she rarely crossed the threshold of home. Though her feeling for the people round was benevolent, intercourse with them she never sought; nor, with very few exceptions, ever experienced. And yet she knew them: knew their ways, their language, their family histories; she could hear of them with interest, and talk of them with detail, minute, graphic, and accurate; but *with* them, she rarely exchanged a word. Hence it ensued that what her mind had gathered of the real concerning them, was too exclusively confined to those tragic and terrible traits of which, in listening to the secret annals of every rude vicinage, the memory is sometimes compelled to receive the impress. Her imagination, which was a spirit more sombre than sunny, more powerful than sportive, found in such traits material whence it wrought creations like Heathcliff, like Earnshaw, like Catherine. Having formed these beings, she did not know what she had done. If the auditor of her work, when read in manuscript, shuddered under the grinding influence of natures so relentless and implacable, of spirits so lost and fallen; if it was complained that the mere hearing of certain vivid and fearful scenes banished sleep by night, and disturbed mental peace by day, Ellis Bell would wonder what was meant, and suspect the complainant of affectation. Had she but lived, her mind would of itself have grown like a strong tree, loftier, straighter, wider-spreading, and its matured fruits would have attained a mellower ripeness and sunnier bloom; but on that mind time and experience alone could work: to the influence of other intellects, it was not amenable.

Having avowed that over much of *Wuthering Heights* there broods "a horror of great darkness;" that, in its storm-heated and electrical atmosphere, we seem at times to breathe lightning: let me point to those spots where clouded daylight and the eclipsed sun still attest their existence. For a specimen of true benevolence and homely fidelity, look at the character of Nelly Dean; for an example of constancy and tenderness, remark that of Edgar Linton. (Some people will think these qualities do not shine so well incarnate in a man as they would do in a woman, but Ellis Bell could never be brought to comprehend this notion: nothing moved her more than any insinuation that the faithfulness and clemency, the long-suffering and loving-kindness which are esteemed virtues in the daughters of Eve, become foibles in the sons of Adam. She held that mercy and forgiveness are the divinest attributes of the Great Being who made both man and woman, and that what clothes the Godhead in glory, can disgrace no form of feeble humanity). There is a dry saturnine humour in the delineation of old Joseph, and some glimpses of grace and gaiety animate the younger Catherine. Nor is even the first heroine of the name destitute of a certain strange beauty in her fierceness, or of honesty in the midst of perverted passion and passionate perversity.

Heathcliff, indeed, stands unredeemed; never once swerving in his arrow-straight course to perdition, from the time when "the little black-haired swarthy thing, as dark as if it came from the Devil," was first unrolled out of the bundle and set on its feet in the farmhouse kitchen, to the hour when Nelly Dean found the grim, stalwart corpse laid on its back in the panel-enclosed bed, with wide-gazing eyes that seemed "to sneer at her attempt to close them, and parted lips and sharp white teeth that sneered too."

Heathcliff betrays one solitary human feeling, and that is *not* his love for Catherine; which is a sentiment fierce and inhuman: a passion such as might boil and glow in the bad essence of some evil genius; a fire that might form the tormented centre—the ever-suffering soul of a magnate of the infernal world: and by its quenchless and ceaseless ravage effect the execution of the decree which dooms him to carry Hell with him wherever he wanders. No; the single link that connects Heathcliff with humanity is his rudely-confessed regard for Hareton Earnshaw—the young man whom he has ruined; and then his half-implied esteem for Nelly Dean. These solitary traits omitted, we should say he was child neither of Lascar nor gipsy, but a man's shape animated by demon life—a Ghoul—an Afreet.

Whether it is right or advisable to create beings like Heathcliff, I do not know: I scarcely think it is. But this I know: the writer who possesses the creative gift owns something of which he is not always master—something that, at times, strangely wills and works for itself. He may lay down rules and devise principles, and to rules and principles it will perhaps for years lie in subjection; and then, haply without any warning of revolt, there comes a time when it will no longer consent to "harrow the valleys, or be bound with a band in the furrow"—when it "laughs at the multitude of the city, and regards not the crying of the driver"—when, refusing absolutely to make ropes out of sea-sand any longer, it sets to work on statue-hewing, and you have a Pluto or a Jove, a Tisiphone or a Psyche, a Mermaid or a Madonna, as Fate or Inspiration direct. Be the work grim or glorious, dread or divine, you have little choice left but quiescent adoption. As for you—the nominal artist—your share in it has been to work passively under dictates you neither delivered nor could question—that would not be uttered at your prayer, nor suppressed nor changed at your caprice. If the result be attractive, the World will praise you, who little deserve praise; if it be repulsive, the same World will blame you, who almost as little deserve blame.

Wuthering Heights was hewn in a wild workshop, with simple tools, out of homely materials. The statuary found a granite block on a solitary moor; gazing thereon, he saw how from the crag might be elicited a head, savage, swart, sinister; a form moulded with at least one element of grandeur—power. He wrought with a rude chisel, and from no model but the vision of his meditations. With time and labour, the crag took human shape; and there it stands colossal, dark, and frowning, half statue, half rock: in the former sense, terrible and goblin-like; in the latter, almost beautiful, for its colouring is of mellow grey, and moorland moss clothes it; and heath, with its blooming bells and balmy fragrance, grows faithfully close to the giant's foot.

—Charlotte Brontë, "Preface,"
Wuthering Heights, 1850

Sydney Dobell (1850)

Dobell was one of Wuthering Heights's early champions. Charlotte was extremely grateful for Dobell's sensitivity to her sister's genius at a time when few reviewers looked favorably on the novel. In a personal letter to him, she thanked him "with a full heart" for "the noble justice he has rendered to one dear to me as myself—perhaps dearer" (quoted in Gaskell, p. 349). While Dobell's critique of Wuthering Heights recognizes Emily's talent, his admiration is not unqualified: If she is a genius, she is one of "exquisite but unconscious art"; her impressive intellectual powers are filtered through a childlike "simplicity." In its vacillations between deference and condescension, the tone of Dobell's review is consistent with his discussion of Charlotte's oeuvre. It is also in line with many contemporary analyses of Emily's poetry, which deemed it to be both brilliant and technically inept.

As he does in the Charlotte Brontë excerpt, Dobell places significant value here on the development of credible characters. In particular, he praises Emily Brontë's sympathetic and subtle depiction of Catherine Earnshaw but suggests that she fails in the portrayal of Heathcliff by making him despicable, rather than enigmatically aloof.

———✺——— ———✺——— ———✺———

Laying aside *Wildfell Hall*, we open *Wuthering Heights*, as at once the earlier in date and ruder in execution. We look upon it as the flight of an impatient fancy fluttering in the very exultation of young wings; sometimes beating against its solitary bars, but turning, rather to exhaust, in a circumscribed space, the energy and agility which it may not yet spend in the heavens—a youthful story, written for oneself in solitude, and thrown aside till other successes recall the eyes to it in hope. In this thought let the critic take up the book; lay it down in what thought he will, there are some things in it he can lay down no more.

That Catherine Earnshaw—at once so wonderfully fresh, so fearfully natural—new, 'as if brought from other spheres,' and familiar as the recollection of some woeful experience—what can surpass the strange compatibility of her simultaneous loves; the involuntary art with which her two natures are so made to co-exist, that in the very arms of her lover we dare not doubt her purity; the inevitable belief with which we watch the oscillations of the old and new elements in her mind, and the exquisite truth of the last victory of nature over education, when the past returns to her as a flood, sweeping every modern landmark from within her, and the soul of the child, expanding, fills the woman?

Found at last, by her husband, insensible on the breast of her lover, and dying of the agony of their parting, one looks back upon her, like that husband, without one thought of accusation or absolution; her memory is chaste as the loyalty of love, pure as the air of the Heights on which she dwelt.

Heathcliff *might* have been as unique a creation. The conception in his case was as wonderfully strong and original, but he is spoilt in detail. The authoress has too often disgusted, where she should have terrified, and has allowed us a familiarity with her fiend which had ended in unequivocal contempt. If *Wuthering Heights* had been written as lately as *Jane Eyre*, the figure of Heathcliff, symmetrised and elevated, might have been one of the most natural and most striking portraits in the gallery of fiction.

Not a subordinate place or person in this novel but bears more or less the stamp of high genius. Ellen Dean is the ideal of the peasant playmate and servant of 'the family.' The substratum in which her mind moves is finely preserved. Joseph, as a specimen of the sixty years' servitor of 'the house,' is worthy a museum case. We feel that if Catherine Earnshaw bore her husband a child, it must be that Cathy Linton, and no other. The very Jane Eyre, of quiet satire, peeps out in such a paragraph as this:—'He told me to put on my cloak, and run to Gimmerton for the doctor and the parson. I went through wind and rain, and brought one, the doctor, back with me: the other said, *he would come in the morning.*' What terrible truth, what nicety of touch, what 'uncanny' capacity for mental aberration in the first symptoms of Catherine's delirium. 'I'm not wandering; you're mistaken, or else I should believe you really *were* that withered hag, and I should think I *was* under Penistone Crags: and I'm conscious it's night, and there are two candles on the table making the black press shine like jet.' What an unobtrusive, unexpected sense of *keeping* in the hanging of Isabella's dog.

The book abounds in such things. But one looks back at the whole story as to a world of brilliant figures in an atmosphere of mist; shapes that come out upon the eye, and burn their colours into the brain, and depart into the enveloping fog. It is the unformed writing of a giant's hand: the 'large utterance' of a baby god. In the sprawling of the infant Hercules, however, there must have been attitudes from which the statuary might model. In the early efforts of unusual genius, there are not seldom unconscious felicities which maturer years may look back upon with envy. The child's hand wanders over the strings. It cannot combine them in the chords and melodies of manhood; but its separate notes are perfect in themselves, and perhaps sound all the sweeter for the Æolian discords from which they come.

We repeat, that there are passages in this book of *Wuthering Heights* of which any novelist, past or present, might be proud. Open the first volume at the fourteenth page, and read to the sixty-first. There are few things in modern prose to surpass these pages for native power. We cannot praise too warmly the brave simplicity, the unaffected air of intense belief, the admirable combination of extreme likelihood with the rarest originality, the nice provision of the possible even in the highest effects of the supernatural, the easy strength and instinct of keeping with which the accessory circumstances are grouped, the exquisite but unconscious art with which the chiaro-scuro of the whole is managed, and the ungenial frigidity of place, time, weather, and persons, is made to heighten the unspeakable pathos of one ungovernable outburst.

—Sydney Dobell, "Currer Bell," 1850,
The Life and Letters of Sydney Dobell,
ed. Emily Jolly, 1878, vol. 1, pp. 169–171

George Henry Lewes (1850)

Lewes's admiration of *Wuthering Heights* came at a time when most readers (and critics) were preoccupied by the novel's offensiveness, not impressed by its "truth" and "conscientiousness." Lewes is also relatively early in his awareness of the sex of the "Bell" authors, marveling that such coarse and powerful works as *Wuthering Heights* and *The Tenant of Wildfell Hall* were produced by "two retiring, solitary, consumptive girls!"

More specifically, Lewes praises Ellis Bell's determination to allow Catherine to love Edgar and Heathcliff, despite (or because of) the great differences between them.

Curious enough it is to read *Wuthering Heights* and *The Tenant of Wildfell Hall,* and remember that the writers were two retiring, solitary, consumptive girls! Books, coarse even for men, coarse in language and coarse in conception, the coarseness apparently of violence and uncultivated men—turn out to be the productions of two girls living almost alone, filling their loneliness with quiet studies, and writing these books from a sense of duty, hating the pictures they drew, yet drawing them with austere conscientiousness! . . .

The power, indeed, is wonderful. Heathcliff, devil though he be, is drawn with a sort of dusky splendour which fascinates, and we feel the truth of his burning and impassioned love for Catherine, and of her inextinguishable love for him. It was a happy thought to make her love the kind, weak, elegant Edgar, and yet without lessening her passion for Heathcliff. Edgar appeals to her love of refinement, and goodness, and culture; Heathcliff clutches her soul in his passionate embrace. Edgar is the husband she has chosen, the man who alone is fit to call her wife; but although she is ashamed of her early playmate she loves him with a passionate abandonment which sets culture, education, the world, at defiance. It is in the treatment of this subject that Ellis Bell shows real mastery, and it shows more genius, in the highest sense of the word, than you will find in a thousand novels.

—George Henry Lewes, *Leader,*
December 28, 1850, p. 953

Dante Gabriel Rossetti (1854)

Dante Gabriel Rossetti (1828–1882) was an English poet, painter, illustrator, and translator, perhaps best known for his collected verse, *Poems by D.G. Rossetti* (1870). He was a founding member of the Pre-Raphaelite

Brotherhood, a group of artists and writers whose works rejected the "mechanistic" direction of art they associated with artists after Raphael. Rossetti's poetry was also considered (by most, negatively) as an example of the "fleshly school of poetry" for its representation of eroticism and physicality.

—✺— —✺— —✺—

I've been greatly interested in *Wuthering Heights,* the first novel I've read for an age, and the best (as regards power and sound style) for two ages, except *Sidonia.* But it is a fiend of a book—an incredible monster, combining all the stronger female tendencies from Mrs. Browning to Mrs. Browning. The action is laid in Hell,—only it seems places and people have English names there.

—Dante Gabriel Rossetti, letter to
William Allingham, September 19, 1854

W. Clark Russell (1871)

William Clark Russell (1844–1911) was an English sailor before he became a full-time author and journalist. He wrote many supernaturally inflected novels with nautical themes, including *The Wreck of the Grosvenor* (1875) and *The Death Ship: A Strange Story* (1888).

—✺— —✺— —✺—

Wuthering Heights is a noble work. Frequent passages haunt one like scenes from *Macbeth* or the *Cenci.* In some points her genius seems superior to her sister's.

—W. Clark Russell, *The Book of Authors,*
1871, p. 499

T. Wemyss Reid (1877)

Reid's damning critique of *Wuthering Heights* makes a historical judgment that was soon to be out of date: The novel, he says, "is now practically unread." But he writes in 1877, when *Wuthering Heights* was beginning to be reassessed by critics who were newly appreciative of its narrative sophistication. Reid, however, firmly represents the mid-Victorian trend in finding *Wuthering Heights* "repulsive and almost ghastly," singling out Heathcliff's characterization as particularly offensive and deciding that the mind of his author was probably "diseased."

—✺— —✺— —✺—

Wuthering Heights, the solitary prose work of Emily Brontë, is now practically unread. Even those who admire the genius of the family, those who have the highest opinion of the qualities displayed in *Jane Eyre* or *Villette,* turn away with something like a shudder from "that dreadful book," as one who knew the Brontës intimately always calls it. But I venture to invite the attention of my readers to this story, as being in its way as marvelous a *tour de force* as *Jane Eyre* itself. It is true that as a novel it is repulsive and almost ghastly. As one reads chapter after chapter of the horrible chronicles of Heathcliff's crimes, the only literary work that can be recalled for comparison with it is the gory tragedy of *Titus Andronicus.* From the first page to the last there is hardly a redeeming passage in the book. The atmosphere is lurid and storm-laden throughout, only lighted up occasionally by the blaze of passion and madness. The hero himself is the most unmitigated villain in fiction; and there is hardly a personage in the story who is not in some shape or another the victim of mental or moral deformities. Nobody can pretend that such a story as this ever ought to have been written; nobody can read it without feeling that its author must herself have had a morbid if not diseased mind.

—T. Wemyss Reid, *Charlotte Brontë:*
A Monograph, 1877, pp. 201–202

A. Mary F. Robinson (1883)

Robinson's analysis of *Wuthering Heights* is an important piece of Brontë criticism for a number of reasons. As Emily Brontë's first biographer, Robinson had the difficult task of bringing Emily from the margins of Charlotte's story (where Gaskell's biography and Charlotte's relative popularity and prolificacy had left her) to the center of her own. To this end, Robinson had to make a powerful case for Emily's artistic genius. She also had to explain pragmatically how "this quiet clergyman's daughter" could write what was thought to be such a strange and morbid novel, an explanation that was more than necessary in the face of persistent rumors that *Wuthering Heights* was the work of Emily's more scandalous sibling, her brother, Branwell.

Thus Robinson's approach to *Wuthering Heights* is heavily biographical; in every aspect of the novel, she finds several broad correlatives to Emily's personal life. She justifies this approach by deferring to two other examples of such criticism: Charlotte's famous biographical notice and Reid's discussion of Emily in his biography of Charlotte. In the biographical notice, which Robinson excerpts, Charlotte draws a strong link between Emily's imaginative life and her immediate environment. Robinson extrapolates from this observation four principal influences on *Wuthering Heights*: "the neighborhood of her home, the character of her disposition, the quality of her experience . . . [and] her acquaintance with German literature." One of Robinson's more interesting critical maneuvers here is her reinterpretation of the darker, more controversial elements of *Wuthering Heights* as manifestations of Emily's internalized religion. This kind of recontextualization may have helped rescue *Wuthering Heights* from damning allegations of immorality. In many instances, Robinson's detective work seems clumsy and overdetermined, but the importance of her criticism still stands.

—◆◆◆— —◆◆◆— —◆◆◆—

A gray old Parsonage standing among graves, remote from the world on its wind-beaten hilltop, all round the neighboring summits wild with moors; a lonely place among half-dead ash-trees and stunted thorns, the world cut off on one side by the still ranks of the serried dead, and distanced on the other by mile-long stretches of heath: such, we know, was Emily Brontë's home.

An old, blind, disillusioned father, once prone to an extraordinary violence of temper, but now grown quiet with age, showing his disappointment with life by a melancholy cynicism that was quite sincere; two sisters, both beloved, one, fired with genius and quick to sentiment, hiding her enthusiasm under the cold demeanor of the ex-governess, unsuccessful, and unrecognized; the other gentler, dearer, fairer, slowly dying, inch by inch, of the blighting neighborhood of vice; one brother, scarce less dear, of set purpose drinking himself to death out of furious thwarted passion for a mistress that he might not marry: these were the members of Emily Brontë's household.

Herself we know: inexperienced, courageous, passionate, and full of pity. Was it wonderful that she summed up life in one bitter line?—

Conquered good and conquering ill.

Her own circumstances proved the axiom true, and of other lives she had but little knowledge. Whom should she ask? The gentle Ellen who seemed of another world, and yet had plentiful troubles of her own? The curates she despised for their narrow priggishness? The people in the village of whom she knew nothing save when sickness, wrong, or death summoned her to their homes to give help and protection? Her life had given only one view of the world, and she could not realize that there were others which she had not seen.

"I am bound to avow," says Charlotte, "that she had scarcely more practical knowledge of the peasantry among whom she lived than a nun has of the country people that pass her convent gates. My sister's disposition was not naturally gregarious; circumstances favored and fostered her tendency to seclusion; except to go to church, or to take a walk on the hills, she rarely crossed the threshold of home. Though her feeling for the people round her was benevolent, intercourse with them she never sought, nor, with very few exceptions, ever experienced; and yet she knew them, knew their ways, their language, their family histories; she could hear of them with interest and talk of them with detail, minute, graphic, and accurate; but with them she rarely exchanged a word. Hence it ensued that what her mind had gathered of the real concerning them was too exclusively confined to those tragic and terrible traits of which, in listening to the secret annals of every rude vicinage, the memory is sometimes compelled to receive the impress. Her imagination, which was a spirit more sombre than sunny, more powerful than sportive, found in such traits materials whence it wrought creations like Heathcliff, like Earnshaw, like Catharine. Having formed these beings, she did not know what she had done. If the auditors of her work, when read in manuscript, shuddered under the grinding influence of natures so relentless and implacable—of spirits so lost and fallen; if it was complained that the mere hearing of certain vivid and fearful scenes banished sleep by night and disturbed mental peace by day, Ellis Bell would wonder what was meant and suspect the complainant of affectation. Had she but lived, her mind would of itself have grown like a strong tree—loftier and straighter, wider spreading—and its matured fruits would have attained a mellower ripening and sunnier bloom; but on that mind time and experience alone could work, to the influence of other intellects it was not amenable."

Yet no human being is wholly free, none wholly independent, of surroundings. And Emily Brontë least of all could claim such immunity. We can with difficulty just imagine her a prosperous heiress, loving and loved, high-spirited and even hoydenish; but with her cavalier fantasy informed by a gracious splendor all her own, we can just imagine Emily Brontë as Shirley Keeldar, but scarcely Shirley Keeldar writing *Wuthering Heights*. Emily Brontë away from her moors, her loneliness, her poverty, her discipline, her companionship with genius, violence, and degradation, would have taken another color, as hydrangeas grow now red, now blue, according to the nature of the soil. It was not her lack of knowledge of the world that made the novel she wrote become *Wuthering Heights,* not her inexperience, but rather her experience, limited and perverse, indeed, and specialized by a most singular temperament, yet close and very real. Her imagination was as much inspired by the circumstances of her life, as was Anne's when she wrote the *Tenant of*

Wildfell Hall, or Charlotte's in her masterpiece *Villette;* but, as in each case the imagination was of a different quality, experience, acting upon it, produced a distinct and dissimilar result; a result obtained no less by the contrariety than by the harmony of circumstance. For our surroundings affect us in two ways; subtly and permanently, tingeing us through and through as wine tinges water, or, by some violent neighborhood of antipathetic force, sending us off at a tangent as far as possible from the antagonistic presence that so detestably environs us. The fact that Charlotte Brontë knew chiefly clergymen is largely responsible for *Shirley,* that satirical eulogy of the Church and apotheosis of Sunday-school teachers. But Emily, living in this same clerical evangelistic atmosphere, is revolted, forced to the other extreme; and, while sheltering her true opinions from herself under the all-embracing term "Broad Church," we find in her writings no belief so strong as the belief in the present use and glory of life; no love so great as her love for earth—earth the mother and grave; no assertion of immortality, but a deep certainty of rest. There is no note so often struck in all her work, and struck with such variety of emphasis, as this: that good for goodness' sake is desirable, evil for evil's sake detestable, and that for the just and the unjust alike there is rest in the grave.

This quiet clergyman's daughter, always hearing evil of Dissenters, has therefore from pure courage and revolted justice become a dissenter herself. A dissenter in more ways than one. Never was a nature more sensitive to the stupidities and narrowness of conventional opinion, a nature more likely to be found in the ranks of the opposition; and with such a nature indignation is the force that most often looses the gate of speech. The impulse to reveal wrongs and sufferings as they really are is overwhelmingly strong; although the revelation itself be imperfect. What, then, would this inexperienced Yorkshire parson's daughter reveal? The unlikeness of life to the authorized pictures of life; the force of evil, only conquerable by the slow-revolving process of nature which admits not the eternal duration of the perverse; the grim and fearful lessons of heredity; the sufficiency of the finite to the finite, of life to life, with no other reward than the conduct of life fulfils to him that lives; the all-penetrating kinship of living things, heather-sprig, singing lark, confident child, relentless tyrant; and, not least, not least to her already in its shadow, the sure and universal peace of death.

A strange evangel from such a preacher; but a faith evermore emphasized and deeper rooted in Emily's mind by her incapacity to acquiesce in the stiff, pragmatic teaching, the narrow prejudice, of the Calvinists of Haworth. Yet this very Calvinism influenced her ideas, this doctrine she so passionately rejected, calling herself a disciple of the tolerant and thoughtful Frederick

Maurice, and writing, in defiance of its flames and shriekings, the most soothing consolations to mortality that I remember in our tongue.

Nevertheless, so dual-natured is the force of environment, this antagonistic faith, repelling her to the extreme rebound of belief, did not send her out from it before she had assimilated some of its sternest tenets. From this doctrine of reward and punishment she learned that for every unchecked evil tendency there is a fearful expiation; though she placed it not indeed in the flames of hell, but in the perverted instincts of our own children. Terrible theories of doomed incurable sin and predestined loss warned her that an evil stock will only beget contamination: the children of the mad must be liable to madness; the children of the depraved, bent towards depravity; the seed of the poison-plant springs up to blast and ruin, only to be overcome by uprooting and sterilization, or by the judicious grafting, the patient training of many years.

Thus prejudiced and evangelical Haworth had prepared the woman who rejected its Hebraic dogma, to find out for herself the underlying truths. She accepted them in their full significance. It has been laid as a blame to her that she nowhere shows any proper abhorrence of the fiendish and vindictive Heathcliff. She who reveals him remembers the dubious parentage of that forsaken seaport baby, "Lascar or Gipsy;" she remembers the Ishmaelitish childhood, too much loved and hated, of the little interloper whose hand was against every man's hand. Remembering this, she submits as patiently to his swarthy soul and savage instincts as to his swarthy skin and "gibberish that nobody could understand." From thistles you gather no grapes.

No use, she seems to be saying, in waiting for the children of evil parents to grow, of their own will and unassisted, straight and noble. The very quality of their will is as inherited as their eyes and hair. Heathcliff is no fiend or goblin; the untrained doomed child of some half-savage sailor's holiday, violent and treacherous. And how far shall we hold the sinner responsible for a nature which is itself the punishment of some forefather's crime? Even for such there must be rest. No possibility in the just and reverent mind of Emily Brontë that the God whom she believed to be the very fount and soul of life could condemn to everlasting fire the victims of morbid tendencies not chosen by themselves. No purgatory, and no everlasting flame, is needed to purify the sins of Heathcliff; his grave on the hillside will grow as green as any other spot of grass, moor-sheep will find the grass as sweet, heath and harebells will grow of the same color on it as over a baby's grave. For life and sin and punishment end with death to the dying man; he slips his burden then on to other shoulders, and no visions mar his rest.

"I wondered how any one could ever imagine unquiet slumbers for the sleepers in that quiet earth." So ends the last page of *Wuthering Heights.*

So much for the theories of life and evil that the clash of circumstance and character struck out from Emily Brontë . It happened, as we know, that she had occasion to test these theories; and but for that she could never have written *Wuthering Heights.* Not that the story, the conception, would have failed. After all there is nothing more appalling in the violent history of that upland farm than many a midland manor set thick in elms, many a wild country-house of Wales or Cornwall, could unfold. Stories more socially painful than the mere brute violence of the Earnshaws; of madness and treachery, stories of girls entrapped unwillingly into a lunatic marriage that the estate might have an heir; legends of fearful violence, of outcast children, dishonored wives, horrible and persistent evil. Who, in the secret places of his memory, stores not up such haunting gossip? And Emily, familiar with all the wild stories of Haworth for a century back, and nursed on grisly Irish horrors, tales of 1798, tales of oppression and misery, Emily, with all this eerie lore at her finger-ends, would have the less difficulty in combining and working the separate motives into a consistent whole, that she did not know the real people whose histories she knew by heart. No memory of individual manner, dominance or preference for an individual type, caught and disarranged her theories, her conception being the completer from her ignorance. This much her strong reason and her creative power enabled her to effect. But this is not all.

This is the plot; but to make a character speak, act, rave, love, live, die, through a whole lifetime of events, even as the readers feel convinced he must have acted, must have lived and died, this demands at least so much experience of a somewhat similar nature as may serve for a base to one's imagination, a reserve of certainty and reassurance on which to draw in times of perplexity and doubt. Branwell, who sat to Anne sorrily enough for the portrait of Henry Huntingdon, served his sister Emily, not indeed as a model, a thing to copy, but as a chart of proportions by which to measure, and to which to refer, for correct investiture, the inspired idea. Mr. Wemyss Reid (whose great knowledge of the Brontë history and still greater kindness in admitting me to his advantages as much as might be, I cannot sufficiently acknowledge)—this capable critic perceives a *bona fide* resemblance between the character of Heathcliff and the character of Branwell Brontë as he appeared to his sister Emily. So much, bearing in mind the verse concerning the leveret, I own I cannot see. Branwell seems to me more nearly akin to Heathcliff's miserable son than to Heathcliff. But that, in depicting Heathcliff's outrageous thwarted love for Catharine, Emily did draw upon her experience of her brother's suffering, this extract from an unpublished lecture of Mr. Reid's will sufficiently reveal:

"It was in the enforced companionship of this lost and degraded man that Emily received, I am sure, many of the impressions which were subsequently conveyed to the pages of her book. Has it not been said over and over again by critics of every kind that *Wuthering Heights* reads like the dream of an opium-eater? And here we find that during the whole time of the writing of the book an habitual and avowed opium-eater was at Emily's elbow. I said that perhaps the most striking part of *Wuthering Heights* was that which deals with the relations of Heathcliff and Catharine after she had become the wife of another. Whole pages of the story are filled with the ravings and ragings of the villain against the man whose life stands between him and the woman he loves. Similar ravings are to be found in all the letters of Branwell Brontë written at this period of his career; and we may be sure that similar ravings were always on his lips as, moody and more than half mad, he wandered about the rooms of the parsonage at Haworth. Nay, I have found some striking verbal coincidences between Branwell's own language and passages in *Wuthering Heights*. In one of his own letters there are these words in reference to the object of his passion: 'My own life without her will be hell. What can the so-called love of her wretched sickly husband be to her compared with mine?' Now, turn to *Wuthering Heights* and you will read these words: 'Two words would comprehend my future—death and hell; existence after losing her would be hell. Yet I was a fool to fancy for a moment that she valued Edgar Linton's attachment more than mine. If he loved with all the powers of his puny being, he couldn't love in eighty years as much as I could in a day.' "

So much share in *Wuthering Heights* Branwell certainly had. He was a page of the book in which his sister studied; he served, as to an artist's temperament all things unconsciously serve, for the rough block of granite out of which the work is hewn, and, even while with difficulty enduring his vices, Emily undoubtedly learned from them those darker secrets of humanity necessary to her tragic incantation. They served her, those dreaded, passionate outbreaks of her brother's, even as the moors she loved, the fancy she courted, served her. Strange divining wand of genius, that conjures gold out of the miriest earth of common life; strange and terrible faculty laying up its stores and half-mechanically drawing its own profit out of our slightest or most miserable experiences, noting the gesture with which the mother hears of her son's ruin, catching the faint varying shadow that the white wind-shaken window-blind sends over the dead face by which we watch, drawing its life from a thousand deaths, humiliations, losses, with a hand in our sharpest joys and bitterest sorrows; this faculty was Emily Brontë's, and drew its profit from her brother's shame.

Here ended Branwell's share in producing *Wuthering Heights*. But it is not well to ignore his claim to its entire authorship; for in the contemptuous silence of those who know their falsity, such slanders live and thrive like unclean insects under fallen stones. The vain boast of an unprincipled dreamer, half-mad with opium, half-drunk with gin, meaning nothing but the desire to be admired at any cost, has been given too much prominence by those lovers of sensation who prefer any startling lie to an old truth. Their ranks have been increased by the number of those who, ignorant of the true circumstances of Emily's life, found it impossible that an inexperienced girl could portray so much violence and such morbid passion. On the contrary, given these circumstances, none but a personally inexperienced girl could have treated the subject with the absolute and sexless purity which we find in *Wuthering Heights*. How *infecte,* commonplace, and ignominious would Branwell, relying on his own recollections, have made the thwarted passion of a violent adventurer for a woman whose sickly husband both despise! That purity as of polished steel, as cold and harder than ice, that freedom in dealing with love and hate, as audacious as an infant's love for the bright flame of fire, could only belong to one whose intensity of genius was rivalled by the narrowness of her experience—an experience limited not only by circumstances, but by a nature impervious to any fierier sentiment than the natural love of home and her own people, beginning before remembrance and as unconscious as breathing.

The critic, having Emily's poems and the few remaining verses and letters of Branwell, cannot doubt the incapacity of that unnerved and garrulous prodigal to produce a work of art so sustained, passionate, and remote. For in no respect does the terse, fiery, imaginative style of Emily resemble the weak, disconnected, now vulgar, now pretty mannerisms of Branwell. There is, indeed, scant evidence that the writer of Emily's poems could produce *Wuthering Heights;* but there is, at any rate, the impossibility that her work could be void of fire, concentration, and wild fancy. As great an impossibility as that vulgarity and tawdriness should not obtrude their ugly heads here and there from under Branwell's finest phrases. And since there is no single vulgar, trite, or Micawber-like effusion throughout *Wuthering Heights;* and since Heathcliff's passion is never once treated in the despicable would-be worldly fashion in which Branwell describes his own sensations, and since at the time that *Wuthering Heights* was written he was manifestly, and by his own confession, too physically prostrate for any literary effort, we may conclude that Branwell did not write the book.

On the other side we have not only the literary evidence of the similar qualities in *Wuthering Heights* and in the poems of Ellis Bell, but the express and reiterated assurance of Charlotte Brontë , who never even dreamed, it would seem, that it could be supposed her brother wrote the book; the testimony of the publishers who made their treaty with Ellis Bell; of the servant Martha who saw her mistress writing it; and—most convincing of all to those who have appreciated the character of Emily Brontë—the impossibility that a spirit so upright and so careless of fame should commit a miserable fraud to obtain it.

Indeed, so baseless is this despicable rumor that to attack it seems absurd, only sometimes it is wise to risk an absurdity. Puny insects, left too long unhurt, may turn out dangerous enemies irretrievably damaging the fertile vine on which they fastened in the security of their minuteness.

To the three favoring circumstances of Emily's masterpiece, which we have already mentioned—the neighborhood of her home, the character of her disposition, the quality of her experience—a fourth must be added, inferior in degree, and yet not absolutely unimportant. This is her acquaintance with German literature, and especially with Hoffmann's tales. In Emily Brontë's day, Romance and Germany had one significance; it is true that in London and in prose the German influence was dying out, but in distant Haworth, and in the writings of such poets as Emily would read, in Scott, in Southey, most of all in Coleridge, with whose poems her own have so distinct an affinity, it is still predominant. Of the materialistic influence of Italy, of atheist Shelley, Byron with his audacity and realism, sensuous Keats, she would have little experience in her remote parsonage. And, had she known them, they would probably have made no impression on a nature only susceptible to kindred influences. Thackeray, her sister's hero, might have never lived for all the trace of him we find in Emily's writings; never is there any single allusion in her work to the most eventful period of her life, that sight of the lusher fields and taller elms of middle England; that glimpse of hurrying vast London; that night on the river, the sun slipping behind the masts, doubly large through the mist and smoke in which the houses, bridges, ships, are all spectral and dim. No hint of this, nor of the sea, nor of Belgium, with its quaint foreign life; nor yet of that French style and method so carefully impressed upon her by Monsieur Heger, and which so decidedly moulded her elder sister's art. But in the midst of her business at Haworth we catch a glimpse of her reading her German book at night, as she sits on the hearthrug with her arm round Keeper's neck; glancing at it in the kitchen, where she is making bread, with the volume of her choice propped up before her; and by the style of the novel jotted down in the rough, almost simultaneously with her reading, we know that to her the study of German was not—like French and music—the mere necessary acquirement of a governess, but an influence that entered her mind and helped to shape the fashion of her thoughts.

So much preface is necessary to explain, not the genius of Emily Brontë, but the conditions of that genius—there is no use saying more. The aim of my writing has been missed if the circumstances of her career are not present in the mind of my reader. It is too late at this point to do more than enumerate them, and briefly point to their significance. Such criticism, in face of the living work, is all too much like glancing in a green and beautiful country at a map, from which one may, indeed, ascertain the roads that lead to it and away, and the size of the place in relation to surrounding districts, but which can give no recognizable likeness of the scene which lies all round us, with its fresh life forgotten and its beauty disregarded. Therefore let us make an end of theory and turn to the book on which our heroine's fame is stationed, fronting eternity. It may be that in unravelling its story and noticing the manner in which its facts of character and circumstance impressed her mind, we may, for a moment, be admitted to a more thorough and clearer insight into its working than we could earn by the completest study of external evidence, the most earnest and sympathizing criticism.

—A. Mary F. Robinson, "*Wuthering Heights:*
Its Origin," *Emily Brontë*, 1883, pp. 206–224

FREDERIC HARRISON (1895)

Harrison was not the only nineteenth-century critic to compare Emily Brontë's work to Coleridge: A. Mary F. Robinson did so in her 1883 biography of the author, but in a reference to Emily's poetry, not *Wuthering Heights*. For Robinson, the Coleridge comparison was also a compliment, whereas Harrison seems to be invoking the opiate haze of *Kubla Khan* quite negatively in this nod to *Wuthering Heights*.

In considering the gifted Brontë family, it is really Charlotte alone who finally concerns us. Emily Brontë was a wild, original, and striking creature, but her one book is a kind of prose *Kubla Khan*—a nightmare of the superheated imagination.

—Frederic Harrison, "Charlotte Brontë's
Place in Literature," *Forum*,
March 1895, p. 32

CLEMENT K. SHORTER
(1896)

The contrast between Shorter's estimation of *Wuthering Heights* as a signal of "the most striking genius that nineteenth-century womanhood has
given us" and Harrison's qualified admission of Emily's originality in the
previous excerpt is a fascinating testament to the critical divergence on
Emily's talents and *Wuthering Heights*'s importance.

—————— —————— ——————

She wrote *Wuthering Heights* because she was impelled thereto, and the
book, with all its morbid force and fire, will remain, for all time, as a monument
of the most striking genius that nineteenth century womanhood has given us.
It was partly her life in Yorkshire—the local colour was mainly derived from
her brief experience as a governess at Halifax—but it was partly, also, the
German fiction which she had devoured during the Brussels period, that
inspired *Wuthering Heights*.

—Clement K. Shorter, *Charlotte Brontë*
and Her Circle, 1896, p. 158

RICHARD D. GRAHAM (1897)

Graham's review of *Wuthering Heights* returns to the biographical and
shows that the fascination with Emily's alleged isolation did not recede
at the *fin de siècle*. Graham considers William Wright's *Brontës in Ireland*
as a plausible account of the family mythos (Irish folklore passed from
Patrick Brontë to his novelist daughters); other critics (notably Reid)
found Wright's "evidence" of the Irish influence on the Brontë daughters
superficial and suspiciously inventive. Still, Graham maintains that our
lack of substantiated knowledge of Emily Brontë qualifies her as "the
Sphinx of Victorian literature."

—————— —————— ——————

Her *Wuthering Heights* is a strange, forbidding tale, and no one can read it
without wondering how characters and incidents so coarse and repulsive
could ever have occurred to a being so retiring and so ignorant of life as
she. We have seen how Dr. Wright in his *Brontës in Ireland* has plausibly
suggested that the knowledge of the seamy side of human character and life
revealed in the work of these sisters came to them from their familiarity
with the legends concerning the older Brontës, with which he supposes
their father's memory to have been stored; but until his theory finds for

itself a firmer basis of authentic fact, Emily Brontë must remain the Sphinx of Victorian literature.

—Richard D. Graham, *The Masters of*
Victorian Literature, 1897, p. 45

Hugh Walker (1897)

Walker, musing about the direction that Emily's art would have taken had she not died so young, speculates that her writing would probably have improved. Yet he asserts that the regard she seems to show for the contemptible Heathcliff reflects certain fundamental flaws in her psyche that aesthetic development could not have eradicated.

Wuthering Heights is her only novel, for she died the year after its publication. It remains therefore uncertain whether she would have mastered her errors, or whether, as in her sister's case, her first work was to be her greatest. The probability is that she would have improved. She was only thirty; and the defects *of Wuthering Heights* are artistic,—faulty construction, want of proportion, absence of restraint. These are defects which experience might be expected to overcome; especially as Emily Brontë's verse showed that she was by no means without taste. There are flaws in the substance too; and it is less likely that these would have disappeared. Even Mrs. Gaskell could not deny that there is some foundation for the charge of coarseness brought against Charlotte; and there is more in the case of Emily. It is not merely that her characters are harsh and repulsive: there are not a few such characters in life, and there were many of them within the experience of the Brontë family. But besides, Emily Brontë appears to sympathise with, and sometimes to admire, the harsher and less lovable features of the characters she draws. Heathcliff is spoilt for most readers by the seemingly loving minuteness with which the author elaborates the worst characteristics of his nature, characteristics familiar to her from family legend.

—Hugh Walker, *The Age of Tennyson,*
1897, p. 103

Wilbur L. Cross (1899)

Cross's somewhat eccentric description of *Wuthering Heights* re-creates Heathcliff's experience from the character's own perspective. In effect,

Cross underscores his description of *Wuthering Heights* as a gothic romance by emphasizing not only Heathcliff's inner torment but also the supreme alienation that Emily imbued him with. Despite the dramatic nature of his description, though, Cross condones the violence of *Wuthering Heights*, claiming that "romantic fiction" has never exceeded "the madness and terror" of the novel.

———— ———— ————

In literary history the precise time order of events is not always the precise logical order. The long vista of the purely Gothic romance, at whose entrance stands the blood-stained castle of Otranto, is closed by a storm and passion beaten house on the Yorkshire moors. The motive of Emily Brontë's *Wuthering Heights* (1847) is vengeance. Relieved of all impertinences of time and place, the situation is this: A man sits down and reflects: I was born in shame; men have denied me education; and they have taken from me the woman I loved, on the ground that I am unworthy of her. I am not responsible for being what I am; I did not preside over my birth; the demon within me that I tried to suppress, others loosed from his bands. The vengeance that the Almighty has allowed to sleep I myself will wake and wreak upon those who have wronged me, and upon their children. After years of appalling success in meting out the punishment of a Jehovah, one obstacle stands in the way to the consummation of the entire scheme of revenge. Face to face with defeat, the will loses none of its tension; the defier of gods and men starves himself into delirium and death; his eyes that will not close still glare in exultation, and his lip is curled in a sneer, displaying sharp white teeth beneath. He is placed in the ground near the woman the side of whose coffin he had long ago in his mad grief torn away, that he might lie the closer to her. Beyond the madness and terror of *Wuthering Heights*, romantic fiction has never gone. Its spiritual counterpart in real life is Emily Brontë, who preserved her inexorable will far into the day on which she died.

—Wilbur L. Cross, *The Development of the English Novel*, 1899, pp. 166–167

WILLIAM DEAN HOWELLS (1900)

William Dean Howells (1837–1920), an American, started his writing career as a journalist and quickly inspired the attention of eminent writers Oliver Wendall Holmes and James Russell Lowell. Early in his career, Howells wrote a campaign biography for Abraham Lincoln that led to his appointment as U.S. consul in Venice (1861–1865). Back in the United States, Howells reentered journalism and soon after became the editor of the *Atlantic Monthly* (1871–1881). During this time, he also began writing novels, including *Their Wedding Journey* (1872), *The Undiscovered Country* (1880), and *Dr. Breen's Practice* (1881). After leaving the *Atlantic Monthly*, Howells published his best-known novel, *The Rise of Silas Lampham* (1885), joined the editorial staff of *Harper's Bazaar*, and continued writing fiction and nonfiction. In the early twentieth century, Howells was known as the foremost literary man in the United States and counted among his friends writers such as Mark Twain and Henry James.

In his assessment of Emily Brontë's heroines, Howells rescues *Wuthering Heights* from its frequent charges of crudity and says that the novel's heroines display an authentic "savagery of nature." Further, Emily's representation of the love between Heathcliff and the first Catherine unobjectionably reflects "the wholesome[ness] and decen[cy]" of a thunderstorm.

Howells tellingly faults the construction of *Wuthering Heights* at the same time that other critics were starting to celebrate the novel's unusually complex narrative design. He also strays from popular opinion in finding the characters of *Wuthering Heights* convincing; despite their luridness and crudity, he contends, "they have an intense and convincing reality." He goes on to praise the relative distance between Emily and her characters, saying that she remains "superior to her material," whereas Charlotte has a tendency to identify herself through her heroines.

The heroines of Emily Brontë have not the artistic completeness of Charlotte Brontë's. They are blocked out with hysterical force, and in their character there is something elemental, as if, like the man who beat and browbeat them, they too were close to the savagery of nature. The sort of supernaturalism, which appears here and there in their story, wants the refinement of the telepathy and presentiment which play a part in *Jane Eyre*, but it is still more effectual in the ruder clutch which it lays upon the fancy.

In her dealing with the wild passion of Heathcliff for the first Catharine, Emily Brontë does not keep even such slight terms with convention as Charlotte does in the love of Rochester and Jane Eyre; but this fierce longing, stated as it were in its own language, is still farther from anything that corrupts or tempts; it is as wholesome and decent as a thunder-storm, in the consciousness of the witness. The perversities of the mutual attraction of the lovers are rendered without apparent sense on the part of the author that they can seem out of nature, so deeply does she feel them to be in nature, and there is no hint from her that they need any sort of proof. It is vouchsafed us to know that Heathcliff is a foundling of unknown origin, early fixed in his hereditary evils by the cruelty of Hindley Earnshaw, whose father has adopted him; but it is not explained why he should have his malign power upon Catharine. Perhaps it is enough that she is shown a wilful, impetuous, undisciplined girl, whose pity has been moved for the outcast before her fancy is taken. After that we are told what happens and are left to account for it as we may.

We are very badly told, in terms of autobiography thrice involved. First, we have the narrative of Heathcliff's tenant, then within his the narrative of the tenant's housekeeper, as she explains the situation she has witnessed at Heathcliff's house, and then within hers the several narratives of the actors in the tragedy. Seldom has a great romance been worse contrived, both as to generals and particulars, but the essentials are all there, and the book has a tremendous vitality. If it were of the fashion of any other book, it might have passed away, but it is of its own fashion solely, and it endures like a piece of the country in which its scenes are laid, enveloped in a lurid light and tempestuous atmosphere of its own. Its people are all of extreme types, and yet they do not seem unreal, like the extravagant creations of Dickens's fancy; they have an intense and convincing reality, the weak ones, such as Heathcliff's wife and son, equally with the powerful, such as Heathcliff himself and the Catharines, mother and daughter. A weird malevolence broods over the gloomy drama, and through all plays a force truly demoniacal, with scarcely the relief of a moment's kindliness. The facts are simply conceived, and stated without shadow of apology or extenuation; and the imagination from which they sprang cannot adequately be called morbid, for it deals with the brute motives employed without a taint of sickly subjectiveness. The author remains throughout superior to her material; her creations have all a distinct projection, and in this, Emily Brontë shows herself a greater talent than Charlotte, who is never quite detached from her heroine, but is always trammelled in sympathy with Jane Eyre, with whom she is united by ties of a like vocation and experience, as governess. You feel that she is present in all Jane's sufferings, small and great, if not in her raptures; but Emily Brontë keeps as sternly aloof from both her Catharines as from Heathcliff himself. She bequeathed the world at her early death a single book of as singular power as any in fiction; and proved herself, in spite of its defective technique, a great artist, of as realistic motive and ideal as any who have followed her. . . .

No one can deny the charm of this, the absolute reality, the consummate art, which is still art, however unconscious. Did the dying girl who wrote the strange book, where it is only one of so many scenes of unfaltering truth, know how great it was, with all its defects? In any case criticism must recognize its mastery, and rejoice in its courage.

—William Dean Howells, "Heroines of Nineteenth-Century Fiction: XIX. The Two Catharines of Emily Brontë," *Harper's Bazaar*, December 29, 1900, pp. 224–230

ALICE MEYNELL (1917)

Alice Christiana Gertrude Thompson Meynell (1847–1922) was a poet, writer, critic, editor, and suffragist. Her first poetry collection was *Preludes* (1875), and later publications (poetry and nonfiction) include *Ruskin* (1900), *Later Poems* (1901), and *The Work of John S. Sargent* (1903). In 1940, Oxford University Press published *The Poems of Alice Meynell*, a compilation of her complete works.

Meynell also worked with her husband, Wilfred Meynell, as owner and editor of newspapers including *The Pen*, *The Weekly Register*, and *Merry England*, to which she also contributed. She was active in the Women Writers' Suffrage League in the second decade of the twentieth century.

Meynell's admiration for *Wuthering Heights* liberates Emily Brontë from some of the conventional expectations of an author, such as the assumed requirement that the reader identify with the novelist's creations. Instead, Meynell classifies Brontë's inventions as figments of her rare and mysterious imagination that most readers cannot hope to fully grasp.

Heathcliff's love for Catherine's past childhood is one of the profound surprises of this unparalleled book; it is to call her childish ghost—the ghost of the little girl—when she has been a dead adult woman twenty years that the inhuman lover opens the window of the house on the Heights. Something is this that the reader knew not how to look for. Another thing known to genius and beyond a reader's hope is the tempestuous purity of those passions. This wild quality of purity has a counterpart in the brief passages of nature that make the summers, the waters, the woods, and the windy heights of that murderous story seem so sweet. The "beck" that was audible beyond the hills after rain, the "heath on the top of Wuthering Heights" whereon, in her dream of Heaven, Catherine, flung out by angry angels, awoke sobbing for joy; the bird whose feathers she—delirious creature—plucks from the pillow of her deathbed ("This—It should know it among a thousand—it's a lapwing's. Bonny bird; wheeling over our heads in the middle of the moor. It wanted to get to its nest, for the clouds had touched the swells and it felt rain coming"); the two only white spots of snow left on all the moors, and the brooks brim-full; the old apple-trees, the smell of stocks and wallflowers in the brief summer, the few fir-trees by Catherine's window-bars, the early moon—I know not where are landscapes more exquisite and natural. And among the signs of death where is any fresher than the window seen from the garden to be swinging open in the morning, when Heathcliff lay within, dead and drenched with rain?

None of these things are presented by images. Nor is that signal passage wherewith the book comes to a close. Be it permitted to cite it here again. It has taken its place, it is among the paragons of our literature. Our language will not lapse or derogate while this prose stands for appeal: "I lingered under that benign sky; watched the moths fluttering among the heath and harebells, listened to the soft wind breathing through the grass, and wondered how anyone could ever imagine unquiet slumbers for the sleepers in that quiet earth."

Finally, of Emily Brontë's face the world holds only an obviously unskilled reflection, and of her aspect no record worth having. Wild fugitive, she vanished, she escaped, she broke away, exiled by the neglect of her contemporaries, banished by their disrespect, outlawed by their contempt, dismissed by their indifference. And such an one was she as might rather have taken for her own the sentence pronounced by Coriolanus under sentence of expulsion; she might have driven the world from before her face and cast it out from her presence as he condemned his Romans: "*I* banish you."

—Alice Meynell, "Charlotte and Emily Brontë," 1911, *Hearts of Controversy*, 1917, pp. 96–99

POETRY

While all the Brontë sisters wrote poetry and published together *Poems, by Currer, Ellis, and Acton Bell* (1846), only Emily Brontë received critical commendation in the nineteenth century as an important poet. She was a far more prolific poet than either of her sisters, and about 200 poems survive that have been identified as hers. These date back to the mid-1830s, when she was in her teens, and extend to shortly before her death in 1848. Much of Emily's poetry (especially the earlier works) portrays her imaginative world of Gondal, and these works have collectively been treated as an epic.

The critical response to Emily's poetry is far more consistent than that to *Wuthering Heights*. Critics frequently commend the strength, stoicism, and grimness of her voice, as well as her ability to embody nature. They often reproach the constructions of her verses, finding them hastily assembled with too little attention to poetic meter and rhythm (Gosse calls some of her poems "disjointed"). As with *Wuthering Heights*, few miss an opportunity to read Emily's later poems (those not overtly tied to Gondal) as explicitly autobiographical statements, treating them as stark testaments to an uncompromising mind. Many critics quite plaintively wonder how exactly the great promise she showed from an early age might have been developed, had she not died so young.

EDMUND GOSSE (1880)

Edmund William Gosse (1849–1928) was an English poet, novelist, and critic of art (especially sculpture) and literature. His scholarly work included literary surveys—*A History of Eighteenth-Century Literature* (1889) and *History of Modern English Literature* (1897). The wide scope of such studies informs his consideration of Emily Brontë's poetry, which draws on earlier nineteenth-century female poets (Felicia Hemans and Letitia Landon). He also takes a biographical approach in incorporating details about Emily's personality, such as her stoicism and strangeness, into her poetic voice.

———— ⌁⌁⌁ —— ⌁⌁⌁ —— ⌁⌁⌁ ————

Not even the unstinted praise of three great and very dissimilar poets has given to Emily Brontë her due rank in popular esteem. Her work is not universally acceptable, even to imaginative readers; her personality is almost repulsive to many who have schooled themselves to endure the vehemence of genius but not its ominous self-restraint. Most people were afraid of Emily Brontë's 'whitening face and set mouth' when she was alive, and even now that she is dead her memory seems to inspire more terror than affection. Against an instinctive repugnance it is in vain to reason, and in discussing her poetical quality we must assume that her power has at least been felt and not disliked by the reader, since 'you must love her, ere to you she should seem worthy to be loved.' Those who have come under the spell of her genius will expect no apology for her intellectual rebellion, her stoic harshness of purpose, her more than manlike strength. She was a native blossom of those dreary and fascinating moorlands of which Charlotte has given, in a few brilliant phrases, so perfect a description, and like the acrid heaths and gentians that flourish in the peat, to transplant her was to kill her. Her actions, like her writings, were strange, but consistent in their strangeness. Even the dreadful incident of her death, which occurred as she stood upright in the little parlour at Haworth, refusing to go to bed, but just leaning one hand upon the table, seems to me to be no unfit ending for a life so impatient of constraint from others, so implacable in its slavery to its own principles.

The poetry of Emily Brontë is small in extent and conventional in form. Its burning thoughts are concealed for the most part in the tame and ambling measures dedicated to female verse by the practice of Felicia Hemans and Letitia Landon. That she was progressing to the last even in this matter of the form is shown by the little posthumous collection of her verses issued by Charlotte, consisting of early, and very weak pieces, and of two poems written in the last year of her life, which attain, for the first time, the majesty of rhythm demanded by such sublime emotions. But it is impossible not to regret that she missed that accomplishment in the art of poetry which gives an added force to the verse of her great French contemporary, Marceline Valmore, the only modern poetess who can fitly be compared with Emily Brontë for power of expressing passion in its simplicity. In the 1846 volume there are but few of the contributions of Ellis Bell in which the form is adequate to the thought. Even 'The Prisoner', certain lines of which have justly called forth Mr. Swinburne's admiration, is on the whole a disjointed and halting composition. The moving and tear-compelling elegy called 'A Death-Scene', in conception one of the most original and passionate poems in existence, is clothed in a measure that is like the livery of a charitable institution. This limitation of style does not interfere with the beauty of her three or four best poems, where indeed it does not exist, but it prevents the poetess in all but these superlative successes from attaining that harmony and directness of utterance which should characterise a song so unflinchingly sincere as hers.

It is difficult to praise Emily's three or four greatest poems without an air of exaggeration. Finest among them all is that outburst of agnostic faith that was found by Charlotte on her desk when she died, a 'last poem' not to be surpassed in dignity and self-reliance by any in the language. 'The Old Stoic' might have prepared us for the 'Last Lines' by its concentrated force and passion. But the 'chainless soul' of the author found its most characteristic utterance in the 'Stanzas'.

—Edmund Gosse, "Emily Brontë,"
The English Poets, ed. Thomas Humphry Ward
1880, vol. 4, pp. 581–582

A.M. WILLIAMS "EMILY BRONTË" (1893)

In the following reading of Emily Brontë's work, A.M. Williams strikes some familiar chords. He expresses surprise that one so inexperienced could write a book of such complexity, he remarks on her excellent characterizations of Heathcliff, Catherine, and others, and he bemoans her premature death.

One of Williams's focuses here is the importance of the Yorkshire landscape to Emily's imaginative life. In both *Wuthering Heights* and the poetry, Williams perceives an extraordinary "susceptibility to nature" that "carries her into veins of thought that recall the imaginings of Shelley." This aspect of Emily's work has been noted by numerous critics (including Charlotte), but Williams identifies it as one of her most striking literary gifts.

Another strain that Williams points out in Emily's poetry is an attitude of resilience and grim hopefulness; even in the face of death, he says, her "brave, strong spirit" defies despair. Like many other posthumous reviews of Emily's work, this piece has a rather melancholic tone.

One can readily see that she could have owed little to influences outside Haworth, and little more to reading; for, situated as she was, she could have had access to only a comparatively small number of books. The question then is, whence came the influences that helped to form the powerful character that confronts us in her writings? One potent influence was the moors. They were to her more than objects of sensuous enjoyment. She loved them with a deep, passionate love; they informed her with their own strong, wild nature; their dreariest, gloomiest aspects found harmonies in her stern spirit; their purple heather glowing in the autumn sun stirred her with full, rich joy. Charlotte has written of her sister's love for the moors, and in Emily's novel, *Wuthering Heights,* a striking passage reveals the pleasure Emily derived from the scenery about Haworth. "He said the pleasantest manner of spending a hot July day was lying from morning till evening on a bank of heath in the middle of the moors, with the bees humming dreamily about among the bloom, and the larks singing high up overhead, and the blue sky and bright sun shining steadily and cloudlessly. That was his most perfect ideal of heaven's happiness; mine was rocking in a rustling green tree, with a west wind blowing and bright white clouds flitting rapidly above, and not only larks, but throstles, and blackbirds, and linnets, and cuckoos, pouring out music on every side, and the moors seen at a distance, broken into cool, dusky dells; but close by great swells of long grass undulating in waves to the breezes, and woods and sounding water, and the whole world awake and wild with joy." The same feeling finds expression in her poems, as in 'The Bluebell,' and in the piece beginning, "Loud without the wind was roaring." Another powerful influence was her father. He is described as a passionate, self-willed, vain, cold, and distant man, stern and determined, ever eager to maintain his opinions, whether or not they harmonised with the popular judgment—a man, indeed, whose instincts were soldierly rather than priestly. This description is so far supported by Charlotte's presentment of him in the Mr. Helstone of *Shirley*. Mr. Brontë had many wild stories and traditions of his native Ireland, and he delighted, by means of them, to excite terror in his children. We may be sure that, despite their terrifying effect, these tales of danger and dread appealed strongly to Emily's bold and fearless mind. Similar stories were told to the children by their aunt, Miss Branwell, who had brought from Cornwall a goodly store of such weird narratives as Mr. Hunt has brought together in his *Romances and Drolls of the West of England*. Tabby was an authority on Yorkshire traditions, and had strange things to tell of old-world doings in the county. The effect of all this was early seen. While still in the nursery the little Brontës were writing romances, and all Emily's stories reflected the wild, creepy tales she had become familiar with.

On a larger scale the same influence is at work in Emily's extraordinary novel, *Wuthering Heights*. For extraordinary it is, whether we regard the form or the substance. There are faults of expression and of treatment; but in *Wuthering Heights* we have the first novel of a young woman with little knowledge either of literature or of life, and yet the story is told with compactness and force, scenery is described with marvellous vividness and sympathy, characters are represented with amazing individuality, while, though incidents and characters are at times so appalling that many readers turn from the book in horror, there is such power, both of personality and of treatment, as positively fascinates even while it terrifies. But it should be noted Emily Brontë had no conscious intention of exciting terror. It is true that, as Heathcliff reveals himself in all his savagery, one stands aghast at his wolfish ferocity; yet one can plainly see that the author is not seeking for means of affecting her readers, but, heedless of readers, is working out her altogether astounding conception.

The promise of the book is found not in the story (though what story there is is clearly told) but in the delineation of character. Heathcliff is a wonderful, if repulsive, creation. His wife asks questions that the reader often asks: "Is Mr. Heathcliff a man? If so, is he mad? And, if not, is he a devil?" It is difficult to say when he is most terrible—when he is behaving like the incarnation of cruelty, when he is raving in the very delirium of passionate love for Catherine Earnshaw, when he is wandering by midnight among the graves out on the moors, haunted by a feeling of the presence of the dead Catherine, when he is calling on her spirit with wailings of intensest agony, or when in the last days he moves like one in a dream, seeing some vision that gladdens him and yet robs him of all power to live, till the morning comes when he is found dead, with fierce and staring eyes. A repulsive creation, and yet it may safely be said that the imagination that conjured up a monster like Heathcliff, and developed his character with such force, was equal to high creative work. But there is more than potential merit of character-drawing. The younger Catherine has some charming traits: her light-heartedness and fearlessness, if at times they seem to verge on recklessness and careless despair, are at other times exceedingly attractive. Isabella Linton, though an inconsistent and somewhat sketchy conception, shows glimpses of a noble dignity when face to face with the dreadful life she has to lead at Wuthering Heights. Edgar Linton, if cast in too weak a mould, is yet in many respects well drawn. Gentleness, courtesy, deep and true affection, and scholarly tastes, make him a strong contrast to the wild and uncultured Heathcliff, that "arid wilderness of furze and whinstone"; and if at times his character is allowed to become ignobly unmanly, enough of excellence remains to show that Emily Brontë could conceive a refined and cultured mind. Probably the strongest assurance that her genius was capable of careful, steady work as well as of wild flights is to be found in the two servants, Nelly Dean and Joseph. Both characters are well conceived, but Joseph is admirable. His faithfulness to the family he had served so long, his rugged nature, his unbending and repellent Calvinism, his certainty as to his own sanctity and his doubt as to every other body's—all these are well set forth. Joseph is interesting in another way: he gives Emily Brontë opportunities of showing that she can handle the ludicrous with considerable effect. There is genuine humour in some of Joseph's appearances, all the more that his efforts as a humorist are quite unconscious.

In strong contrast to the gloom cast over the story by Heathcliff is the beauty of those passages that tell how Catherine Linton does all she can to soften the ruggedness in Hareton Earnshaw's disposition, and to raise him above the degraded level to which Heathcliff had depressed him, and of those that reveal the author's susceptibility to nature under all aspects. She is alive to the beauty of darkening moors and bright blue skies, of bare hillside and wooded valley, of carolling birds and whispering trees and murmuring streams. Her love of nature carries her into veins of thought that recall the imaginings of Shelley. Lockwood had gone to visit the lonely churchyard where lay Heathcliff, Edgar Linton, and Catherine Earnshaw, and he thus concludes the story of *Wuthering Heights:* "I lingered round them under that benign sky; watched the moths fluttering among the heath and harebells, listened to the soft wind breathing through the grass, and wondered how anyone could ever imagine unquiet slumbers for sleepers in that quiet earth."

Charlotte Brontë compares her sister's novel to a figure rudely carved from a granite block: "There it stands, colossal, dark, and frowning—half statue, half rock; in the former sense terrible and goblin-like, in the latter almost beautiful, for its colouring is of mellow grey, and moorland moss clothes it, and heath, with its blooming bells and balmy fragrance, grows faithfully close to the giant's foot." Rude *Wuthering Heights* is, but it *has* power and it *has* beauty, and when its author died our literature lost a novelist of great promise.

Emily Brontë's poetry is equally full of power, but is perhaps equally unlikely to find readers. This is not because of anything in it so repellent as what is to be found in *Wuthering Heights*. On the contrary, its feeling for nature, its pensiveness, above all the grandeur of thought and the strength of soul in the finest passages, are in themselves attractive. The fatal defect is the want of form; only now and again is the expression worthy of the conception. Something, too, might be said against a certain gloom in the poems, due to their renunciation of hope and love and joy, were this not fully redeemed by their passion for nature and their lofty resolution. If joy leaves us, never to return, we are not to despair.

There should be no despair for you
    While nightly stars are burning;
While evening pours its silent dew,
    And sunshine gilds the morning.
There should be no despair—though tears
    May flow down like a river:

Are not the best beloved of years
    Around your heart for ever?
They weep, you weep, it must be so;
    Winds sigh as you are sighing,
And Winter sheds its grief in snow
    Where Autumn's leaves are lying:
Yet, these revive, and from their fate,
    Your fate cannot be parted:
Then, journey on, if not elate,
    Still, *never* broken-hearted!

Of Emily Brontë it may be truly said she was never broken-hearted. Even sorrow and deadly sickness could not subdue the unbending firmness of her soul. When death was coming very near, she wrote in her wonderful last lines:

O God within my breast,
Almighty, ever-present Deity!
    Life—that in me has rest,
As I—undying Life—have power in thee!
. . .
    There is no room for Death,
Nor atom that his might could render void:
    Thou—Thou art Being and Breath,
And what Thou art may never be destroyed.

Here is what supremely fascinates the admirers of Emily Brontë's poems—the brave, strong spirit that, even when cabined and confined by conventional verse-forms, flames and dances in its bounds.

    I'll walk where my own nature would be leading;
      It vexes me to choose another guide,

she cries in proud independence, and echoes the prayer of 'The Old Stoic':

    Riches I hold in light esteem,
      And Love I laugh to scorn;
    And lust of fame was but a dream,
      That vanished with the morn:
    And if I pray, the only prayer
      That moves my lips for me
    Is, 'Leave the heart that now I bear,

And give me liberty!'
Yes, as my swift days near their goal,
'Tis all that I implore;
In life and death a chainless soul,
    With courage to endure.

In this there is the very abandon of self-reliance, the uncontrolled utterance of fearlessness.

The softer qualities of the poems are seen in compositions like 'Remembrance' (though it contains a characteristic note of strength), 'The Outcast Mother,' 'A Death Scene,' 'The Wanderer from the Fold.' What the author had achieved in the way of pure melody is fairly represented in these lines:

Blow, west wind, by the lonely mound,
    And murmur, summer streams—
There is no need of other sound
    To soothe my lady's dreams.

Careful reading of Emily Brontë's poetry deepens the regret that, after perusing *Wuthering Heights,* one feels for her early death. She passed away before her rare powers had time fully to reveal themselves, though not before she had written enough to indicate the richness of her promise. How rich was not recognised in her lifetime, though of this she never complained. She complained, indeed, of nothing. Yet appreciation would doubtless have given her pleasure, self-controlled and self-reliant as she was. Praise of the highest kind has been freely bestowed on her work, but too late to gratify her, for, in her own fine words:

The dweller in the land of death
    Is changed and careless too.

—A.M. Williams, "Emily Brontë," *Temple Bar,* July 1893

CLEMENT K. SHORTER (1897)

... her best verse is perhaps the greatest ever written by a woman. "Last Lines" and "The Old Stoic" will rank with the finest poetry in our literature.

—Clement K. Shorter, *Victorian Literature:*
Sixty Years of Books and Bookmen,
1897, p. 47

ANGUS M. MACKAY (1898)

MacKay's approbation of the Brontë family's talents is usually generous, praising their collection of novels as "some of the best" in the English language. It is as poet, however, that he situates Emily Brontë, and he considers *Wuthering Heights* to be more akin to a tragedy than a novel.

While MacKay, writing in 1898, is in the midst of a revival of interest in and appreciation for Emily's work, he still considers her gifts in poetry underrated. MacKay attributes this critical oversight to a number of factors, including the average reader's failure to give her poems due attention. Another element is Emily's seeming preference for emotional emphasis over "elegant expression," to which MacKay speculates that "Had she lived she probably would have learnt to value more highly the technique of her art."

But the greatest reason for the underestimation of Emily Brontë's talents, MacKay believes, is the assumption that her verses render a world obscure to most readers. Undoubtedly, this assumption owes much to the popular notion that Emily was a true eccentric, difficult to understand even by members of her own family. But MacKay calls for a reevaluation of her poems from a point of view that takes "the circumstances and environment of Emily's life" into consideration and does not automatically assume that she was an isolated romantic, "independent of [her] environment," and mysterious to even the sympathetic reader. After this objective, he urges the reader to consider Emily's work alongside her deep and consistent affinity for Haworth and the moors. Her engagement with the harsh and unpopulated world around her offers interpretative opportunity in its very focus.

For all of his attention to Emily's poetry, MacKay still uses *Wuthering Heights* as the best evidence of her literary gifts. But again, MacKay considers *Wuthering Heights* as a "prose drama" reminiscent of Shakespeare's tragedies, rather than in comparison to other Victorian novels.

Though Haworth Parsonage was not like Somersby Rectory in Tennyson's youth, "a nest of singing birds," it produced among its five versifiers one gifted singer. As if Nature would show how much she could accomplish with a single stock, the family which afforded material for some of the most fascinating biographies in the English language, and gave us some of the best novels, produced also a remarkable poet. Emily Brontë's right to the title is stamped upon all her work, and perhaps even more clearly upon her romance than upon her verse. For *Wuthering Heights,* if we have regard to its essential qualities rather than its accidental form, is not a novel, but a tragedy. Emily's place is not with Scott and Thackeray, George Eliot and Charlotte Brontë, but with the poets: her prose drama links her with Shakespeare, as her affinities in her verse are with Coleridge and Blake. Until this is clearly perceived much criticism of *Wuthering Heights* will be misdirected. In literature, as in science, comparison is only fruitful when the subject is placed in its right genus and class.

My concern in this paper, however, is chiefly with the poems of Emily Brontë, which even now have not attained to a full measure of appreciation. The little book in which they appeared, it is well known, fell stillborn from the press. And when, later, the Brontë novels attracted attention to them anew, the critics, from Lockhart downwards, were, as Charlotte bitterly complained, "blind as bats, insensate as stones" to Emily's merits. The lapse of half a century has brought about a certain quickening of this critical insensibility. Her swan-song, the pantheistic hymn she wrote as she stood on the threshold of the grave, now finds a place in every anthology of English verse, and lovers of literature are aware that several others of her poems are remarkable. But the impression still remains that the bulk of her verse possesses little merit.

This inadequate estimate is due to a variety of causes. It is accounted for in part by the inclusion of one or two pieces, probably written very early in life, which really are of small value. The average reader, who finds most of the poems a little difficult to understand, sees the defects of these at a glance, and passes judgment accordingly. A more patient examination, however, would have shown how small the amount of dross really is. Once we have been at the pains to grasp their meaning there are few of the poems of Emily Brontë we should care to part with. Another cause of the undervaluing of Emily's verse is to be found in the careless rhymes and faulty construction by which they are often disfigured. Sometimes these are obviously due to the printer's carelessness; but also it would seem that Emily Brontë, like the Brownings, affected to despise ornamental capitals and gilt edges, valuing rather weighty thought than elegant expression. Had she lived she probably would have learnt to value more highly the technique of her art. And in any case it would be a mistake to suppose she could not be mistress of sound as well as sense when she chose. A few of her lyrics are even exquisitely musical; some have the spontaneousness and inevitableness of an Elizabethan snatch, others the childlike grace and charm of Blake at his best. Let any one with an ear for the melody of words read "Hope was but a timid friend," or "The linnet's in the rocky dells" (correcting the obvious misprints of the first verse), or "The Lady to her Guitar," and he will not doubt that the gift of musical expression was a part of this poet's original equipment.

But the main obstacle to the wider recognition of Emily Brontë's poetical gifts is the prevailing notion that much of her work is hopelessly obscure. Those who grant her some of Blake's charm charge her also with much of his mad inconsequence. Even so sympathetic a critic as Miss Mary F. Robinson supports this notion: she speaks of the "incoherence" of the poems, likens them to scenes in a dream "rapidly succeeding each other without logical connection," speaks of their "uncertain outline bathed in a vague golden mist of imagination," and seems to think that many of them contain no meaning whatever: we may admire the vivid colour, but they are blotches of paint, not pictures! Can any one who has appreciated the masterly power of *Wuthering Heights* suppose that when its author turns to verse she becomes an intellectual sloven and incapable of logical expression? I believe, on the contrary, that, putting aside the few stanzas which are immature, there is not one of Emily's poems in which she has not some definite thought or thoughts to express, or in which she fails to utter them with precision. The obscurity vanishes once we are able to place ourselves in the position the poet occupied when she wrote them. Charlotte printed explanatory headings to one or two of the poems which were published after her sister's death. One of these runs:

> The genius of a solitary region seems to address his wandering and wayward votary, and to recall within his influence the proud mind which rebelled at times even against what it most loved.

Without these words the poem would have been as "obscure," as "incoherent" as any which bears Emily's name; but with them all becomes clear, and we read the verses with singular interest. I believe it would be possible to prefix similar elucidations to all the poems; and if it be asked how the clues may be found which will guide us to their meaning, I reply, by the very simple process of considering the circumstances and environment of Emily's life.

There is a superstition that Emily was independent of environment, that all her powers were self-evolved, and were unmodifiable by circumstance. This is not true of Emily, because it is not true of any author. On lately visiting Haworth I turned into a little dissenting burial-yard containing a few score graves. The first tombstone my eye fell on was inscribed with the name of Murgatroyd, and, glancing round, the names Earnshaw, Barraclough, Moore, Malone—all to be found in the Brontë novels—were met with in rapid succession; a proof that in small things as in great we are acted upon irresistibly by our surroundings. As nature can change sand into opals and clay into sapphires, and can transmute ordure into the fragrance and loveliness of the rose, so imagination can vivify and transfigure the commonplace experiences of which ordinary existence is made up, and bathe them in "the light that never was on land or sea"; but nevertheless the dictum holds true of the creative forces of nature and of imagination alike—*ex nihilo nihil*. Therefore, however wonderful was the magic wand which Emily's imagination wielded, her character and surroundings cannot but afford some clue to the nature of her thoughts and creations.

It is true that in a sense we know little of Emily Brontë; but this is because externally there was little to know. The world for her was comprised in Haworth Vicarage and the moors beyond it; humankind was represented by her own family circle. Charlotte tells us in the preface to *Wuthering Heights* that Emily hardly spoke to a soul in her father's parish, and during her short sojourn at the Brussels pensionnat she remained equally aloof. That her life was thus limited was not, perhaps, a matter to be deplored. Confined within such narrow walls, the stream of her imagination wore itself a deep channel. Had her experience been more varied that stream would have been wider, but also shallower and more like other streams: it would have reflected more things in heaven and earth, but there would have been none of those dark fathomless pools which have such a fascination for us. Nor does the narrowness of Emily's life make it more difficult to use it as a guide to the interpretation of her work. A career full of change and incident would have been too complex for our purpose; but here the clues are so few that it is easy to follow them out. The influences which shaped her work are easily catalogued. There was the intense attachment to her home and people, which made even a short separation positive agony; there was the tragedy of her only brother's moral ruin; the passionate love of nature; the shyness of character and loneliness of life which intensified the pleasures of imagination and caused her to brood deeply over the problems of existence. To one or other of these influences almost all her poems may be traced. . . .

It is hoped that the endeavour here made to interpret these fascinating but enigmatical poems by means of the traits of their author's character and the circumstances of her life may help, in some slight degree, to a better appreciation of them. But, as I have already said, Emily Brontë's rank as a poet is to be measured, not by her verse, but by her single romance. The quantity as well as the quality of work must needs be taken into account in estimating the genius of a writer, and it may seem that a beginner's first volume forms a slender foundation for a claim to high rank. But if we look only to the *quality* of the imagination displayed in *Wuthering Heights*—its power, its intensity, its absolute originality—it is scarcely too much to say of Emily that she might have been Shakespeare's younger sister. To the many, of course, this will seem merely fantastic; but the few who have really learnt to appreciate *Wuthering Heights* will see no exaggeration in the title. Putting aside the clumsiness of the framework—the only mark of the prentice-hand in the whole book—what is there comparable to this romance except the greater tragedies of Shakespeare? The single peasant in the story, Joseph, is of the kin of Shakespeare's clowns, and yet is quite distinct from them. Heathcliff is one of the most vivid creations in all literature; he fascinates the imagination, and in some scenes almost paralyses us with horror, and yet that subtle human touch is added which wrings from us pity and almost respect. He reminds us of Shylock and Iago—not, indeed, by any likeness to their characters, but by the sense of wonder he awakens in us at the power that could create such a being. Catharine Earnshaw, again, and Catharine Linton—are not these by their piquancy and winsomeness almost worthy of a place in Shakespeare's gallery of fair women? The whole story has something of the pathos of *King Lear* and much of the tragic force of *Macbeth*, and yet both characters and story are, perhaps, as absolutely original as any that can be named in English literature. It is not, of course, meant that Emily Brontë achieved anything comparable to Shakespeare's greatest work: Shakespeare lived to become a great artist, while Emily only once tried her prentice-hand; Shakespeare knew the world in all its phases, while Emily passed her life in the seclusion of a remote village: but the material out of which the two wrought their work, the protoplasm of their creations, so to speak, was the same. Suppose Shakespeare had died, as Emily did, after completing his first work—*Love's Labour's Lost*—would he have lived in men's memories at all? Or suppose the great dramatist's career to have closed at the same age as Emily's—twenty-nine: he would then have written a group of five complete plays, many of them comparatively immature, and none of them of the first rank as showing the real supremacy of his genius. Thus considered, the claim that Emily Brontë's creative power had something of the nature of Shakespeare's will not appear extravagant to those who can justly estimate what she has accomplished in *Wuthering Heights*.

It would be profitless, perhaps, to speculate on the work which this powerful imagination might have achieved had time been granted; let us rather be grateful for the imperishable work with which she has enriched our literature, and cherish the careless preludes which show how great a poet was lost to the world when Emily Brontë died.

—Angus M. MacKay, from "On the
Interpretation of Emily Brontë,"
Westminster Review, August 1898,
pp. 203–206, 217–218

THEODORE WATTS-DUNTON (1906)

Watts-Dunton's glowing appraisal of Emily's poetry is less critically specific than that of many fellow critics; he ranks her "very high" among nineteenth-century poets and refers, mostly without example, to her influence on later poets. He does mention one poem (W.E. Henley's "Invictus"), which he claims was inspired by Emily's emotionality, but otherwise only broadly connects her pessimism to a similar strain among late-century poetry.

[Emily Brontë's] claim to a place among the poets of England is beyond all question.

It may be said, indeed, that if the influence a poet has exercised upon subsequent singers is to be taken into account in finding his or her position in the literary firmament, Emily Brontë must rank very high among the poets of the nineteenth century. . . . As regards Emily Brontë, the remarkable thing is that notwithstanding the undoubted excellence of such poems as 'The Old Stoic,' 'Remembrance,' and 'A Death-Scene,' her influence upon succeeding poets has been principally, if not entirely, gained by one poem—the poem written just before she died. This 'outburst of agnostic faith,' as it is admirably called by Mr. Gosse (who was the first to include it in an anthology), is so brief that I can quote it here in full—

No coward soul is mine,
No trembler in the world's storm-troubled sphere:
I see Heaven's glories shine,
And faith shines equal, arming me from fear.

O God within my breast.
Almighty, ever-present Deity!
Life—that in me has rest,
As I—Undying Life—have power in Thee!

Vain are the thousand creeds
That move men's hearts: unutterably vain;
Worthless as withered weeds,
Or idlest froth amid the boundless main,

To waken doubt in one
Holding so fast by Thine infinity;
So surely anchored on
The steadfast Rock of immortality.

With wide-embracing love
Thy Spirit animates eternal years,
Pervades and broods above,
Changes, sustains, dissolves, creates, and rears.

Though earth and man were gone,
And suns and universes ceased to be,
And Thou wert left alone,
Every existence would exist in Thee.

There is not room for Death,
Nor atom that his might could render void:
Thou—Thou art Being and Breath,
And what Thou art may never be destroyed.

It may be confidently affirmed that no poem written by the acknowledged master-singers of the nineteenth century has had such an effect upon certain subsequent poets as the poem given above—the late group of poets whose note is a pessimism of the 'cheery' order. . . . The pagan stoicism breached through every line of this noble poem has had an extraordinary and widespread influence upon some of the most noticeable work of the later poets of our own time. Over and over again its particular accent has been caught up and repeated—repeated, we may be sure, not with any desire on the part of the poets to appropriate what is not their own (for it is a mistake to think that poets consciously feed upon the 'sprouts' of other men's minds) —but repeated because they found the grand and startling temper of the lines irresistible—so irresistible that their own feebler and paler personalities have sunk before it. I will mention only one of them, and this is the most striking of them all. I allude to a poem called 'Invictus' by Mr. W.E. Henley—a poem which is so good and is so well and so deservedly know that at the present moment the original poem by Emily Brontë seems among critics to be forgotten . . . [It] is to the wonderful and true outpouring of Emily Brontë's heart that all the inspiration of 'Invictus' is to be traced.

—Theodore Watts-Dunton, introduction
to *The Professor, to which are added
the poems of Charlotte, Emily, and
Anne Brontë*, Oxford, 1906, pp. xii–xiv

ANNE BRONTË

BIOGRAPHY

ANNE BRONTË
(1820–1849)

Anne Brontë, the sixth and last child of Patrick and Maria Brontë, was born on January 17, 1820, in Thornton. A few months later, the family moved to Haworth, and the following year, Maria Brontë died. Unlike her older sisters, Anne was educated at home by their father and aunt until 1832, when Charlotte took over most of her sisters' lessons. Accounts of Anne's childhood describe her relationship with Emily as exceptionally close, and the two collaborated on a series of fantastic stories set in the imaginary land of Gondal well into adulthood.

In 1835, Anne attended Roe Head School, where Emily had briefly studied and where Charlotte was currently teaching. Anne suffered a serious illness in 1837, which may have inspired in her a sense of spiritual renewal; she was the most religious of the Brontë siblings. Anne returned to Haworth to recuperate and stayed there until 1839, when she took her first position as a governess to the Ingram family. In 1840 she went to work for the Robinson family, where she stayed until 1845.

Again returning to Haworth, Anne, along with her sisters, began writing poetry and together they published *Poems* (1946) under the names of Currer, Ellis, and Acton Bell. Anne published *Agnes Grey* in 1847, which received mediocre reviews, and *The Tenant of Wildfell Hall* was published the next year. *Tenant* scandalized many readers and critics for its frank portrayal of a violent alcoholic.

Anne's life was tragically cut short; she contracted tuberculosis and died in May 1849, while visiting Scarborough with Charlotte and their friend Ellen Nussey.

PERSONAL

The historical record of Anne Brontë's life is slim. In the nineteenth century, her two novels, *Agnes Grey* (1847) and *The Tenant of Wildfell Hall* (1848), were considered by most critics to be inferior to her sisters' works. The biographical records of Charlotte's life, especially by Gaskell and Reid, eclipse Anne in their consideration of the other sisters: Her novels were less popular than Charlotte's and less idiosyncratic than Emily's, and her placid personality inspired relatively little speculation or interest. Most treatments of Anne, then, emphasize her sweetness and piety and, if only by comparison, suggest that she was the least interesting and least talented of the Brontë sisters.

Anne's life, somewhat ironically, is most fully documented at its very end. Charlotte (who was still mourning Emily and Branwell), along with her school friend Ellen Nussey, accompanied a tubercular Anne to Scarborough, a coastal town in Yorkshire, in May 1849. It was hoped that the sea air of Scarborough could have a tonic effect on Anne's health. But Anne died after only four days in Scarborough, and the description of her death (by both Charlotte and Ellen) depicts her martyrlike forbearance.

Charlotte Brontë (1841)

This excerpt from a letter to Ellen Nussey describes Anne's trials as a governess in the Robinson family, where she worked from 1840 until 1845. The experience of Anne's heroine Agnes Grey at Horton Lodge is thought to be drawn from Anne's lonely and taxing tenure with the Robinsons at Thorp Green, Scarborough. Branwell joined Anne to tutor the Robinsons' son Edmund in 1843 and began what appears to be an inappropriate relationship with Mrs. Robinson. Not much is known about this liaison, but it led to Branwell's dismissal from his post in 1845 and certainly precipitated Anne's in the same year.

I have one aching feeling in my heart (I must allude to it, though I had resolved not to). It is about Anne; she has so much to endure: far, far more than I have. When my thoughts turn to her, they always see her as a patient, persecuted stranger. I know what concealed susceptibility is in her nature, when her feelings are wounded. I wish I could be with her, to administer a little balm. She is more lonely, less gifted with the power of making friends, even than I am. Drop the subject.

—Charlotte Brontë, 1841, letter to Ellen Nussey,
from *The Brontës*, Clement Shorter, 1896

Anne Brontë (1841)

Anne wrote this diary paper from her position as governess in the Robinson family home. Her record of her life is striking in its summational quality; she reports the ages of herself and her siblings, and their various locations, with brusque precision. But the diary paper also hints at a more abstract level of thinking in Anne's preoccupation with the future. Moreover, Anne's focus on her siblings clarifies the closeness of the family and the relative exclusion of other people.

This is Emily's birthday. She has now completed her 23rd year, and is, I believe, at home. Charlotte is a governess in the family of Mr. White. Branwell is a clerk in the railway station at Luddenden Foot, and I am a governess in the family of Mr. Robinson. I dislike the situation and wish to change it for another. I am now at Scarborough. My pupils are gone to bed and I am hastening to finish this before I follow them.

We are thinking of setting up a school of our own, but nothing definite is settled about it yet, and we do not know whether we shall be able to or not. I hope we shall. And I wonder what will be our condition and how or where we shall all be on this day four years hence; at which time, if all be well, I shall be 25 years and 6 months old, Emily will be 27 years old, Branwell 28 and 1 month, and Charlotte 29 years and a quarter. We are now all separate and not likely to meet again for many a weary week, but we are none of us ill that I know of, and all are doing something for our own livelihood except Emily, who, however, is as busy as any of us, and in reality earns her food and raiment as much as we do.

How little know we what we are
How less what we may be!

Four years ago I was at school. Since then I have been a governess at Blake Hall, left it, come to Thorp Green, and seen the sea and York Minster. Emily has been a teacher at Miss Patchet's school, and left it. Charlotte has left Miss Wooler's, been a governess at Mrs. Sidgwick's, left her, and gone to Mrs. White's. Branwell has given up painting, been a tutor in Cumberland, left it, and become a clerk on the railroad. Tabby has left us, Martha Brown has come in her place. We have got Keeper, got a sweet little cat and lost it, and also got a hawk. Got a wild goose which has flown away, and three tame ones, one of which has been killed. All this diversities, with many others, are things we did not foresee in the July of 1837. What will the next four years bring forth? Providence only knows. But we ourselves have sustained little alteration since that time. I have the same faults I had then, only I have more wisdom and experience, and a little more self-possession than I then enjoyed. How will it be when we open this paper and the one Emily has written? I wonder whether *Gondaland* will still be flourishing, and what will be their condition. I am now writing the fourth volume of *Solala Vernon's Life*.

For some time I have looked upon 25 as a sort of era in my existence. It may prove a true presentiment, or it may be only a superstitious fancy; the latter seems most likely, but time will show.

—Anne Brontë, July 30, 1841

Anne Brontë (1845)

This second diary paper responds to the preceding one with information about the four years that have passed. The conflict that Anne alludes to as a "very unpleasant and undreamt-of experience of human nature" is thought to be Branwell's improper relationship with Mrs. Robinson, Anne's employer, that precipitated her resignation from the post and inspired the emotional anguish and instability she explored in *The Tenant of Wildfell Hall*. But, as in the diary paper of 1841, her focus on the group of siblings is consistent, despite the various occupations and postings that have broadened their experiences away from Haworth.

When Anne again closes this record with speculations about the future, our retrospective reading brings a tragic perspective. While 1848 marked the publication of *The Tenant of Wildfell Hall* (June) followed by Charlotte and Anne's trip to London (July) to reveal their real identities to their publishers, the rest of the year was grim. Branwell's death in September was followed by Emily's in December. Anne then died the following May, in 1849.

— — — — — —

Yesterday was Emily's birthday, and the time when she should have opened our 1841 paper, but by mistake we opened it today instead. How many things have happened since it was written—some pleasant, some far otherwise. Yet I was then at Thorp Green, and now I am only just escaped from it. I was wishing to leave it then, and if I had known that I had four years longer to stay how wretched I should have been; but during my stay I have had some very unpleasant and undreamt-of experience of human nature. Others have seen more changes. Charlotte has left Mr. White's, and been twice to Brussels, where she stayed each time nearly a year. Emily has been there too, and stayed nearly a year. Branwell has left Luddendon Foot, and been a tutor at Thorp Green, and had much tribulation and ill health. . . . This is a dismal, cloudy, wet evening. We have had so far a very cold, wet summer. Charlotte has lately been to Hathersage, in Derbyshire, on a visit of three weeks to Ellen Nussey. She is now sitting sewing in the dining-room. Emily is ironing upstairs. I am sitting in the dining-room in the rocking-chair before the fire with my feet on the fender. Paper is in the parlour. Tabby and Martha are, I think, in the kitchen. Keeper and Flossy are, I do not know where. Little Dick is hopping in his cage. When the last paper was written we were thinking of setting up a school. The scheme has been dropt, and long after taken up again, and dropt again, because we could not get pupils. Charlotte is thinking about getting another situation. She wishes to go to Paris. Will she go? She has let Flossy in, by-the-by, and he is now lying on the sofa. Emily is engaged in writing the Emperor Julius's Life. She has read some of it, and I want very much to hear the rest. She is writing some poetry, too. I wonder what it is about? I have begun the third volume of

Passages in the Life of an Individual. I wish I had finished it. This afternoon I began to set about making my grey figured silk frock that was dyed at Keighley. What sort of a hand shall I make of it? E. and I have a great deal of work to do. When shall we sensibly diminish it? I want to get a habit of early rising. Shall I succeed? We have not yet finished our *Gondal Chronicles* that we began three years and a half ago. When will they be done? [. . .] I wonder how she shall all be, and where and how situated, on the thirtieth of July 1848, when, if we are all alive, Emily will be just 30. I shall be in my 29th year, Charlotte in her 33rd, and Branwell in his 32nd; and what changes shall we have seen and known; and shall we be much changed ourselves? I hope not, for the worse at least. I for my part, cannot well be flatter or older in mind than I am now. Hoping for the best, I conclude.

—Anne Brontë, July 31, 1845

CHARLOTTE BRONTË (1849)

This excerpt is taken from a letter that Charlotte wrote to W.S. Williams during Anne's increasingly serious—and eventually fatal—illness.

———— ———— ————

Anne and I sit alone and in seclusion as you fancy us, but we do not study. Anne cannot study now, she can scarcely read; she occupies Emily's chair; she does not get well. A week ago we sent for a medical man of skill and experience from Leeds to see her. He examined her with the stethoscope. His report I forbear to dwell on for the present—even skillful physicians have often been mistaken in their conjectures.

My first impulse was to hasten her away to a warmer climate, but this was forbidden: she must not travel; she is not to stir from the house this winter; the temperature of her room is to be kept constantly equal. . . .

When we lost Emily I thought we had drained the very dregs of our cup of trial, but now when I hear Anne cough as Emily coughed, I tremble lest there should be exquisite bitterness yet to taste. However, I must not look forwards, nor must I look backwards. . . .

Anne is very patient in her illness, as patient as Emily was unflinching. I recall one sister and look at the other with a sort of reverence as well as affection—under the test of suffering neither has faltered.

—Charlotte Brontë, January 18, 1849,
from a letter to W.S. Williams, from
The Brontës, Clement Shorter, 1896

ELLEN NUSSEY (1849)

Ellen Nussey, Charlotte's close friend from Roe Head School, went with Charlotte and Anne to Scarborough, where Anne had visited as a governess, and where—as this record minutely documents—she died a peaceful if abrupt death.

Accounts of Anne's life from people other than Charlotte are rare. While Nussey's testimony does not diverge from the persona that Charlotte also depicted (they both render Anne as patient, selfless, and retiring), it is valuable for confirming a sister's perspective, which we could plausibly expect to be sentimental or partisan. Nussey's letter also underscores the strong religious faith identified in Anne, even (or especially) as she faces her imminent death.

The "Minster" that Nussey refers to here is the gothic cathedral, York Minster, which dates back to the fourteenth century.

―――

She left her home May 24th, 1849—died May 28th. Her life was calm, quiet, spiritual: *such* was her end. Through the trials and fatigues of the journey, she evinced the pious courage and fortitude of a martyr. Dependence and helplessness were ever with her a far sorer trial than hard, racking pain.

The first stage of our journey was to York; and here the dear invalid was so revived, so cheerful, and so happy, we drew consolation, and trusted that at least temporary improvement was to be derived from the change which *she* had so longed for, and her friends had so dreaded for her.

By her request we went to the Minster, and to her it was an overpowering pleasure; not for its own imposing and impressive grandeur only, but because it brought to her susceptible nature a vital and overwhelming sense of omnipotence. She said, while gazing at the structure, 'If finite power can do this, what is the . . . ?' and here emotion stayed her speech, and she was hastened to a less exciting scene.

Her weakness of body was great; but her gratitude for every mercy was greater. After such an exertion as walking to her bed-room, she would clasp her hands and raise her eyes in silent thanks, and she did this not to the exclusion of unwonted prayer, for that too was performed on bended knee, ere she accepted the rest of her couch.

On the 25th we arrived at Scarborough; our dear invalid having, during the journey, directed our attention to every prospect worthy of notice.

On the 26th she drove on the sands for an hour; and lest the poor donkey should be urged by its driver to a greater speed than her tender heart thought right, she took the reins, and drove herself. When joined by her friend, she was charging the boy-master of the donkey to treat the poor animal well. She was ever fond of dumb things, and would give up her own comfort for them.

On Sunday, the 27th, she wished to go to church, and her eye brightened with the thought of once more worshipping her God amongst her fellow-creatures. We thought it prudent to dissuade her from the attempt, though it was evident her heart was longing to join in the public act of devotion and praise.

She walked a little in the afternoon, and meeting with a sheltered and comfortable seat near the beach, she begged we would leave her, and enjoy the various scenes near at hand, which were new to us but familiar to her. She loved the place, and wished us to share her preference.

The evening closed in with the most glorious sunset ever witnessed. The castle on the cliff stood in proud glory gilded by the rays of the declining sun. The distant ships glittered like burnished gold; the little boats near the beach heaved on the ebbing tide, inviting occupants. The view was grand beyond description. Anne was drawn in her easy chair to the window, to enjoy the scene with us. Her face became illumined almost as much as the glorious scene she gazed upon. Little was said, for it was plain that her thoughts were driven by the imposing view before her to penetrate forwards to the regions of unfading glory. She again thought of public worship, and wished us to leave her, and join those who were assembled at the House of God. We declined, gently urging the duty and pleasure of staying with her, who was now so dear and so feeble. On returning to her place near the fire, she conversed with her sister upon the propriety of returning to their home. She did not wish it for her own sake, she said; she was fearing others might suffer more if her decease occurred where she was. She probably thought the task of accompanying her lifeless remains on a long journey was more than her sister could bear—more than the bereaved father could bear, were she borne home another, and a third tenant of the family-vault in the short space of nine months.

The night passed without any apparent accession of illness. She rose at seven o'clock, and performed most of her toilet herself, by her expressed wish. Her sister always yielded such points, believing it was the truest kindness not to press inability when it was not acknowledged. Nothing occurred to excite alarm till about 11 a.m. She then spoke of a feeling of change. 'She believed she had not long to live. Could she reach home alive, if we prepared immediately for departure?' A physician was sent for. Her address to him was made with perfect composure. She begged him to say 'How long he thought she might live;—not to fear speaking the truth, for she was not afraid to die.' The doctor reluctantly admitted that the angel of death was already arrived and that life was ebbing fast. She thanked him for his truthfulness, and he departed to come again very soon. She still occupied her easy chair, looking so serene, so reliant: there was no opening for grief as yet, though all knew the separation was at hand. She clasped her hands, and reverently invoked a blessing from on high; first upon her sister, then upon her friend, to whom she said, 'Be a sister in my stead. Give Charlotte as much of your company as you can.' She then thanked each for her kindness and attention.

Ere long the restlessness of approaching death appeared, and she was borne to the sofa; on being asked if she were easier, she looked gratefully at her questioner, and said, 'It is not *you* who can give me ease, but soon all will be well, through the merits of our Redeemer.' Shortly after this, seeing that her sister could hardly restrain her grief, she said, 'Take courage, Charlotte; take courage.' Her faith never failed, and her eyes never dimmed till about two o'clock, when she calmly and without a sigh passed from the temporal to the eternal. So still and so hallowed were her last hours and moments. There was no thought of assistance or of dread. The doctor came and went two or three times. The hostess knew that death was near, yet so little was the house disturbed by the presence of the dying, and the sorrow of those so nearly bereaved, that dinner was announced as ready, through the half-opened door, as the living sister was closing the eyes of the dead one. She could now no more stay the welled-up grief of her sister with her emphatic and dying 'Take courage,' and it burst forth in brief but agonizing strength. Charlotte's affection, however, had another channel, and there it turned in thought, in care, and in tenderness. There was bereavement, but there was not solitude;—sympathy was at hand, and it was accepted.

—Ellen Nussey, written to Elizabeth Gaskell,
from *The Life of Charlotte Brontë*, p. 372–376

Elizabeth Gaskell (1857)

This anecdote recorded by Gaskell in her biography of Charlotte refers to a "young lady" visiting the Brontës at Haworth. This is Ellen Nussey. It is rare, if thirdhand, evidence of Anne's pride in her writing.

During the time that the negotiations with Messrs. Aylott and Co. (about the poems of C., A., and E. Bell) was going on [1846], Charlotte went to visit her old school-friend, with whom she was in such habits of confidential intimacy; but neither then nor afterwards, did she ever speak to her of the publication of the poems; nevertheless, this young lady suspected that the sisters wrote for Magazines; and in this idea she was confirmed when, on one of her visits to Haworth, she saw Anne, with a number of *Chambers' Journal*, and a gentle smile of pleasure stealing over her placid face as she read.

"What is the matter?" asked the friend. "Why do you smile?"

"Only because I see they have inserted one of my poems," was the quiet reply; and not a word more was said on the subject.

—Elizabeth Gaskell, *The Life of
Charlotte Brontë*, 1857, pp. 290–291

ELLEN NUSSEY (1871)

Ellen Nussey's reminiscences of a visit to the Brontë parsonage at Haworth in 1832 recall Anne at age twelve.

⸺⁘⸺ ⸺⁘⸺ ⸺⁘⸺

Anne—dear, gentle Anne—was quite different in appearance from [her siblings]. She was her aunt's favorite. Her hair was a very pretty light brown, and fell on her neck in graceful curls. She had lovely violet-blue eyes, fine penciled eyebrows, and clear, almost transparent complexion. She still pursued her studies, and especially her sewing, under the surveillance of her aunt.

—Ellen Nussey, *Scribner's Magazine*, May 1871

CLEMENT K. SHORTER (1896)

Shorter's account of Anne is also secondhand, an alleged comment by Arthur Bell Nicholls, Charlotte's husband. Again, we see substantiation of Anne as a sweet and gentle person, but little in the way of biographical complexity comes through.

⸺⁘⸺ ⸺⁘⸺ ⸺⁘⸺

Gentleness is a word always associated with [Anne] by those who knew her. When Mr. Nicholls saw what professed to be a portrait of Anne in a magazine article, he wrote: 'What an awful caricature of the dear, gentle Anne Brontë!' Mr. Nicholls has a portrait of Anne in his possession, drawn by Charlotte, which he pronounces to be an admirable likeness, and this does convey the impression of a sweet and gentle nature. . . .

Apart from the correspondence we know little more than this—that Anne was the least assertive of the three sisters, and that she was more distinctly a general favorite. We have Charlotte's own word for it that even the curates ventured upon 'sheep's eyes' at Anne. We know all too little of her two experiences as governess, first at Blake Hall with Mrs. Ingham, and later at Thorp Green with Mrs. Robinson. . . . With the exception of these two uncomfortable episodes as governess, Anne would seem to have had no experience of the larger world.

—Clement K. Shorter, *Charlotte Brontë*
and Her Circle, 1896, p. 181–182

MARY AUGUSTA WARD (1900)

Ward also refers to Nicholl's comment about the inaccurate portrait of Anne. She does, however, venture toward a more substantive treatment of Anne in recalling Gaskell's description of Anne's childhood precocity and creativity.

Many years after Anne's death her brother-in-law protested against a supposed portrait of her, as giving a totally wrong impression of the 'dear, gentle Anne Brontë.' 'Dear' and 'gentle' indeed she seems to have been through life, the youngest and prettiest of the sisters, with a delicate complexion, a slender neck and small, pleasant features. Notwithstanding, she possessed in full the Brontë seriousness, the Brontë strength of will. When her father asked her at four years old what a little child like her wanted most, the tiny creature replied—if it were not a Brontë it would be incredible!—'Age and experience.' When the three children started their 'Island Plays' together in 1827, Anne, who was then eight, chose Guernsey for her imaginary island, and peopled it with 'Michael Sadler, Lord Bentinck, and Sir Henry Halford.' She and Emily were constant companions, and there is evidence that they shared a common world of fancy from very early days to mature womanhood.

—Mary Augusta Ward, *The Life and Words of*
Charlotte Brontë and Her Sisters,
Haworth, 1900, pp. ix–x

GENERAL

Anne Brontë's critical reputation in the nineteenth century relied almost entirely on her status as a Brontë. As a novelist (or poet) independent of her more famous sisters, she is discussed rarely. While late-twentieth-century critics have "rediscovered" the youngest Brontë in substantive ways, the dismissive treatment she received during her lifetime and in the later decades of the Victorian age is reflected here by the paucity of comments about her artistry and place in the literary canon. Indeed, "general" treatments of Anne's work are difficult to locate, as the nineteenth-century interest in her largely centered on her membership in a famous family.

PETER BAYNE (1857)

Peter Bayne's courteous disregard of Anne Brontë follows the precedent set by most nineteenth-century critics of the sisters' work.

━━━ ━━━ ━━━

Of Anne Brontë, known as Acton Bell, we have scarce a remark to make. In her life, too, sadness was the reigning element, but she possessed no such strong genius as her sister.

... It may well be doubted whether any more than a faint and mournful reminiscence of Ellis and Acton Bell will survive the generation now passing away.

—Peter Bayne, *Essays in Biography and Criticism* (1857), p. 419.

T. WEMYSS REID (1877)

Reid writes with the confidence of firsthand knowledge of Anne, which he did not have, when he claims that her life and her fiction (or at least *The Tenant of Wildfell Hall*) was overdetermined by the example of Branwell's degradation. This association—or Anne's witnessing Branwell's "fall"—is to many nineteenth-century critics the most interesting thing about the youngest and most diffident Brontë sister.

━━━ ━━━ ━━━

It is with a feeling of curious disappointment that one rises from the perusal of the writings of Anne Brontë. She wrote two novels, *Agnes Grey* and *The Tenant of Wildfell Hall*, neither of which will really repay perusal. In the first she sought to set forth some of the experiences which had befallen her in that patient placid life which she led as a governess. They were not ordinary experiences, the reader should know. I have resolutely avoided, in writing this sketch of Charlotte Brontë and her sisters, all unnecessary reference to the tragedy of Branwell Brontë's life. But it is a strange sad feature of that story, that the pious and gentle youngest sister was compelled to be a closer and more constant witness of his sins and sufferings than either Charlotte or Emily. She was living under the same roof with him when he went astray and was thrust out in deep disgrace. I have said already that the effect of his career upon her own was as strong and deep as Mrs. Gaskell represents it to have been. Branwell's fall formed the dark turning point in Anne Brontë's life. So it was not unnatural that it should colour her literary labours. Accordingly, whilst *Agnes Grey* gives us some of the scenes of her governess life, dressed up in the fashion of the ordinary romances of thirty years ago,

The Tenant of Wildfell Hall presents us with a dreary and repulsive picture of Branwell Brontë's condition after his fall.

—T. Wemyss Reid, *Charlotte Brontë:*
A Monograph, 1877, p. 217

Clement Shorter (1896)

It can scarcely be doubted that Anne Brontë's two novels, *Agnes Grey* and *The Tenant of Wildfell Hall*, would have long since fallen into oblivion but for the inevitable association with the romances of her two greater sisters. While this may be taken for granted, it is impossible not to feel, even at the distance of half a century, a sense of Anne's personal charm.

—Clement Shorter, *Charlotte Brontë*
and Her Circle, 1896, p.181

Mary Augusta Ward (1900)

Like Reid, Ward considers the example of Branwell's crisis at Thorp Green to be the shaping factor of Anne Brontë's life. This is the "experience and grief" to which Ward here refers. She further determines that Branwell's problems inspired or at least extended Anne's deep "religious melancholy."

Not only is such speculation about the influence of Branwell on Anne impossible to substantiate, but it also creates a portrait of Anne as one who is passively acted on by her troubled brother rather than someone with an autonomous will of her own.

Anne was not strong enough, her gift was not vigorous enough, to enable her thus to transmute experience and grief. The probability is that when she left Thorp Green in 1845 she was already suffering from that religious melancholy of which Charlotte discovered such piteous evidence among her papers after her death. It did not much affect the writing of *Agnes Grey*, which was completed in 1846, and reflected the minor pains and discomforts of her teaching experience, but it combined with the spectacle of Branwell's increasing moral and physical decay to produce that bitter mandate of conscience under which she wrote *The Tenant of Wildfell Hall*.

—Mary Augusta Ward, *The Life and Words*
of Charlotte Brontë and Her Sisters,
Haworth, 1900, pp. xiii–xiv

WORKS

AGNES GREY

Agnes Grey, Anne's first novel, published under her pseudonym Acton Bell, tells the story of a hardworking governess who is harassed by the demands of her employers and the unruliness of their children. Agnes eventually finds happiness with an upstanding curate who rescues her from such degrading labor.

The novel garnered middling reviews when it was first published in 1847 as an appendage to *Wuthering Heights.* That latter novel was much more controversial and innovative and, in most reviews (which discussed both novels), commanded the majority of the critics' discussion. Knowledge of and interest in the Brontë family later inspired some renewed interest in the novel for what it may suggest about Anne's own life and her experience as a Brontë. This is evident in both Roscoe's and Montegut's readings.

It is not known when Anne started writing *Agnes Grey,* but she finished her first copy of the manuscript in 1846, and it was accepted (for publication with *Wuthering Heights*) by Thomas Cautley Newby. This publisher treated both books carelessly, allowing numerous errors in the printed edition and even misspellings of Anne's novel as *"Anges Grey"* in the third volume. After Anne's death, Charlotte corrected much of the first edition and Smith, Elder & Company published a second edition (still attached to *Wuthering Heights*) in 1850, followed by a third edition in 1858.

CHARLOTTE BRONTË (1847)

In this letter to W.S. Williams, Charlotte briefly refers to *Agnes Grey,* then specifying the way that the novel was poorly served by Newby's editorial negligence.

You are not far wrong in your judgment respecting *Wuthering Heights* and *Agnes Grey.* . . . *Agnes Grey* is the mirror of the mind of the writer. The orthography and punctuation of the book are mortifying to a degree—almost all the errors that were corrected in the proof-sheets appear intact in what should have been the fair copies. If Mr. Newby always does business in this way, few authors would like to have him for their publisher a second time.

—Charlotte Brontë, letter to
W.S. Williams, December 21, 1847

HENRY F. CHORLEY (1847)

In a familiar vein, Chorley's review of *Wuthering Heights* and *Agnes Grey* regrets the gloominess of the Bells's creations. He advises the authors, should they take to fiction again, to dispense with the "eccentric and unpleasant." It is interesting to note that Anne did not heed this advice, as her next novel, *The Tenant of Wildfell Hall*, certainly exceeds *Agnes Grey* in its portrayal of domestic disharmony and social defiance.

Here are two tales so nearly related to *Jane Eyre* in cast of thought, incident, and language as to excite some curiosity. All three might be the work of one hand,—but the first issued [*Jane Eyre*] remains the best. In spite of much power and cleverness, in spite of its truth to life in the remote corners and nooks of England, *Wuthering Heights* is a disagreeable story. . . . If the Bells, singly or collectively, are contemplating future or frequent utterances in fiction, let us hope that they will spare us further interiors so gloomy as the one here [in *Wuthering Heights*] elaborated with such dismal minuteness. In this respect *Agnes Grey* is more acceptable to us, though less powerful. It is the tale of a governess who undergoes much that is the real bond of a governess's endurance;—but the new victim's trials are of a more ignoble quality than those which awaited Jane Eyre. In the household of the Bloomfields the governess is subjected to torment by Terrible Children (as the French have it); in that of the Murrays she has to witness the ruin wrought by false indulgence on two coquettish girls, whose coquetries jeopardize her own hearts' secret. In both these tales there is so much feeling for characters, and nice marking of scenery, that we cannot leave them without once again warning their authors against what is eccentric and unpleasant. Never was there a period in our history of Society when we English could so ill afford to dispense with sunshine.

—Henry F. Chorley, *The Athenaeum*, 1052,
December 25, 1847, pp. 1,324–1,325

W.C. ROSCOE (1857)

William Caldwell Roscoe (1825–1859) was an English poet, essayist, and critic. His mention here of *Agnes Grey* is excerpted from a long essay that reviews Gaskell's biography of Charlotte. What is typical about this notice, then, is the marginalization of *Agnes Grey* in the context of the more famous works by (or about) the other Brontës. He also follows convention in considering *Agnes Grey* for what it reveals about Anne personally. Unlike others, Roscoe praises Anne's first novel for its perceptual deftness and artistry and for its realistic representation of several male characters.

———— ———— ————

Agnes Grey reflects so accurately all we hear of [Anne], that we can scarcely be wrong in supposing it shadows forth her character as well as a part of her experiences. Without wishing to seem paradoxical, we cannot help thinking that Anne had more of the artist's faculties than either of her sisters. Her stories are much more homogenous in their structure, her characters more consistent, and, though less original and striking, conducted with a nicer perception of dramatic propriety. Grimsby, Hattersley, and Lord Lowborough—unfilled outlines as they are—are more of real men than Heathcliff, Rochester, or Dr. John.

—W.C. Roscoe, *National Review*
June 1857, p. 127

ÉMILE MONTÉGUT (1857)

Émile Montégut was a French critic and writer who wrote frequently on English literature. His books include *Essais sur la littérature anglais* (1883) and a series, *Écrivains modernes de l'Angleterre* (1882–1892).

Montégut's sense of the "sharp angles of reality" that inform *Agnes Grey* are somewhat modified by his other primary comment about the novel: that it signifies passivity and resignation.

———— ———— ————

To read Anne's book, *Agnes Grey*, is a painful and harrowing experience. In it, she writes on the constant family theme, the sufferings of dependence, for Agnes Grey—like Jane Eyre—is a governess. It is fundamentally a realistic novel; none of the sharp angles of reality have been softened, no coarse or wounding detail has been omitted. One feels that the sensibility of the author is too highly strung and too exhausted for her to engage in even a shadow of a struggle. A dull half-light illumines these pages which are filled with accounts of small unhappinesses suffered without murmur, small happinesses accepted with a gentle gratitude with scarcely the strength to smile. Resignation is the soul of this little book.

—Émile Montégut, *Revue des deux mondes*,
July 1, 1857, p. 139

THE TENANT OF WILDFELL HALL

The Tenant of Wildfell Hall (1848), Anne Brontë's second and final novel, angered many critics for its stark and harrowing portrayal of an alcoholic, Arthur Huntingdon. The novel, which is presented as a compilation of letters and diary entries, concerns the trials of Helen Huntingdon, Arthur's wife. Helen tries and fails to reform her husband and, in desperation, adopts a pseudonym and leaves him, taking their young son with her. Much of the story concerns Helen's relationship with Gilbert Markham, a young farmer to whom she gradually confides her past with Huntingdon, and whom she eventually marries after her first husband's death.

Huntingdon is famously and notoriously modeled on the tragic figure of Branwell Brontë, whose disgrace and profligacy Anne witnessed firsthand when they were both employed by the Robinson family at Thorp Green. Helen's strong Christian faith is also biographical, drawn from Anne's own feelings.

Anne wrote the novel shortly after finishing *Agnes Grey* and was under contract to publish it also with Thomas Newby. It appeared in July 1848 and exposed the same editorial sloppiness that Newby evinced with *Agnes Grey* (spelling and punctuation errors, for instance). Worse, Newby conflated Acton Bell's name with Currer Bell's, hoping that the inference that *Tenant*'s author was the author of *Jane Eyre* would boost its sales. To correct this misrepresentation, Charlotte and Anne made their well-known trip to London to disclose their identities (see Ward's description of this trip, included in this section).

———⚬⚬⚬⚬— —⚬⚬⚬— —⚬⚬⚬—

ANNE BRONTË (1848)

The following is Anne Brontë's preface to the second edition of *The Tenant of Wildfell Hall* and functions as her explanation for the vivid and disturbing portrait of the alcoholic Huntingdon. Lest her readers think that she enjoyed the melodrama of Huntingdon's behavior, as several critics at the time implied, Anne explains that the illustration was taken from life. By this she refers, if elliptically, to the unfortunate example of her brother, Branwell, during their time together in the Robinsons' home at Thorp Green.

———⚬⚬⚬— —⚬⚬⚬— —⚬⚬⚬—

While I acknowledge the success of the present work to have been greater than I anticipated, and the praises it has elicited from a few kind critics to have been greater than it deserved, I must also admit that from some other quarters it has been censured with an asperity which I was as little prepared to expect, and which my judgment, as well as my feelings, assures me is more bitter than just. It is scarcely the province of an author to refute the arguments of his censors and vindicate his own productions; but I would have prefaced the first edition, had I foreseen the necessity of such precautions against the misapprehensions of those who would read it with a prejudiced mind or be content to judge it by a hasty glance.

My object in writing the following pages was not simply to amuse the Reader; neither was it to gratify my own taste, not yet to ingratiate myself with the Press and the Public: I wished to tell the truth, for truth always conveys its own moral to those who are able to receive it. But as the priceless treasure too frequently hides at the bottom of a well, it needs some courage to dive for it, especially as he that does so will be likely to incur more scorn and obloquy for the mud and water into which he has ventured to plunge, than thanks for the jewel he procures. . . .

As the story of *Agnes Grey* was accused of extravagant overcolouring in those very parts that were carefully copied from the life, with a most scrupulous avoidance of all exaggeration, so, in the present work, I find myself censured for depicting *con amore*, with 'a morbid love of the coarse, if not of the brutal,' those scenes which, I will venture to say, have not been more painful for the most fastidious of my critics to read than they were for me to describe. I may have gone too far; in which case I shall be careful not to trouble myself or my readers in the same way again; but when we have to do with vice and vicious characters, I maintain it is better to depict them as they really are than as they would wish to appear. To represent a bad thing in its least offensive light is, doubtless, the most agreeable course for a writer of fiction to pursue; but is it the more honest, or the safest? Is it better to reveal the snares and pitfalls of life to the young and thoughtless traveler, or to cover them with branches and flowers? Oh, reader! If there were less of this delicate concealment of facts—this whispering, 'Peace, peace,' when there is no peace, there would be less of sin and misery to the young of both sexes who are left to wring their bitter knowledge from experience.

I would not be understood to suppose that the proceedings of the unhappy scapegrace, with his few profligate companions I have here introduced, are a specimen of the common practices of society—the case is an extreme one, as I trusted none would fail to perceive; but I know that such characters do exist and if I have warned one rash youth from following in their steps, or prevented one thoughtless girl from falling into the very natural error of my heroine, the book has not been written in vain. . . .

One word more, and I have done. Respecting the author's identity, I would have it be distinctly understood that Acton Bell is neither Currer nor Ellis Bell, and therefore let not his faults be attributed to them. . . . As to whether the name be real or fictitious, it cannot greatly signify to those who know him only by his works. As little, I should think, can it matter whether the writer so designated is a man, or a woman, as one or two of my critics professed to have discovered. . . . I am satisfied that if a book is a good one, it is so whatever the sex of the author may be. All novels are, or should be, written for both men and women to read, and I am at a loss to conceive how a man should permit himself to write anything that would be really disgraceful to a woman, or why a woman should be censured for writing anything that would be proper and becoming for a man.

> —Anne Brontë, preface to the second edition
> of *The Tenant of Wildfell Hall*, July 22, 1848

Charlotte Brontë (1848)

In this letter to W.S. Williams, Charlotte thanks the editor for critiquing *The Tenant of Wildfell Hall*, and she also indicates a sense of ownership over her sister's novel when she assures Williams that his review will receive "our most careful attention."

Charlotte questions Williams's comparison of Huntingdon to Rochester, from her own *Jane Eyre*, and in the following discussion, she reorients the subject of her letter from *The Tenant of Wildfell Hall* to *Jane Eyre*. Such critical agency perhaps helps to explain why Anne was so consistently overshadowed by her more assertive elder sister.

My sister Anne thanks you, as well as myself, for your just critique on *Wildfell Hall*. It appears to me that your observations exactly hit both the strong and weak points of the book, and the advice which accompanies them is worthy of, and shall receive, our most careful attention. . . .

You say Mr. Huntingdon reminds you of Mr. Rochester. Does he? Yet there is no likeness between the two; the foundation of each character is entirely different. Huntingdon is a specimen of the naturally selfish, sensual, superficial man, whose one merit of a joyous temperament only avails him while he is young and healthy, whose best days are his earliest, who never profits by experience, who is sure to grow worse the older he grows. Mr. Rochester has a thoughtful nature and a very feeling heart; he is neither selfish nor self-indulgent; he is ill-educated, misguided; errs, when he does err, through rashness and inexperience: he lives for a time as too many other men live, but being radically better than most men, he does not like that degraded life, and is never happy in it. He is taught the severe lessons of experience and has sense to learn wisdom from them. Years improve him; the effervescence of youth foamed away, what is really good in him still remains. His nature is like wine of a good vintage, time cannot sour, but only mellows him. Such at least was the character I meant to portray.

—Charlotte Brontë, letter to W.S. Williams, August 14, 1848

E.P. WHIPPLE (1848)

Whipple believes that Acton Bell is not only the author *of The Tenant of Wildfell Hall* but of *Wuthering Heights* and, "if we mistake not, of certain offensive but powerful portions of *Jane Eyre*." While many critics and publishers were misled or misinformed about the discrete identities of the Bells, Whipple's proof of this claim seems to be that he considers Acton the most likely of the Bell family of authors to be responsible for the "spiritual wickedness" evinced in these texts. Here he compares *The Tenant* to *Wuthering Heights*.

The Tenant of Wildfell Hall is altogether a less unpleasant story [than *Wuthering Heights*], though it resembles it in the excessive clumsiness with which the plot is arranged, and the prominence given to the brutal element of human nature. The work seems a convincing proof that there is nothing kindly or genial in the author's powerful mind, and that, if he continues to write novels, he will introduce into the land of romance a larger number of hateful men and women than any other writer of the day. Gilbert, the hero, seems to be a favorite with the author, and to be intended as a specimen of manly character; but he would serve as the ruffian of any other novelist. His nature is fierce, proud, moody, jealous, revengeful, and sometimes brutal. We can see nothing good in him except a certain rude honesty; and that quality is seen chiefly in his bursts of hatred and his insults to women. Helen, the heroine, is doubtless a strong-minded woman, and passes bravely through a great deal of suffering; but if there be any loveable or feminine virtues in her composition, the author has managed to conceal them. She marries a profligate, thinking to reform him; but the gentleman, with a full knowledge of her purpose, declines reformation, goes deeper and deeper into vice, and becomes at last as fiendlike as a very limited stock of brains will allow. This is a reversal of the process carried on in *Jane Eyre*; but it must be admitted that the profligate in *The Tenant of Wildfell Hall* is no Rochester. He is never virtuously inclined, except in those periods of illness and feebleness which his debaucheries have occasioned, thus illustrating the old proverb,—

"When the devil was sick, the devil a monk would be,
When the devil was well, the devil a monk was he."

He has almost constantly by him a choice coterie of boon companions, ranging from the elegant libertine to the ferocious sensualist, and the reader is favored with exact accounts of the drunken orgies, and with numerous scraps of their profane conversation. All the characters are drawn with great power and precision of outline, and the scenes are as vivid as life itself. Everywhere is seen the tendency of the author to degrade passion into appetite, and to give prominence to the selfish and malignant elements of human nature; but while he succeeds in making profligacy disgusting, he fails in making virtue pleasing. His depravity is total depravity, and his hard and imprudent debauchees seem to belong to that class of reprobates whom Dr. South considers "as not so much born as damned into the world." The reader of Acton Bell gains no enlarged view of mankind, giving a healthy action to his sympathies, but is confined to a narrow space of life, and held down, as it were, by main force, to witness the wolfish side of his nature literally and logically set forth. But the criminal courts are not the places in which to take a comprehensive view of humanity, and the novelist who confines his observations to them is not likely to produce any lasting impression, except of horror and disgust.

—E.P. Whipple, "Novels of the Season,"
The North American Review,
October 1848, cxli, pp. 358–360

CHARLES KINGSLEY (1849)

Kingsley's review is valuable for its fair-minded and accurate predic-
tion of what "the world" will object to in *The Tenant of Wildfell Hall*: the
unpleasant (and unpleasantly realistic) portrayal of a violent man.

Kingsley's own objections are not altogether dissimilar, as he faults
Anne Brontë for her thoroughness in portraying Huntingdon's sins.

Kingsley does not deny the accuracy of her representation but rather its painstaking precision, as he argues that a novelist can be truthful without indulging in so much ugly detail.

He also complains that the character of Gilbert Markham is not sufficiently appealing to justify Helen's love for him. To Kingsley, Gilbert bears some uncomfortable resemblance to the masculine villains of the story at the same time that he, unconvincingly, attracts the gentle and cerebral Helen. Kingsley thereby claims that Gilbert's characterization is comprised of "two opposite poles."

A people's novel of a very different school is *The Tenant of Wildfell Hall.* It is, taken altogether, a powerful and an interesting book. Not that it is a pleasant book to read, nor, as we fancy, has it been a pleasant book to write; still less has it been a pleasant training which could teach an author such awful facts, or give courage to write them. The fault of the book is coarseness of subject which will be the stumbling-block of most readers, and which makes it utterly unfit to be put into the hands of girls; of that we do not complain. There are foul and accursed undercurrents in plenty, in this same smug, respectable, whitewashed English society, which must be exposed now and then; and Society owes thanks, not sneers, to those who dare to shew her the image of her own ugly, hypocritical visage. We must not lay Juvenal's coarseness at Juvenal's door, but at that of the Roman world which he stereotyped in his fearful verses. But the world does not think so. It will revile Acton Bell for telling us, with painful circumstantiality, what the house of a profligate, uneducated country squire is like, perfectly careless whether or not the picture be true, only angry at having been disturbed from its own self-complacent doze. . . .

But taking this book as a satire, and an exposure of evils, still all unnecessary coarseness is a defect,—a defect which injures the real useful and real worth of the book. The author introduces, for instance, a long diary, kept by the noble and unhappy wife of a profligate squire; and would that every man in England might read and lay to heart that horrible record. But what greater mistake, to use the mildest term, can there be than to fill such a diary with written oaths and curses, with details of drunken scenes which no wife, such as poor Helen is represented, would have the heart, not to say the common decency, to write down as they occurred? Dramatic probability and good feeling are equally outraged by such a method. The author, tempted naturally to indulge her full powers of artistic detail, seems to have forgotten that there are silences more pathetic than all words.

A cognate defect, too, struck us much; the splenetic and bitter tone in which certain personages in the novel are mentioned, when really, poor souls, no deeds of theirs are shown which could warrant such wholesale appellations as 'brute' and 'demon.' One is inclined sometimes to suspect that they are caricatures from the life, against whom some private spite is being vented; though the author has a right to reply, that the whole novel being the autobiography of a young gentleman farmer, such ferocities are to be charged on him, not on her. True, but yet in his mouth as much as in any one's else they want cause for them to be shewn, according to all principles of fiction; and if none such exists on the face of the story, it only indicates a defect in the youth's character which makes his good fortune more improbable. For the book sets forth how the gallant Gilbert wins the heart, and after her husband's death, the hand of the rich squire's well-born and highly-cultivated wife. . . .

But the novelist, especially when he invents a story, instead of merely giving a dramatic life to one ready made, which is the Shakespearan, and, as we suspect, the higher path of art, must give some internal and spiritual probability to his outward miracles; and this, we think, Acton Bell has in this case failed to do. We cannot see any reason why Gilbert Markham, though no doubt highly attractive to young ladies of his own caliber, should excite such passionate love in Helen, with all her bitter experiences of life, her painting, and her poetry, her deep readings and deep thoughts—absolutely no reason at all, except the last one in the world, which either the author or she would have wished, namely, that there was no other man in the way for her to fall in love with. We want to see this strange intellectual superiority of his to the general run of his class (for we must suppose some such); and all the characteristics we do find, beyond the general dashing, manful spirit of a young farmer, is a very passionate and somewhat brutal temper, and, to say the least, a wanton rejection of a girl to whom he has been giving most palpable and somewhat rough proofs of affection, and whom he afterwards hates bitterly, simply because she rallies on him having jilted her for a woman against whose character there was every possible ground for suspicion. This is not to be counterbalanced by an occasional vein of high-flown sentimentalism in the young gentleman (and that, too, not often) when he comes in contact with his lady-love. If the author had intended to work out the noble old Cymon and Iphigenia myths, she ought to have let us see the gradual growth of the clown's mind under the influence of the accomplished woman; and this is just what she has not done. Gilbert Markham is not one character oscillating between his old low standard and his higher new one, according as he comes in contact with his own countrified friends or his new lady-love, but two different men, with no single root-idea of character to unite and explain the two opposite poles of his conduct.

—Charles Kingsley, *Fraser's Magazine*,
April 1849, xxxix, pp. 423–425

MARY A. WARD (1900)

Ward cites the ambiguity surrounding the authorship of *The Tenant of Wildfell Hall* and Charlotte and Anne's trip to London to correct it. She considers Anne's novel to be admirable in many ways: in its "narrative ability," moral force, and realistic representation. But in this last category, Ward argues that Anne Brontë has gone too far, imbuing the novel with a tractlike didacticism that compares poorly with *Jane Eyre*'s more imaginative style. Ward believes that this fault results from Anne writing descriptively about Branwell's behavior, rather than creatively styling a work of fiction.

Wildfell Hall seems to have attained more immediate success than anything else written by the sisters before 1848, except *Jane Eyre*. It went into a second edition within a very short time of its publication, and Messrs. Newby informed the American publishers with whom they were negotiating that it was the work of the same hand which had produced *Jane Eyre*, and superior to either *Jane Eyre* or *Wuthering Heights*! It was, indeed, the sharp practice connected with this astonishing judgment which led to the sisters' hurried journey to London in 1848—the famous journey when the two little ladies in black revealed themselves to Mr. Smith, and proved to him that they were not one Currer Bell, but two Miss Brontës. It was Anne's sole journey to London—her only contact with a world that was not Haworth, except that supplied by her school-life at Roe Head and her two teaching engagements.

And there was and is a considerable narrative ability, a sheer moral energy in *Wildfell Hall*, which would not be enough, indeed, to keep it alive if it were not the world of a Brontë, but still betray its kinship and source. The scenes of Huntingdon's wickedness are less interesting but less improbable than the country-house scenes of *Jane Eyre*; the story of his death has many true and touching passages; the last love-scene is well, even in parts admirably, written. But the book's truth, so far as it is true, is scarcely the truth of imagination; it is rather the truth of a tract or a report. There can be little doubt that many of the pages are close transcripts from Branwell's conduct and language,—so far as Anne's slighter personality enabled her to render her brother's temperament, which was more akin to Emily's than to her own.

—Mary Augusta Ward, *The Life and Words of Charlotte Brontë and Her Sisters*, Haworth, 1900, pp. xiii–xiv

Chronology

〜〜〜 〜〜〜 〜〜〜

1812 Reverend Patrick Brontë marries Maria Branwell on December 29.

1814 Maria Brontë, their first child, is born on April 23.

1815 Elizabeth Brontë is born on February 8.

1816 Charlotte Brontë is born on April 21.

1817 Patrick Branwell Brontë, the only son, is born in June.

1818 Emily Jane Brontë is born on July 30.

1820 Anne Brontë is born on January 17. The Brontë family moves to the parsonage at Haworth, near Bradford, Yorkshire.

1821 Maria Brontë dies of cancer in September. Her sister Elizabeth Branwell takes charge of the household.

1824 Maria and Elizabeth attend the Clergy Daughters' School at Cowan Bridge. Charlotte follows them in August and Emily in November.

1825 The two oldest girls, Maria and Elizabeth, contract tuberculosis at school. Maria dies on May 6; Elizabeth dies June 15. Charlotte and Emily are withdrawn from the school on June 1. Charlotte and Emily do not return to school until they are in their teens; in the meantime, they are educated at home.

1826 Reverend Brontë brings home a box of wooden soldiers for his son; this is the catalyst for the creation of the Brontës' juvenile fantasy worlds and writings. Charlotte and Branwell begin the Angrian stories and magazines, and Emily and Anne work on the Gondal saga.

1831 Charlotte attends Miss Wooler's school. She leaves the school seven months later to tend to her sisters' education. In 1835, she returns as governess, accompanied by Emily.

1835 After only three months, Emily leaves Miss Wooler's school because of homesickness. Anne arrives in January 1836 and remains until December 1837.

1837 In September, Emily becomes a governess at Miss Patchett's school, near Halifax.

1838 In May, Charlotte leaves her position at Miss Wooler's school.

1839 Anne becomes governess for the Ingram family at Blake Hall, Mirfield. She leaves in December. Charlotte becomes governess to the Sidgwick family, at Stonegappe Hall, near Skipton. She leaves in July after two months.

1840 All three sisters live at Haworth.

1841 Anne becomes governess to the Robinson family, near York. Charlotte becomes governess to the White family and moves to Upperwood House, Rawdon. She leaves in December. The sisters plan to start their own school. The scheme, attempted several years later, fails for lack of inquiries.

1842 Charlotte and Emily travel to Brussels to study at the Pensionnat Héger. There, Charlotte develops unrequited love for the master of the school, Monsieur Héger. After the death of their aunt in November, they return to Haworth.

1843 Branwell joins Anne in York as tutor to the Robinson family. Charlotte returns to Brussels and remains until January 1844.

1845 Charlotte discovers Emily's poetry and suggests that a selection be published along with Anne's and her own verse.

1846 *Poems, by Currer, Ellis, and Acton Bell* is published by Aylott & Jones. Two copies are sold. Charlotte's *The Professor,* Emily's *Wuthering Heights,* and Anne's *Agnes Grey* are all completed. The latter two are accepted by T.C. Newby, but *The Professor* is rejected. Charlotte's *Jane Eyre* is begun in August and immediately accepted by Smith, Elder & Company when it is completed in August 1847.

1847 *Jane Eyre* is published. *Wuthering Heights* and *Agnes Grey* are published by T.C. Newby.

1848 Anne's *The Tenant of Wildfell Hall* is published by T.C. Newby, which tries to sell it to an American publisher as a new book by Currer Bell, author of the immensely popular *Jane Eyre.*

Smith, Elder & Company requests that Charlotte bring her sisters to London to prove that there are three Bells. Charlotte and Anne visit London. Branwell dies of tuberculosis on September 24. Emily dies of the same on December 19.

1849 Anne dies of tuberculosis on May 28. Charlotte's *Shirley* is published by Smith, Elder & Company. Charlotte meets Thackeray and Harriet Martineau in London.

1850 Charlotte meets G.H. Lewes and Elizabeth Gaskell in London. She edits her sisters' work. Smith, Elder & Company publishes a new edition of *Wuthering Heights* and *Agnes Grey,* along with some of Anne's and Emily's poetry and a "Biographical Notice" of her sisters' lives by Charlotte.

1852 Reverend A.B. Nicholls proposes marriage to Charlotte. Her father objects, and Nicholls is rejected. Eventually, Charlotte's father relents, and she marries in June 1854.

1853 Charlotte's *Villette* is published in January.

1855 Charlotte dies of pregnancy-related toxemia on March 31.

1857 Charlotte's *The Professor* is published posthumously with a preface written by her husband. Elizabeth Gaskell's *Life of Charlotte Brontë* is published in March.

1860 "Emma," a fragment of a story by Charlotte, is published in *The Cornhill Magazine,* with an introduction by Thackeray.

1861 Reverend Patrick Brontë, having survived all his children, dies.

Index

Charlotte, Emily, and Anne Bronte are represented by initials CB, EB, and AB, respectively. Names of characters are followed by the work in which they appear.